VOICES FROM THE
PAGAN CENSUS

Studies in Comparative Religion
Frederick M. Denny, Series Editor

VOICES FROM THE PAGAN CENSUS

A National Survey of Witches and
Neo-Pagans in the United States

HELEN A. BERGER, EVAN A. LEACH,
AND LEIGH S. SHAFFER

University of South Carolina Press

© 2003 University of South Carolina

Published in Columbia, South Carolina, by the
University of South Carolina Press

Manufactured in the United States of America

07 06 05 04 03   5 4 3 2 1

Library of Congress Cataloging-in-Publication Data

Berger, Helen A., 1949–
   Voices from the pagan census : a national survey of witches and neo-pagans in the
United States / Helen A. Berger, Evan A. Leach, Leigh S. Shaffer.
      p. cm. — (Studies in comparative religion)
   Includes bibliographical references and index.
   ISBN 1-57003-488-5 (alk. paper)
   1. Witchcraft—United States. 2. Neopaganism—United States. I. Leach, Evan A.
II. Shaffer, Leigh S. III. Title. IV. Studies in comparative religion (Columbia, S.C.)
BF1573.B48 2003
299—dc21   2003001347

To our parents

In memory of Frieda M. Berger and Nathan Berger
To Joyce Leach and Edward Leach
In memory of Ruth D. Shaffer and Edward W. Shaffer

CONTENTS

TABLES

SERIES EDITOR'S PREFACE

One of the most arresting developments in American religious life in recent decades is the emergence of a religious movement with a variety of forms that may be clustered under the umbrella term "Neo-Paganism." *Voices from the Pagan Census* is a report on the first national survey of Neo-Pagans, conducted between 1993 and 1995. This book is a sequel to coauthor Helen A. Berger's earlier book in this series, *A Community of Witches: Contemporary Neo-Paganism and Witchcraft in the United States* (1999), which analyzed ethnographic and textual data and included some demographic data from the census as well.

Voices from the Pagan Census reports on the survey results of more than two thousand respondents, of whom more than half provided valuable written remarks beyond what the lengthy questionnaire requested. Although the survey was not based on a random sample —issues of confidentiality and privacy made that infeasible—the snowball sampling process that was followed did contain refinements that increased the census's soundness.

The six Neo-Pagan movements covered in the census included the three most popular: Wiccans, Pagans, Goddess-Worshipers, and three smaller but distinctive movements: Druids, Shamans, and Unitarian-Universalist Pagans. The topics covered by the census included magic, mysticism, politics, spiritual paths, practices, regional variations, families, children, sexuality, popularization, institutional changes, and festivals. Among the most controversial and politically sensitive topics was whether the term "witch" should continue to be used, with three-quarters of respondents insisting that it should.

In addition to its principal aim as a detailed, comprehensive report of the survey sampling, *Voices from the Pagan Census* can also serve as a reliable introductory survey of Neo-Paganism in the United States. Neo-Pagans are increasingly visible and active throughout the country, and the census responses show interesting regional variations in their beliefs, attitudes, and practices. And since the survey's results are compared with parallel findings in the general society, we are fortunate to have for the first time a reliable representation of significant similarities as well as differences between Neo-Pagans and their fellow citizens.

FREDERICK M. DENNY

PREFACE

Voices from the Pagan Census is an analysis of the data collected in a national survey of Neo-Pagans titled The Pagan Census, conducted between 1993 and 1995. Our intent in writing this book is to provide scholars with data that may inform their research on Neo-Pagans, give Neo-Pagans some insights into their community, and provide the general reader with an overview of this new religion. The Pagan Census provides a rich source of data, including information about Neo-Pagans' lives, their political opinions and activities, their spiritual beliefs, and opinions about some of the important issues facing the Neo-Pagan movement today. To enable us to compare Neo-Pagans with other Americans, we include questions from the National Opinion Research Center's (NORC's) General Social Survey (GSS). Ours is the first published large-scale survey that was not conducted primarily at Neo-Pagan festivals and which also includes questions that permit us to directly compare Neo-Pagans with the general American public. This book provides a voice to the over two thousand individuals who answered this survey and through them a unique view into the Neo-Pagan community.

Our analysis of the data portrays Neo-Pagans as sharing many characteristics with their non–Neo-Pagan neighbors but, nonetheless, as a distinct community. Regardless of region of residence, Neo-Pagans tend to have a similar high level of education. This similarity is true even in regions of the United States where the average level of education is relatively low. Neo-Pagans also tend to be more politically liberal and more politically active than their neighbors. Although Neo-Pagans' images of the afterlife and their reported frequency of paranormal experiences differ from other Americans', there are surprising overlaps as occult and paranormal beliefs have become more widespread and accepted throughout American society.

Neo-Pagans on the whole have more nontraditional life-styles than other Americans—that is, high rates of cohabitation or ritual but not legal marriages; significant proportions of their population that is gay, lesbian, or bisexual; and a high acceptance, if not practice, of group marriage. Neo-Pagans who live in more conservative regions of the United States are more likely to be legally married and not cohabiting than are Neo-Pagans living in more liberal areas. Those living in more conservative regions also are less likely than other Neo-Pagans to be politically active, although they tend to hold similar liberal political views.

Although there are overriding similarities among Neo-Pagans, there are also distinctions and differences within the religion. Our respondents define themselves as participating in more than twenty different spiritual paths. Very few individuals claim some of these paths as their primary form of practice. We compare and contrast six spiritual paths—those of Wiccans, Pagans, Goddess Worshipers, Druids, Shamans, and Unitarian Universalist (UU) Pagans. We selected the first three spiritual paths, or sects, because they are the most popular. Druids, Shamans, and UU Pagans were chosen, on the other hand, because they are the most distinctive of the remaining forms of Neo-Paganism.

Among the sects examined, we find some notable differences and many similarities. With some exceptions, Neo-Pagans, regardless of sect, hold similar political views, education and income levels, and are politically active. Goddess Worshipers have the largest proportion of women and indicate the most concern about issues of gender and sexual orientation equity. On the whole, they tend to be more politically active than all except UU Neo-Pagans.

Those Neo-Pagans who choose to participate in a UU church are not only more politically active than other Neo-Pagans but also more likely than other Neo-Pagans to involve their children in their spiritual path. They also report having the most conservative life-style among all Neo-Pagans. All sects, other than Druids, have a disproportionate number of women to men. Shamans, contrary to their image as loners, are as likely as other Neo-Pagans to involve their romantic partner and their children in their spiritual path.

Just over half of those answering our survey are "solitaries"—that is, they practice their religion alone. The religion as it initially developed focused on individuals being trained in groups. However, with the growth of how-to manuals, more people are becoming Neo-Pagans without ever joining a group. Others choose to work on their own after the group they train with dissolves or they leave the group. Our data indicate that solitaries form a distinct cohort among Neo-Pagans. On the whole, solitaries are younger, less politically active, less likely to attend festivals, and less concerned with issues of gender and sexual orientation equity. Those who have children are less likely to involve them in their spiritual path than are those who work in groups or with a partner. The growth of solitary practice among Neo-Pagans may either change the face of the religion or result in a bifurcation as those who work in groups or with a partner might move toward institutionalization of their religion while solitaries may resist that development.

A portion of the demographic material from The Pagan Census is included in Helen A. Berger's *A Community of Witches: Contemporary Neo-Paganism and Witchcraft in the United States* (1999a). At the time she wrote that book, the rest of the data had not been completely processed, cleaned, and analyzed. Some of the questions in the survey grew out of her participant observation study of Witches and Neo-Pagans. Unlike that book, which relied primarily on her ethnographic research in the northeastern United States and an analysis of journals, books, and newsletters written by Neo-Pagans, this one is based primarily on the survey data. Books and articles written by scholars and Neo-Pagans are relied on only to provide a background in which to understand the data and to put the survey findings in context.

Methods

Our survey, like others whose results have been published, is not based on a random sample. Witches and Neo-Pagans represent what social scientists call a hidden population (Eland-Goossensen et al. 1997). Because they fear discrimination and persecution, many Neo-Pagans are apprehensive about making public their identification with this movement. Thus, traditional probability sampling procedures that require an adequate sampling frame are not possible for studying the group. It is not that materials for constructing such sampling frames do not exist—subscription lists for the many magazines and newsletters that cater to the interests of Neo-Pagans would provide raw materials for constructing such a frame. But these lists and similar materials (such as lists of attendees at regional festivals) are kept confidential by publishers and organizers alike. Thus, the best procedures for recruiting representative samples are simply impractical for the study of such groups.

Snowball sampling has been the alternative to probability sampling methods for the study of hidden populations (Babbie 2000; Eland-Goossensen et al. 1997). As the metaphoric term suggests, the snowball sample starts with a small number of elements from the statistical population of interest and then grows larger by drawing in more elements that are identified by a peer-nomination process. Traditional approaches start with an initial list of contacts (which often correspond to an anthropologist's concept of informants) and ask each contact to name as many other members of the target group as possible. If necessary, the initial contacts are often asked to approach nominees on behalf of the researcher in order to maximize the credibility of the researcher and the likelihood that the nominee will cooperate. The sample then grows through a series of chains of respondent to referral to new respondents and so forth. Ordinarily, each member of the chain serves as a respondent. Since such snowball samples are not probability samples, researchers have not attempted to use any random selection processes in identifying potential new respondents. Rather, researchers have tried to maximize the size of the snowball sample as the way to generate the most useful data. If the population of interest is inherently small, and the snowball approach is successful in locating and securing the cooperation of a high proportion of elements as respondents, then the result looks something like a census. As with a traditional census, accuracy of parameter estimation is related to the proportion of population elements ultimately included. In any case, researchers are well aware that they cannot speak with any degree of certainty about the representativeness of a snowball sample.

Recent theoretical and empirical work has been conducted to try to improve upon the representativeness of snowball samples by incorporating random selection into the procedure at each link in a chain of respondents. For example, at each stage in the snowball sampling process, the actual elements of the population contacted for research purposes can be selected at random from the total list of nominees. In this way, some of the advantages of probability sampling can be built into the snowball process, and the sample can be representative of all of the elements nominated. The final list of nominees then becomes analogous to a sampling frame. Another proposal is a procedure known as site sampling (Eland-Goossensen et al. 1997). In this technique the patterns of residence of a population of interest must be identified so that research sites can be selected at random. In this approach the number of elements to be selected at each site is determined by a weighted formula that takes into account the estimated size of the population, the number of elements present at each site, and the estimated frequency of exchange among sites. Both approaches have advantages over the traditional snowball sampling approach, although both are subject to biases associated with the fact that peer-nomination procedures cannot duplicate true random selection. The social networks of respondents are not random, and the probability of any one element being selected using these procedures is not equal to that of other elements. Thus, the representativeness of snowball samples remains problematic, even with these refinements.

In our study the data reported are the result of a process that is a compromise between the best practices known to the researchers and the practical restrictions of the hidden population of interest. Helen A. Berger and Andras Corban Arthen had the initial idea of surveying Neo-Pagans to learn more about their demographic characteristics as well as their beliefs and practices. Arthen, as a founder and director of the EarthSpirit Community—which was then located in Medford, Massachusetts—hoped to gain information about the Neo-Pagan community, and he provided credibility among Neo-Pagans to launch an empirical study. A paper-and-pen survey instrument called "The Pagan Census Project" was created. Some groups who had agreed to cooperate with the project mailed copies of the survey to their membership and others published it in their magazines and newsletters that circulate among interested readers around the United States. Readers were invited to participate in the census project by completing the survey and returning it to the EarthSpirit Community by mail. Thus, the project began as a published survey of interested readers and recipients of the survey. However, it soon became apparent that readers had chosen to treat the project as an invitation to participate in a snowball process. Without direction from the authors of the survey, respondents took it upon themselves to inform and recruit other participants by photocopying and distributing the questionnaire to friends, acquaintances, and coven mates. Some enterprising individuals posted the survey on websites to encourage the participation of an even broader readership. As one such participant informs us: "I've posted the survey on the local BBS. . . . I've also forwarded a copy to friends in the Seattle area who have Circles within Circles and Connections within Connections. . . . My copy came from a youthful Online correspondent" (Survey 3343).[1] The responses we received in the return mail and through e-mail give testimony to the power of interested social networks to encourage participation and to take over the practical administration of the "sampling" process.

In some interesting ways, the process of survey distribution and the content of the survey itself unintentionally dovetailed. For example, research on improved techniques for snowball sampling has identified potential biases in the methodology, which correspond to some of the research questions of the survey. Snowball sampling is subject to an "island" effect: subgroups of a population may exist within which connections are rich and the probability of being nominated may be nearly random, but among which connections may be limited (Eland-Goossensen et al. 1997). The research team believes this to be the case, especially among the most visible subgroups of the Neo-Pagan movement. Demographic questions of residence, practical questions about attending regional festivals, and personal questions about the teachers or publications that have influenced a respondent's path were intended to help identify and describe these islands of Neo-Pagan community, belief, and practice. In our study the islands were visibly at work in the snowballing number of respondents even before we were able to analyze the data and report what respondents tell us about their experiences of community. Similarly,

Eland-Goossensen notes that bias also is created in snowball sampling by overlapping circles of acquaintance. If subgroups were literal islands unto themselves, snowball sampling could not work as a means of reaching the hidden population as a whole. However, these overlaps affect the peer-nomination process in nonrandom ways, producing bias in the final snowball sample. In our case individuals who read eclectically, have access to or have a friend or acquaintance who has access to Neo-Pagan magazines or newsletters, or are on a participating-organizations mailing list provide us with responses from a wide range of participants from many sources. These participants are important both for their contributions to the successful efforts to increase the number of respondents and for the insight their cases offer on the nature of the Neo-Pagan experience.

Acknowledgments

Our greatest debt is to all the Neo-Pagans throughout the United States who took the time to complete our survey, which is four double-sided legal-sized pages in length. More than half of these individuals additionally provide us with sometimes lengthy typed or handwritten comments on issues that they believe are important to their own spiritual development or to the Neo-Pagan community. Andras Arthen and the EarthSpirit Community were instrumental in the creation and distribution of the survey. We have shared all the data with them but not our analysis of the data. All the views and analysis in this book are those of the authors.

West Chester University is thanked for granting Helen Berger a sabbatical to write this book. The College of Arts and Sciences provided two grants to help with the printing and distribution of the survey and cleaning of the data. The Management Department and the School of Business and Public Affairs provided additional funds for data entry and cleaning. Over fifty students worked on data entry and cleaning. Among these students, Melanie Noble and Duane Miller stand out for their significant contribution to the work. Charles McGee, chair of the Management Department, gave his enthusiastic support to this project. Denise Gonazales, administrative assistant to the Management Department, deserves special recognition for her significant assistance in data entry and in the creation of tables.

The book benefited from the continuing support of the editor of this series, Frederick M. Denny. Richard J. Wolff helped us negotiate our way through the NORC's GSS database. Helen Berger's husband, John H. Wolff, deserves special thanks for his willingness to read rough drafts, pick up more than his share of household chores, and support her through all the trials and tribulations of creating a book from data. Evan Leach is indebted to his parents, Edward and Joyce Leach, for their support and encouragement and to his wife, Sarah Tishkoff, for her inspiration and support. Leigh Shaffer is grateful to his wife, Barbara Anne Shaffer, for her support and encouragement as well.

ABBREVIATIONS

CUUPS   Covenant of the Unitarian Universalist Pagans
ELF   Elf Lore Family
ERA   Equal Rights Amendment
GNPP   General Neo-Pagan Population
GSS   General Social Survey
NORC   National Opinion Research Center
NRDNA   New Reformed Druids of North America
RDNA   Reformed Druids of North America
UU(s)   Unitarian Universalist(s)
UUA   Unitarian Universalist Association

1

THE PAGAN CENSUS,
NEO-PAGANISM, AND NEO-PAGANS

> I do consider myself "Pagan" because it is the closest belief, a lifestyle
> that fits me. I practice Witchcraft, candle burning—wax reading. But,
> not by books or publications. It is just a part of me. Astral-projection
> is something I've experienced without even knowing what it was,
> since I found a name for it, I read on it and improve my travels. I do
> astrology and card readings, crystals, pyramids and pendulums. I
> believe very strongly in reincarnation. (Survey 1015)

This is one of the over two thousand respondents to The Pagan Census (see appendix) a nationwide survey that asked Neo-Pagans questions about their beliefs, practices, and everyday lives.[1] *Neo-Pagan* is
an umbrella term covering sects of a new religious movement, the
largest and most important form of which is Witchcraft, or as it is
also called, Wicca. The term *Neo-Pagan* was first used in the United
States by Tim O'tter Zell to describe members of this new religion
who were not initiated through a coven system and who rejected the
labels *Witch* and *Wiccan* (Melton 1992).[2] O'tter Zell, the founder of
the Church of All Worlds, publishes one of the largest and most
influential Neo-Pagan journals, *Green Egg*. The term *Neo-Pagan,* or
Pagan, has become commonplace for practitioners of this new religion. To emphasize their connection to pre-Christian religions, many

practitioners prefer to use the name *Pagan*. Throughout this text, except for direct quotes, we use the term Neo-Pagan to indicate that the religions we are discussing are relatively new, even if some of their practices may be taken directly from or related to older pagan religions.

The Pagan Census

The Pagan Census is a survey conducted by Helen A. Berger and Andras Corbin Arthen, one of the leaders of the largest Neo-Pagan organization in New England, EarthSpirit Community. Arthen was among the first Neo-Pagans Berger met when she began her participant observation study of this religion in New England.[3] The decision to work together on the survey came from a desire to share their strengths, specifically Arthen's knowledge of the Neo-Pagan community and Berger's social science research skills. Initially, Arthen hoped to do a census of the entire Neo-Pagan community. Through his contacts, major Neo-Pagan leaders and organizations in the United States gave their support to The Pagan Census. Nonetheless, it was impossible to do an accurate census. We subsequently hoped to do a random sample. But this too became impossible because Neo-Pagan organizations were unwilling to give us their membership lists, as they felt this would violate their members' privacy. Furthermore, some Neo-Pagans were so anxious to have the voices of their community heard that they photocopied and distributed copies of the survey to others and also placed copies of the survey on the Internet. The result is 2,089 completed surveys.

Like most surveys, ours is not a random sample. However, these data are the largest and most varied of published survey results. All previous surveys have been distributed in a small local area or at festivals—that is, Neo-Pagan gatherings that usually take place at a campground and last a weekend or a week—that attract a small percentage of Neo-Pagans (see, for example, Kirkpatrick 1986; Adler 1986; Jorgensen and Russell 1999; Orion 1995).

This book provides an analysis and interpretation of the data collected from The Pagan Census. Our intention is to give a voice to those who completed The Pagan Census and through them to provide a new look into the Neo-Pagan community. In responding to the survey, people were asked to complete four legal-sized pages of questions in four sections: demographics, political information, religious spiritual beliefs, and Pagan-related information. Space was provided for adding free responses about any issues or concerns. About half of our respondents wrote additional information—some typed, some handwritten, often pages long.

Several questions taken directly from the General Social Survey (GSS) of the National Opinion Research Center (NORC) are worded in ways that are not reflective of Neo-Pagans' discourse or worldview. However, the ability to, at least on some scales, compare and contrast Neo-Pagans with their neighbors makes the awkwardness of the wording for our audience worthwhile. We added a note in the introduction of the survey explaining the inclusion of these questions. Both the free responses and the statistical information about Neo-Pagans—where they live, what they do for a living, their political beliefs and activities, and their religious and spiritual beliefs—are used in our overview of Neo-Paganism. Throughout the text we have recorded the statistical data in percentages; in some instances converting frequencies into percentages introduced some rounding errors, which are never greater than two-tenths of one percent.

What Is Neo-Paganism?

Neo-Pagans define themselves as practicing an earth-based spirituality. As the religion has no dogma, bureaucracy, or acknowledged leaders to determine orthodoxy, people can simply declare themselves to be Pagans or Witches, as has the respondent quoted at the beginning of this chapter. Some Neo-Pagans, however, participate in a rigorous training program through covens or from those Neo-Pagan organizations that offer courses. Because of the ambiguity of boundaries within Neo-Paganism, this process of self-definition does not result in anyone being excluded or viewed as outside the religion. However, the disparity in training results in some Neo-Pagans questioning others' credentials.

It is possible for each individual to have her or his own brand of Neo-Paganism. In practice, however, there is a good deal of similarity, as Neo-Pagans share information and ideas on the Internet, at festivals, and in books and journals (H. Berger 1999a). This means that on the one hand, it is almost always possible to find at least one

Neo-Pagan who is the exception to any generalization about the group. On the other hand, there is a growing similarity in practices, imagery, and language used in rituals and descriptions of mystical experiences.

Neo-Pagans can practice alone as solitaries, or as members of a group—which, among Wiccans, is referred to as a coven—or with a spiritual partner. Most Neo-Pagans, at least for some period of their lives, are solitaries. Some people prefer to practice alone, others are solitaries for a short period when they first enter the religion or when their coven or group disintegrates. Solitaries can remain connected to the larger Neo-Pagan community by attending public rituals and festivals, reading Neo-Pagan magazines, and participating in online Neo-Pagan chat groups.

For Neo-Pagans, Mother Earth, the seasonal cycle of the year, and the phases of the moon are all ritually and symbolically important. The year is spiritually divided by eight sabbats—ritual celebrations of the season—six weeks apart that are related to the myth of the changing relationship between the goddess and the god. The goddess is eternal but changes from maid to mother to crone. The god is born of the goddess at Yule (December 21). He grows to manhood and becomes the goddess's consort, the horned god, at Beltane (May 1), and in the fall (October 31) he dies, to be reborn the next year. In rituals this mythology is related to the changes that are occurring in nature and by analogy in individuals' lives. For example, at Beltane, when the natural world is in bloom, and according to Neo-Pagan mythology, the goddess and the god are lovers; there is a celebration of fertility. The Maypole is danced as a celebration of sexuality, fertility (of thought and action, not necessarily that which results in procreation), and growth—in nature and in people's lives.

The mythology of the changing relationship of goddess and god has been transfigured by women-only groups to the waxing and waning of the earth rhythms or a movement from inward to outward energy (Eller 1993). This alternative mythology is reflected in these groups' sabbat rituals. The phases of the moon, which are commemorated as the three aspects of the goddess—maid, mother, and crone—are celebrated as the esabats by both inclusive and women-only groups.

The goddess is a central image within Neo-Paganism that can be spoken of either as a single deity or as many. Some Neo-Pagans claim that the goddess is not one but that throughout history she has been given many faces and names by different cultures. The god force is similarly viewed as multifaceted. Most Neo-Pagans venerate the goddess or goddesses and the god force or the gods. Some groups, usually women-only groups, focus completely on the goddess or goddesses to the exclusion of the gods. Even in groups in which both the female and male deities are venerated, the goddess is seen as more important than the gods. Although the deities are regularly called upon in rituals, it is not inconsistent to be both an atheist and a Neo-Pagan. Within Neo-Paganism the deities are viewed in several distinct ways: supernatural beings, forces of nature, symbols, or aspects internal to each person. Participants are not always consistent in their image of the deities. The same person may speak of the deities as supernatural beings at one time or as symbols at another.

It is because dogma is unimportant to Neo-Pagans that the meaning of the deities can diverge among people and groups. Neo-Paganism is an experiential religion in which having a mystical experience of the Divine or of infinity is central. The use of drumming, dancing, and guided meditations in rituals creates altered states of consciousness so that participants can have mystical or magical experiences. It is because the emphasis is on experiencing the Divine, not dogma or practice, that Neo-Pagans are comfortable borrowing aspects of rituals and mythology from one another, other cultures, literature, movies, and science fiction. Pragmatically, Neo-Pagans suggest, "If it works, use it." This eclecticism has resulted in some conflicts over the use of elements of Native American spirituality, such as sweat lodges, smudging, or the calling of Native American goddesses or gods into Neo-Pagan circles. Although some Native Americans choose to share their spiritual teachings with outsiders, others claim that their religion is being misused and expropriated (Rose 1992). Some Neo-Pagans are concerned about (and sensitive to) the issue and refrain from using Native American elements in their rituals, focusing instead on historical European paganism or the paganism of other indigenous groups. Others believe they are using the borrowed elements respectfully and hence are not harming

Native Americans but honoring them, their traditions, and Mother Earth. Some Neo-Pagans, furthermore, claim they are part Native American, or were Native Americans in a previous life and that, therefore, these rituals or elements thereof are theirs by birthright (Pike 2001).

Most Neo-Pagan rituals have the same basic format, which is English in origin. Rituals normally begin with the casting of a circle to create sacred space. Because most Neo-Pagan rituals occur in public parks, participants' living rooms, or rented rooms, the creation of sacred space from the mundane is important. There are variations in how the circle is cast. Among Wiccans the space is usually created with the use of a ritual knife called an athama. Some women-only groups create the circle by sending the "energy" from one person to the next hand to hand around the circle. The specific chants or words used to consecrate the space vary. Some groups use the same chant for every ritual; others may change the words or even the specifics of casting the circle either for different rituals, or based on who is leading the ritual.

After the circle is cast, the forces or deities of the four directions are called into the space. Again, the actual words and deities called vary among groups. The choices of a ritual to follow and the deities called upon are related to the purpose of the circle. At sabbats there is normally a reading, an enactment, or a guided meditation that focuses on the season and the corresponding relationship between the goddess and the god or for women-only groups, the changing image of the goddess. Esabats rituals focus on the moon cycles. Magical energy is raised at rituals through dancing, chanting, or meditation and cast into the world to enact a change for an individual or the larger community. These magical workings include such practices as healing a member of the group, a friend, or relative; helping someone find a job, an apartment, or a lover; and aiding the larger community by calling for rain during a drought or helping heal the rain forest or other endangered natural areas. Such rituals can be performed in groups or by individuals. Neo-Pagans, even those who are members of groups, often perform private rituals, particularly if they have a specific problem that they want either help to overcome or the psychological strength to endure.

Neo-Pagans often emphasize the differences in traditions that are reflected in their rituals, mythology, and beliefs. Although there clearly are differences, the basic structure of rituals is almost universal among groups. This universal structure exists because all the sects stemmed from or were influenced by Wicca as it developed in England and was transformed in the United States. Furthermore, most Neo-Pagans read the same books and journals and share information at festivals and on the Internet (H. Berger 1999a). As an experiential religion, the specifics of the ritual are less important than the effect they have on the participants. Nonetheless, there are several strands of Neo-Paganism, which are recognized as having significant differences in ritual practice and mythology—most notably women-only groups and some forms of ethnic-specific Neo-Paganism.

Some scholars have questioned whether Neo-Paganism is a real religion, because it is playful and lacks such typical religious features as a dogma, recognized bureaucracies and churches, and an unambiguous definition of the deities. Neo-Pagans self-consciously create rituals and mythology often using bits and pieces from diverse cultures. Many Neo-Pagans simultaneously participate in the rituals and stand outside of them to the degree that they can reflect on the rituals as something that they created. Neo-Pagans often joke about their own rituals and seem to be taking themselves and their religious practice with a grain of salt, at the same time viewing their spiritual practices as serious. Helen Berger (1999a), Loretta Orion (1995), Melissa Raphael (1996), and Howard Eilberg-Schwartz (1989) argue that it is the playfulness, emphasis on the individual as the ultimate authority, and pastiche of rituals that make Neo-Paganism a religion of its time—late modernity or postmodernity.[4] All these authors argue that although Neo-Paganism does not fit the Judeo-Christian model, it is a religion—one that is reflective of the historic era in which it developed.

History of Neo-Paganism

Gerald Gardner is credited with developing the basic principles of Wicca, or Witchcraft, in the 1940s in Great Britain. He claimed that he was initiated into a coven of Witches that had survived from antiquity. His story has been questioned by scholars (Hutton 1999;

Luhrmann 1989) and academically oriented Neo-Pagans alike (Adler 1986; Kelly 1991). Nonetheless, many contemporary Neo-Pagans still claim that theirs is the old religion. For some this statement is figurative. They contend that they are returning to older practices and to an older form of religion, at the same time acknowledging that their religion is relatively new. Others quite literally argue that they are practicing the religion of antiquity that has been secretly handed down generation to generation in their families or through their covens. Scholars have found no evidence to support the notion of an unbroken link between ancient European pagan religions and modern Neo-Pagan practices (Hutton 1999). The notion of Wicca being an old religion—or *the* old religion—is part of the mythology of this new religion. It is common for new religions to attempt to gain legitimacy by defining themselves as old. For Neo-Pagans, their appeal to the past, however, is also part of their critique of the present, which they view as too materialistic, lacking a spiritual core, in disharmony with nature, and one in which there is discord among people.

The notion that an ancient fertility religion survived in Europe until the early modern period was put forth first by Jules Michelet (1939) and was further developed and popularized by Margaret Murray (1971), an Egyptologist and folklorist. Both authors argue that the witch trials that swept through most of Europe in the fifteenth through seventeenth centuries were the result of first the Catholic and subsequently both the Catholic and Protestant churches attempting to eliminate the last vestiges of the older pagan religion that had flourished throughout Europe. Murray and Michelet describe the old pagan religion as a fertility cult and the witches as kindly individuals, primarily women, who used magic to aid their neighbors. Murray's writings initially gained widespread acceptance but were subsequently discredited.[5] Nonetheless, during the period in which her work was receiving acclaim, Murray's image of a pan-European old fertility religion was absorbed into Wicca in its early years. She wrote the preface to Gerald Gardner's book *Witchcraft Today* (1954), which was published shortly after the 1951 repeal of the English witchcraft statute. Ronald Hutton (1999), in his history of contemporary Pagan Witchcraft, describes Margaret Murray as the godmother of Wicca. Her analysis of the witch trials helped to justify the belief in a hidden coven in England that had survived the witch trials and the spread of Christianity. Clearly, Gardner developed from her work the notion that the old religion was based on the cycles of nature in which magic was practiced and in which the god of the hunt and the goddess of fertility were venerated.

Wicca, according to Hutton, also has a godfather, Aleister Crowley, a ceremonial magician who, with the help of Dion Fortune, presented a coherent system of magic based on nineteenth- and early-twentieth-century European and American occult practices (Hutton 1999; Luhrmann 1989).[6] Crowley defines magic as "the art or science of causing change in conformity with will," a definition that is commonly used today within Neo-Pagan circles (Hutton 1999:174). Furthermore, his methods of practicing magic and his view of magic as a science that manipulates natural forces are the basis of contemporary Neo-Pagan magical practices. Crowley was a controversial figure whom some have described as a Satanist, a claim Hutton disputes.

Although Murray and Crowley are the two most important and immediate influences on Gardner, they must be understood within a larger historical and cultural context. There were several trends within British society that influenced Murray, Crowley, and Gardner, most notably the development of Freemasonry, a growing interest in folklore and the occult, the popularity of Theosophy, and a history of popular magic in England and Wales (Hutton 1999). The Freemasons originated in Scotland in the seventeenth century and flowered in the early eighteenth century in England. By the nineteenth century the Freemasons had given rise to a number of secret societies, each of which believed it preserved and was handing down knowledge from antiquity. Many of these societies, like the Freemasons, used the symbol of the pentagram—a symbol that is now used by Neo-Pagans. These organizations became particularly important within British society in the nineteenth century (Hutton 1999).

At the same time that secret societies were popular among men of all social classes in England, there was a growing interest in the occult, in part fueled by the growth of Theosophy, a religion that first developed in the United States in 1875 (Hutton 1999). This religion, which was founded in New York City by Helena Petrovna Blavatsky and Henry Steel Olcott, claims that all religions share a common base—that is, an understanding and appreciation of the mystical. Blavatsky argues that Western religions lost much of their mysticism as they gained in bureaucratic structure. According to Blavatsky, Eastern religions more clearly display their mystical basis and hence the underpinning of all religions. Blavatsky and Olcott were instrumental in bringing Eastern mystical practices to the West. They took these practices out of their cultural context, arguing that they could be understood as much as a science as a form of spirituality (Webb 1974; Ellwood 1986).

The Hermetic Order of the Golden Dawn, a group that many consider the direct forerunner of modern Wicca, was developed by individuals influenced by both the Masonic tradition and Theosophy. The founders of the Golden Dawn asserted that their rituals and magical practices were based on recently found ancient Rosicrucian documents. Like the Theosophists before them, they claimed to place magical or occult beliefs within a scientific framework. Unlike previous Masonic orders, the Golden Dawn was open to both men and women (Hutton 1999). Two of the most famous members were Dion Fortune and Aleister Crowley (Luhrmann 1989). Like the Golden Dawn, Wicca, as initially developed by Gardner had elements of a secret society. These elements include covens being initiatory societies with three degrees of attainment indicating increased knowledge, rituals that are kept secret, and practitioners taught a series of allegedly ancient rituals and magical techniques. Within Wiccan covens in the United States, some elements of an initiatory society remain, such as the existence of three degrees of attainment or knowledge. Other aspects of an initiatory society have been eliminated or modified. Although some groups still contend that their rituals are secret, in reality few—if any— seem to be. The growth of "how-to" books by initiated Witches has resulted in there being very few, if any, secret rituals.

Although the Golden Dawn played an important role in the creation of Wicca, Hutton places equal importance on two other trends in English society: the existence of an indigenous magical tradition that remained alive through the nineteenth century and the growth of the romantic movement. Based on the extensive research of folk-lorists, Hutton concludes that cunning women and men who pre-formed magic for cures, to find lost objects, or to ensure a good harvest were common in England through the nineteenth century. These individuals were, on the whole, Christians who went to church and did not consider themselves to be practicing an alterna-tive religion. Hutton conjectures that some contemporary individu-als who claim to be hereditary Witches may be the descendants of these folk practitioners. He argues that many of the practices of these wise women and men have been incorporated into the magi-cal practices of Wicca. He notes, however, that the folk magical practices of the rural English population were not part of an organ-ized religion, and hence these people were not practicing the old religion. Nonetheless, some Witches may have a family history of magical practices, including books of charms.

Interest in magical folk practices grew in England with the devel-opment of romanticism, which looked back to traditional societies as more authentic and caring than modern industrial society. This movement also helped change the way the educated elite viewed ancient and indigenous paganism. In the early part of the nineteenth century, paganism had been perceived as an inferior religion of primi-tive peoples. Within romantic literature, to the contrary, paganism of the classical period became an object of interest and study. It is in this literature that the triple goddess—maid, mother, and crone—was conceptualized and developed. In the same literature, Pan, the god of the hunt, appeared as a major figure. Romantic literature com-bined with Theosophy's interest in pagan religions as more authentic forms of spiritual understanding resulted in the development of a new and more positive image of paganism. It was in this milieu that the English Folklore Society developed. Margaret Murray was a member of this society.

Although Gardner's rituals, mythology, and magical practices can all be seen as having roots in earlier movements, he nonetheless cre-ated something new—a religion that eventually grew, divided into sects, and was exported to all the English-speaking countries as well as to Germany, Holland, and France. Although the roots of Neo-Paganism can be found most immediately in nineteenth-century

England, the broader appeal of the religion did not manifest itself until the twentieth century, as it was in the 1960s and 1970s that the religion became a large and international movement. The religion has been changed significantly by its popularity, the development of a number of sects in England and the United States, and perhaps most importantly by its growth and transformation in the United States.

Neo-Paganism in the United States

Raymond Buckland is credited with bringing Wicca to the United States. Once on American soil, the religion was influenced by a number of features of American culture in the 1960s and 1970s, including the growing women's movement, the counterculture, the environmental movement, and American individualism. Initially, the religion in the United States, as in Britain, was composed of groups in which initiates took a vow of secrecy about their practices and rituals. Secrecy, hierarchy, and the more formal elements of ceremonial magic, which were part of Wicca in England, became less pronounced in the United States. The publication of how-to manuals in the United States, which helped to decrease if not eliminate the secrecy that marked British Wiccan covens, also resulted in the development of solitary practitioners and of covens that formed around the reading of these books. In our survey 50.9 percent of the respondents state that they are currently solitary practitioners. Although some of these individuals were undoubtedly coven trained, others were self-initiated. The development and growth of solitary practitioners has changed the face of Neo-Paganism. Groups that form after participants read books on the goddess and on creating covens also have helped to transform this new religion. These groups on the whole are less formal and less hierarchical than traditional Wiccan covens.

The link that developed in the United States between feminism and Witchcraft also has had a profound influence on this new religion. In 1968 WITCH—Women's International Conspiracy from Hell—was formed in New York City by Mary Daly and Andrea Dworkin.[7] This group, which is possibly best known for hexing the Pentagon during a protest against the United States's involvement in Vietnam, was a political group, not a religious or magical group. The hexing was part of political drama that drew media attention to their cause and was not a serious magical act. The group helped to popularize the theory that the witch trials of the early modern period were an attack on strong independent women who had continued to practice the old religion. They also reclaimed the word *witch*, redefining it as a term for rebellious, brave, and independent women. Both the reclaiming of the word and the reinterpretation of the historic witch trials helped to set the path for the development of women-only Witchcraft groups.

The Susan B. Anthony coven, the first women-only Witchcraft group, was formed in California in 1971 by Zsuzsanna Budapest, a Hungarian immigrant, and six other women. Although she claimed that she brought the religion with her from Hungary, it is clear that Budapest was influenced by other sources, including Gardner's Wicca and WITCH. In creating a feminist form of Witchcraft, Budapest took the basic structure of Gardner's rituals and mythology and changed them to exclude men. Wicca, as it came from England, requires the balancing of male and female polarities in rituals and involves the veneration of the gods and goddesses. Witchcraft as developed by Budapest, and as it is still practiced by women-only groups, acknowledges the goddess to the exclusion of the gods, or god force. Polarity is not viewed as necessary—or even desirable—for rituals (Eller 1993).

Budapest viewed Witchcraft as a feminist form of spirituality that directly attacks what she defines as patriarchal religions. From the WITCH manifesto Budapest took and further developed the mythology of an ancient, pre-Christian pagan religion in which the goddess was worshiped in her triple aspect, women were the central organizers, and all people lived in concert with one another (Eller 1993). Budapest's vision might have remained obscure and confined to the West Coast of the United States if it were not for her arrest and conviction for fortune telling, which brought her national attention when the story was picked up by the press. *MS.* magazine presented her as a martyr for feminist spirituality. Publication of her book *The Holy Book of Women's Mysteries* in 1979 furthermore made her coven's teachings available to women throughout the English-speaking world (Griffin 2003).

Budapest was a major figure in the creation of what came to be called Dianic, or separatist, Witchcraft, but she was not alone. Women in her original coven were also part of this movement, as were other women throughout the United States who independently created links between feminism and Wicca (Eller 1993). For example, Ruth Rhiannon Barrett, one of the women in Budapest's original coven, created Circle of Aradia, which provides classes and open rituals to women in the general public. In Wisconsin the Reformed Congregation of Goddess-International (RCG) was formed in 1984 to provide women with training in goddess spirituality. Today the RCG furnishes training in seven states and Washington, D.C., for women who want to become priestesses in the Dianic tradition (Griffin 2003).

Dianics are a small percentage of Witches and Neo-Pagans but have had an important influence on the development of the religion in the United States and abroad through their emphasis on the links between feminism and Witchcraft. Traditional Wicca as presented by Gardner had within it both the seeds of questioning traditional gender roles and the incorporation of an essentialist and romanticized notion of womanhood and manhood. It was in the United States that this religion became more clearly and openly feminist. Many of the people attracted to this religion were women seeking a female face to the Divine as part of their feminism. Some of these women became Dianics; others joined more traditional covens that were inclusive of men and women.

Starhawk, the most widely read Witch in the English language, serves as an important bridge between more traditional Wicca and Dianics because she incorporates both strains into her vision of the religion. Her first book, *The Spiral Dance* (1979), which provides rituals, information on forming and running covens, and the mythology of the new religion, is one of the first books on practicing Witchcraft. Unlike the Dianics, Starhawk is not a separatist. The group she helped to found in San Francisco is inclusive of both men and women. Her popular books have helped to influence the Witchcraft movement in the United States and ultimately throughout the English-speaking world. Starhawk not only incorporates a strong feminist perspective, which places greater emphasis on the goddess than the god force, but also advocates direct political action for environmental, gay and lesbian, and women's issues (Hutton 1999).

Although there are links between inclusive and women-only Witchcraft groups, tensions also exist. Some individuals who practice traditional Wicca object to the elimination of polarity within women-only groups. In turn, some members of women-only groups are concerned about the sexism that they believe is displayed by male Witches and Neo-Pagans (Jencson 1998). Nonetheless, there is a growing interaction among Neo-Pagan groups at festivals where they participate in each other's rituals, teach, or attend workshops on preparing rituals, running covens, or performing magic. These gatherings, which have grown in number and popularity, provide an arena for Neo-Pagans to meet one another and share information. They also provide a venue for the religion to homogenize—as individuals learn ritual and magical practices from one another—and for Neo-Pagans to question each other's and their own gender roles and life-style choices. The Internet provides another avenue for Neo-Pagans to find one another and to discuss rituals, practices, and ethical issues (H. Berger 1999a).

The women-only groups that grew out of traditional Wicca have, in turn, influenced the way in which Wicca is practiced in the United States and to a lesser degree in the rest of the English-speaking world. Nonetheless, women-only groups remain distinct from inclusive groups by focusing on the mythology of a matriarchal prehistory, having a less formal ritual structure, and excluding men. Other traditions, such as that of the Druids and the Odinists, also distinguish themselves from Wiccans or Dianics by re-creating the pagan practices of a particular European country or region.

On the Margins of Neo-Paganism

Because Neo-Paganism is an amorphous religion in which there are no clear criteria of membership, it is difficult to speak of anyone or any group who claims membership as being outside the religion. Nonetheless, in speaking about their religion, most Neo-Pagans distinguish themselves from Satanists, New Agers, and those who are intolerant of diversity. For that reason we are surprised to find a small percentage of respondents who identify themselves as Satanists and New Agers. Among Neo-Pagans whose spiritual path is based on a particular European tradition, Odinists, who are also called Heathens, have raised the most controversy because a segment of this group are neo-Nazis. A closer look at these three groups, that is, Odinists, Satanists, and New Agers, will permit us to explore the margins and hence the borders of Neo-Paganism.

Odinists

Odinists venerate the Old Norse and Germanic warrior gods and fertility goddesses. Although most Odinists in the United States are not neo-Nazis or racists, there are neo-Nazi groups who self-define as Odinists. These groups are currently reviving Nazi Aryan paganism and its racial agenda. Kaplan (1996) documents the growth of Odinists in the United States and the link between one branch's history and ideology with older Nazi literature. He notes that there is a division between Odinists, who are drawn to Nazi ideology, and those who are responding to "an awakening of childhood memories," which was created by popular children's books of the 1950s and 1960s (Kaplan 1996:197). Kaplan claims that the latter are not racists and are more likely to be members of the Ásatrú Alliance.

Based on his qualitative research, Kaplan estimates that there are between five hundred and one thousand members of the Ásatrú Alliance. He notes that most Odinists are men with a college education who work in a variety of blue- and white-collar professions. We received sixty responses from individuals who identify themselves as Odinists. Our data support Kaplan's conclusions. We find that Odinists are predominately male (65 percent men and 35 percent women), which is the reverse of what we see in the larger Neo-Pagan community. The majority of Odinists in our survey reports that they have completed college, although they are somewhat less likely than other Neo-Pagans to either have completed or to be attending graduate school (19 percent of Odinists are in or have completed graduate school as compared with 26 percent of Neo-Pagans). The median income for Odinists is between twenty and thirty thousand dollars, ten thousand less than the median income of Neo-Pagans.

Harvey (1997), whose research is centered in Europe, agrees with Kaplan that there is a range of political views among Odinists. The neo-Nazis are at one end of the spectrum. Closer to the center are

Odinists who are not neo-Nazis but who still "object strongly to multi-culturalism and the blend of cultures and traditions caused by the mix of peoples in the contemporary world" (Harvey 1997:65). At the other end of the spectrum are those who view their spirituality as one among many and are opposed to any ethnic group being portrayed as superior to others. Harvey claims that although there is variation, Odinists tend to be more politically and socially conservative than other Neo-Pagans. Our research substantiates this claim, although it must be noted, as shown in chapter 2, that most Neo-Pagans are more liberal than the general American population. Therefore, although Odinists are more conservative than other Neo-Pagans, they are still relatively liberal.

In addition to asking respondents' political party affiliation, our survey includes two sets of questions about their political views, the first of which were adopted from the GSS. The first set asks respondents to comment on government spending for a series of social problems. The second set questions how strongly the respondents agree or disagree with a series of statements pertaining to gender and sexual preference equity. The most popular party affiliation is Democratic, with 43 percent of the general Neo-Pagan population and 26 percent of Odinists claiming to be registered Democrats. The second most popular designation is Independent, with 28 percent Neo-Pagans and 24 percent of Odinists in this category. Republicans are third, with 7 percent of Neo-Pagans and 15 percent of Odinists reporting that they are members of this party.

In responding to questions about government spending, Odinists on the whole support traditional liberal causes, although not as strongly as the general Neo-Pagan population. Odinists do not present themselves, in our study, as racists. For example, 36 percent of Neo-Pagans and 39 percent of Odinists claim that too little money is being spent on improving conditions of African Americans in the United States. We would expect any group that is disproportionately composed of racists to view the government as spending too much money on solving the problems of African Americans.

Similarly, on issues of sexual orientation and gender equality, Odinists report being somewhat more conservative than the general Neo-Pagan population but, nonetheless, are still quite liberal.

TABLE 1: Comparison of Political Opinions of the General Neo-Pagan Population (GNPP) and Odinists on Issues of Gender Equality and Sexual Orientation

There Should Be an Equal Rights Amendment

Response	Non-Odinist GNPP %	Odinist %	No Response %
Strongly disagree	1.5	4.3	0.0
Disagree	1.2	2.9	0.0
Qualified disagree	2.0	4.3	0.0
No opinion	5.3	5.8	8.3
Qualified agree	7.7	10.1	0.0
Agree	17.1	14.5	0.0
Strongly agree	63.6	53.6	75.0
No response	1.5	4.3	16.7

Women Should Not Be Included in the Draft

Response	Non-Odinist GNPP %	Odinist %	No Response %
Strongly disagree	22.8	31.9	8.3
Disagree	20.5	20.3	16.7
Qualified disagree	17.9	11.6	8.3
No opinion	10.5	4.3	25.0
Qualified agree	9.3	11.6	8.3
Agree	7.1	5.8	0.0
Strongly agree	9.6	11.6	8.3
No response	2.4	2.9	25.0

Same-Sex Marriage Should Be Legal

Response	Non-Odinist GNPP %	Odinist %	No Response %
Strongly disagree	1.6	4.3	0.0
Disagree	0.9	2.9	0.0
Qualified disagree	0.9	1.4	0.0
No opinion	6.1	14.5	0.0
Qualified agree	5.3	4.3	8.3
Agree	24.1	24.6	16.7
Strongly agree	60.4	47.8	58.3
No response	0.7	0.0	16.7

There Should Be Preferential Hiring of Women

Response	Non-Odinist GNPP %	Odinist %	No Response %
Strongly disagree	14.1	23.2	16.7
Disagree	17.7	21.7	8.3
Qualified disagree	20.9	13.0	0.0
No opinion	7.2	14.5	8.3
Qualified agree	20.8	18.8	33.3
Agree	7.7	2.9	0.0
Strongly agree	10.4	4.3	8.3
No response	1.2	1.4	25.0

Women in the Military Should Be Included in Combat Positions

Response	Non-Odinist GNPP %	Odinist %	No Response %
Strongly disagree	4.3	1.4	0.0
Disagree	2.7	1.4	0.0
Qualified disagree	5.8	4.3	0.0

TABLE 1 (*continued*)

Women in the Military Should Be Included in Combat Positions

Response	Non-Odinist GNPP %	Odinist %	No Response %
No opinion	8.6	8.7	8.3
Qualified agree	23.0	23.2	16.7
Agree	29.6	20.3	25.0
Strongly agree	24.5	37.7	25.0
No response	1.5	2.9	25.0

There Should Be Nondiscrimination on the Basis of Sexual Preference

Response	Non-Odinist GNPP %	Odinist %	No Response %
Strongly disagree	0.8	4.3	0.0
Disagree	0.7	2.9	0.0
Qualified disagree	1.2	0.0	0.0
No opinion	2.3	1.4	0.0
Qualified agree	4.9	10.1	8.3
Agree	21.6	27.5	0.0
Strongly agree	67.4	50.7	75.0
No response	1.0	2.9	16.7

Odinists support same-sex marriage, gays in the military, and the Equal Rights Amendment (ERA), although by a smaller percentage than in the general Neo-Pagan community. Odonists give even weaker support for preferential hiring to redress previous discrimination for women than does the general Neo-Pagan population. They give stronger support, however, for women being included in the draft and women in the military being included in combat positions (see table 1). Our data on the whole supports Harvey's assertion that Odinists are more conservative than the larger Neo-Pagan community, although the difference in the United States is extremely small. Clearly, Odinists who responded to our survey are not neo-Nazis or even right wing. Nonetheless, the existence of neo-Nazi Neo-Pagans has the potential of challenging the flexibility of boundaries within this new religion. Margot Adler, a journalist and Wiccan high priestess, contends that Neo-Pagans "embrace the values of spontaneity, nonauthoritarianism, anarchism, pluralism, polytheism, animism, sensuality, passion, a belief in the goodness of pleasure, in religious ecstasy, and in the goodness of this world, as well as the possibility of many others. They have abandoned the 'single vision' for a view that upholds the richness of myth and symbol" (1986:179–80). Neo-Nazis, whether Pagan or Christian, would not embrace most of these values. Many Neo-Pagans, like the Theosophists, believe that all spiritual paths are valid and provide an avenue to the Divine. But can this belief include neo-Nazis? The general openness to difference that is celebrated by Neo-Pagans makes it difficult to create clear boundaries of who is and who is not a Neo-Pagan. The small number of neo-Nazis within the Neo-Pagan movement makes the issue unimportant at this time. But if the number of neo-Nazis grows, or if the group gains negative publicity, the issue of who is and who is not to be considered a Neo-Pagan may become more pressing.

Satanists

The link created between witchcraft and Satanism in the historic witch trials during the early modern period of Europe and colonial America continues to influence popular images of contemporary Witchcraft.[8] To counteract these images, Witches and Neo-Pagans usually differentiate themselves quite forcefully from Satanists. One respondent to our survey states: "To believe in Satan one must first believe in the Christian worldview . . . as the concept of Satan is directly related to the Judeo-Christian (and their off shoots') concepts of duality of Good vs. Evil. Satanism is therefore a subset of Christianity and not a 'Pagan' religion" (Survey 1524). Another respondent agreeing that Satanism is an offshoot of Christianity adds: "Allowing Satanists to affiliate themselves with us simply because they work magic (which many people with no connection to Paganism do) is in the end detrimental to our efforts to show the Christian dominated public that we are as selfless and spiritually benign as the rest of them. Therefore, they [Satanists] should not even be included in this and future Pagan surveys" (1558). Most of our survey participants agree with the sentiments of these two respondents. When asked if Satanism can be a valid form of Paganism, 79.9 percent of our respondents say no, with 56.6 percent strongly disagreeing. Only 12 percent state that Satanism may be a valid Neo-Pagan path, with most (6.9 percent) of those giving a qualified agreement (8.1 percent have no opinion, and 2 percent do not answer this question). One respondent who is in the minority of supporting Satanism as a valid path offers the opinion, "If we look upon Satanism as a non-valid form of Paganism or a non-acceptable religion then doesn't religious tolerance fly out the window? If we pick and choose what we feel people can believe then doesn't that make 'us' as bad as 'them,' whoever 'them' may be?" (Survey 2640). For this respondent, the openness of Neo-Pagans' boundaries is a central issue, one requiring that no spiritual path be excluded—even Satanism. We received more written comments on the issue of the appropriateness of including Satanist within the umbrella of Neo-Pagans than on any other single issue other than the survey itself. Almost all of these comments maintain that Satanism is not a valid Neo-Pagan spiritual path.

In all, we received twenty-six surveys from individuals who define themselves as Satanists, which represents only 0.01 percent of our respondents. Although those who identify themselves as Satanists are a very small minority of our sample, it is interesting that we received any responses at all from these individuals. Studies of contemporary Satanists such as LaVey's Church of Satan conclude that these groups celebrate selfishness, self-interest, and an extreme form of individualism but are neither harmful nor particularly frightening (Moody 1974; Alfred 1976; Bambridge 1978). The portrait of Satanists created by our statistics is that of a group of disproportionately young white men who are well educated, employed, and in stable relationships. The greatest percentage of this group live in urban or suburban areas. The group differentiates itself most clearly from the larger American population and even the more sexually experimental Neo-Pagan population by having 45 percent of its members self-describe as homosexual or bisexual. Like the Odinists, this group is most likely to be composed of men (65 percent of Satanist in our sample are men). The group is politically active, votes in elections, works in political campaigns, and participates in direct political action, such as protests. Satanists are as likely to be registered as Independents as they are to be Democrats (31 percent). Twelve percent of Satanists are Republicans.

Satanists express even stronger support for issues of sexual orientation or gender equity than the general Neo-Pagan population. Although such issues are difficult to gauge in our survey, we find no indication that Satanists are particularly self-interested or individualistic. For example, in response to questions about government spending, they are more likely than Neo-Pagans to support money being spent on education, the environment, and improving conditions for African Americans.

The Satanists who answered our survey may not be typical of all Satanists. Those who chose to respond to the survey are sufficiently within Neo-Pagan circles to have access to and self-identified enough with Neo-Paganism to participate in The Pagan Census. Although those Satanists who answered our survey distinguish themselves in some ways from the larger Neo-Pagan community, most notably by having more men and more homosexual members, their political and social beliefs are not appreciably different from the larger Neo-Pagan community. Our data do not permit us to say what being a Satanist means specifically to members of this group. Do they, for instance, actually worship Satan and the forces of evil? Or do they view Satan as a pagan god who has been maligned by two thousand years of Christian writings?

The New Age

The New Age and Neo-Paganism are often categorized together, as participants in both religions share a mystical worldview, an interest in rituals from other cultures—particularly those of indigenous peoples—a desire to develop their psychic abilities, a belief in the divinity of the individual, a notion of personal responsibility for the environment, and an emphasis on personal growth as developed in the Human Potential movement (York 1995; Heelas 1996). Some Neo-Pagans have entered the religion from New Age movement. As one respondent to our survey states, "I've come to explore the Pagan movement (Neo-Pagan, Wicca, etc) through an ongoing interest in the New-Age movement. It was through New Age seminars and the like that I found myself drifting to something else a little more grounded" (Survey 3019). Members of both groups tend to be interested in many of the same techniques, such as astral projection, divination, drumming, and drum making. Those involved in the New Age normally pay to learn these techniques at New Age centers, bookstores or other venues. Traditionally among Wiccans and within some other Neo-Pagan traditions, these techniques were taught for free within the coven or group. Although coven training still remains free, there are now more Witches and other Neo-Pagans who are teaching courses at occult bookstores or adult education centers for a fee. Nonetheless, the cost of these courses, on the whole, is less than similar ones at New Age centers. The differences between the two groups, however, are more significant than the cost of lessons. New Agers, unlike Neo-Pagans, do not necessarily follow the wheel of the year nor venerate alternative deities. Furthermore, there is no coven or group tradition within the New Age movement.

There are 204 respondents (9.8 percent of our sample) whose primary identification is as members of the New Age. Shoshanah Feher (1992) and James Lewis (1992) contend that asking individuals to identify themselves with the New Age movement is not useful, because many deny the label while adhering to New Age beliefs—including planetary consciousness, holistic healing, and Karma. As Lewis notes, some New Agers are dropping the label, which they believe has become viewed negatively in the press and by the general population. However, those respondents to The Pagan Census who claim to be New Agers do accept the label.

Although New Agers and Neo-Pagans can be seen as distinct groups in terms of their spiritual worldview, we find that the New Agers are very similar to Neo-Pagans demographically. New Agers differentiate themselves from New-Pagans by being somewhat less likely to be married or to have children. Among those who report having children, New Agers are less likely to claim that they are training their children to follow their spiritual path.

One respondent, who self-identifies as a member of the New Age, remarks, "I enjoy very much my involvement with the Pagan community but many of my beliefs conflict with the Pagans, specifically my 'New Age' tendencies which are really held in contempt [by

Neo-Pagans]—so I am forced to keep my mouth shut at times so as not to go against the grain" (Survey 1882).

Michael York notes that although Neo-Pagans see overlaps between their spiritual practices and those of the New Age, they also view these paths as distinct. In reviewing a survey conducted by the Pagan Spirit Alliance, he describes the negative images of the New Age presented by Neo-Pagans. "It [the New Age] is considered more expensive, more superficial (its roots being less deep), commercial, consumerist, fraudulent, spiritual marketing schemes, a Yuppie phenomenon, gameplaying for shock value, mostly Christian, more generalized, undisciplined, insensitive, ungrounded and seeking a quick fix, the instant answer" (York 1995:157). Although negative notions of the New Age exist, these are not universal among the Neo-Pagans in our survey. We asked our respondents the degree to which they agree or disagree with the statement "Witches and Pagans should actively seek connections with the 'New Age' community." As seen in table 2, we find that our respondents are almost equally split among those having no opinion, those agreeing to some degree, and those disagreeing to some degree. Slightly more (36.9 percent) of our respondents support than disapprove (30.8 percent) of links being made between Neo-Paganism and the New Age. Neo-Pagans continue to distance themselves from the New Age movement, viewing their own spiritual path as more serious, more rigorous, and more clearly differentiated from the Judeo-Christian tradition. Nonetheless, our data suggest that there is some interest among a notable portion of Neo-Pagans in exploring similarities and developing connections with the New Age movement.

A Demographic View of Neo-Pagans

The portrait of Neo-Pagans in statistical studies portray a group that is disproportionately composed of white middle-class women, although it has been noted that men participate in significant numbers as well. Our research supports this raw outline but helps to modify and develop it. Danny Jorgensen and Scott Russell (1999), Loretta Orion (1995), and Margot Adler (1986) conducted their survey research at festivals, which appear to provide a natural venue for the distribution of questionnaires. To ensure that a geographically diverse population be reached, each of these studies distributed

TABLE 2: Attitudes toward the New Age

Response	%
Strongly disagree	5.1
Disagree	11.7
Qualified disagree	14.0
No opinion	30.1
Qualified agree	19.8
Agree	11.8
Strongly agree	5.3
No response	2.2

surveys at several festivals in different parts of the United States. However, by relying on festivals for the distribution of surveys, these surveyors may have biased their samples. In our survey we find that 51 percent of respondents had not attended a festival in the previous year. Jorgensen and Russell speculate that the most committed members are the ones who attend festivals. However, our survey data indicate that men are more likely to attend festivals and to attend more of them per year than are women. We find a number of potentially important differences between those Neo-Pagans who report attending festivals and those who do not. Those who hold graduate degrees are more likely to attend festivals than those who are less educated. Never-married and legally married Neo-Pagans are less likely to attend festivals than those who are divorced, living with their lovers, or ritually married. Solitaries—that is, those who practice alone—are least likely to attend festivals while those who work in groups or with one partner are most likely to attend festivals.

Our survey received the largest return. As previously noted, we received 2,089 responses. Jorgensen and Russell distributed 2,123 surveys at eleven gatherings of which 643, approximately one-third, were returned. Orion does not disclose how many surveys she distributed at festivals throughout the United States for which she received 189 responses. Adler distributed 450 questionnaires at three festivals and received 195. Although each survey asks somewhat different questions, there are sufficient similarities to profitably compare our research to previous studies.

Age, Gender, Sexual Orientation, and Martial Status and Cohabitation

As seen in table 3, most Neo-Pagans report being between the ages of twenty and forty-nine with the greatest frequency being reported between the ages of thirty and thirty-nine. Jorgensen and Russell (1999), the only other study to report ages for Neo-Pagans, similarly find that most Neo-Pagans are between the ages of twenty-six and forty-one. The difference between our and Jorgensen and Russell's findings can be attributed to differences in the way the ages are clustered. To be consistent, we use the same age clusters as the GSS. Both our study and Jorgensen and Russell's study, however, indicate that there are more adults practicing Neo-Paganism than adolescents or people in their early twenties.

Like previous studies, we find that Neo-Pagans are disproportionately female: 64.8 percent of our sample are women, 33.9 percent are men, and 1.3 percent do not answer this question. Jorgensen

TABLE 3: Age Distribution

Age	N	%
8–9	2	0.1
10–19	72	3.6
20–29	582	29.1
30–39	685	34.3
40–49	490	24.5
50–59	157	7.9
60–69	42	2.1
70–79	4	0.2
80 and older	0	0.0
No response	56	2.7
Total	2,089	100.0

and Russell's sample is composed of 56.8 percent women, 42.3 percent men, with 9 percent not answering. Similarly, Orion's sample is composed of 58 percent females, 38 percent males, and 4 percent who identify themselves as androgynous. The disparity between men's and women's participation can be explained by more women than men being drawn to the celebration of the feminine divine. Jorgensen and Russell note that some well-known Neo-Pagans, such as Margot Adler, Dennis Carpenter, and Selena Fox, suggest that men are entering the religion at almost as high a rate as women. Some of the statistical differences between men's and women's rates of participation can be explained by the existence of all-women groups that exclude men. Our data on Wiccan groups, which are traditionally composed of women and men, indicate a disparity of participation between men and women, albeit less than in the general Neo-Pagan population. Within these groups 58.9 percent are female, 39.7 percent are male, and 1.3 percent do not answer the question. Although men do report participating in significant numbers, even in inclusive groups, they remain a minority. This is consistent with research on other religions, which indicate that women have a higher rate of religious participation than men (Chaves 1997, Wallace 1992).

Neo-Pagans have been characterized as culturally and sexually experimental. In her survey, Orion finds that 61 percent of Neo-Pagans are heterosexual, 11 percent homosexual and 28 percent bisexual. In our study we find that 67.8 percent of the population are heterosexual, 4.8 percent lesbians, 4.5 percent gay men, and 19 percent bisexual. The large number of bisexual respondents in both studies is an indication of Neo-Pagans' openness to alternatives—including sexual alternatives.

Over half of the Neo-Pagans in our sample are in stable relationships. As seen in table 4, one-third of our respondents are legally married, another 4.8 percent are handfasted (that is, ritually but not legally married), and another 13.8 percent are cohabiting. Only nine people state that they participate in a group marriage. A large number of respondents, 41.2 percent, have children. The picture drawn by these statistics is of a group whose members—although sexually experimental—are living in stable relationships and in which a large proportion of the population are parents.

TABLE 4: **Marital Status**

Status	N	%
Never married	545	26.1
Married legally	696	33.3
Married ritually	100	4.8
Live with lover	288	13.8
Divorced	318	15.2
Widow/er	20	1.0
Separated	51	2.4
Group marriage	9	0.4
Other	36	1.7
No response	26	1.2

Ethnicity and Geography

Our study, like all previous research on Neo-Paganism, finds that most Neo-Pagans are Caucasian (see table 5). The second most common designation is Native American. Because of their earth-based spirituality and polytheism, Native American spirituality is of popular interest among Neo-Pagans. This interest may result in some respondents choosing to self-define as Native American even if they are not registered with a known tribe. The Neo-Pagan movement does not have many African American or Latina/Latino participants. African Americans and Latinas/Latinos who are drawn to magical polytheistic religions usually join Yorba (or, as it is also called, Santeria), an Afro-Caribbean religion. There are attempts among Neo-Pagans to reach out to members of both the Yorba and Voodoo communities. These attempts have met with some success, but on the whole all three religions remain distinct and separate.

Like previous studies, we find that the largest proportion of Neo-Pagans lives in metropolitan areas. Orion reports that 81 percent of her sample live in urban or suburban areas. Because previous studies indicate that Neo-Pagans are primarily urbanites or suburbanites, Jorgensen and Russell do not include a question about residential

TABLE 5: Race

Race	N	%
White	1,896	90.8
African American/Black	5	0.2
Asian	5	0.2
Native American	19	0.9
Hispanic or Latino	15	0.7
Other	50	2.4
No response	99	0.2

area. About half of our respondents are urban or suburban dwellers. A considerable proportion (16.6 percent) reports that they live either in a secluded area or in a rural community. Another 13.5 percent describe their place of residence as a large town. Residential patterns of Neo-Pagan are reflective of those of other Americans, most of whom live in greater metropolitan areas. Although our study does not negate the view that Neo-Paganism is largely an urban and suburban phenomenon, it does suggest that Neo-Paganism is not a religion that is shunned by those who live close to nature, which is suggested frequently.

Neo-Pagans report living throughout the United States. Multiple formats can be used to divide the country and the states into regions. We follow the format used by the GSS, so that we can compare not only differences among Neo-Pagans but also how those differences correspond to the regional ones reported in the GSS. The nine regions used by the GSS with the states that are included in each region in rank order and with the percentage of respondents we received from each are:

1. Pacific: Alaska, California, Hawaii, Oregon, and Washington (22.8 percent)
2. South Atlantic: Delaware, Florida, Georgia, Maryland, North Carolina, South Carolina, Virginia, West Virginia, Washington, D.C. (16.7 percent)

3. East North Central: Illinois, Indiana, Michigan, Ohio, Wisconsin (14.6 percent)
4. New England: Connecticut, Maine, Massachusetts, New Hampshire, Rhode Island, Vermont (13.5 percent)
5. Middle Atlantic: New Jersey, New York, Pennsylvania (12.8 percent)
6. Mountain: Arizona, Colorado, Idaho Montana, Nevada, New Mexico, Utah, Wyoming (7.8 percent)
7. West South Central: Arkansas, Louisiana, Oklahoma, Texas (5.8 percent)
8. West North Central: Iowa, Kansas, Minnesota, Missouri, Nebraska, North Dakota (3.9 percent)
9. East South Central: Alabama, Kentucky, Mississippi, Tennessee (2.3 percent)

Although Neo-Pagans live throughout the United States, some areas have a larger density of Neo-Pagans.

Socioeconomic Characteristics

The median income level of our respondents is between $30,001 and $40,000. This level is equivalent to the national average for the United States, which since 1989 has been in the mid-$30,000 a year range (United States Census Bureau 2001). This average is somewhat surprising, because Neo-Pagans on the whole have higher education levels than the general American population. Only 7.8 percent of Neo-Pagans report having a high school education or less. This education level can be compared with the general American population in which 51 percent have no more than a high school education (Jorgensen and Russell 1999:332). Scholars who previously note this disparity between educational attainment and income among Neo-Pagans suggest that they are underemployed, possibly because of their greater interest in self or spiritual development than in career advancement. However, another interpretation is possible. Both nationally and in our survey, women, on the average, earn less than men. The median income of women in our survey is between $20,001 and $30,000, as compared with men, whose income is $40,001 to $50,000. The greater proportion of women within the religion helps to explain at least some of the apparent

TABLE 6: Education Level

Level	N	%
Less than high school	50	2.4
High school diploma	113	5.4
Some college	531	25.4
College diploma	534	25.6
Professional or technical school	243	11.6
Postgraduate work	239	11.4
Postgraduate degree	333	15.9
Other	33	1.6
No response	13	0.6

disparity between education level and income. Furthermore, we find that 16 percent who answered the question list their primary occupation as student, the most commonly chosen occupational listing. Another 7.4 percent list their primary occupation as homemaker. Both students and homemakers would be expected to have no or low incomes (see table 7).

The second most popular employment designation is a professional within the computer industry. This response corresponds to Adler's and Jorgensen and Russell's findings. Orion, to the contrary, finds most Neo-Pagans to be in the healing or helping professions. Although these professions rank much lower in our results, if added together, therapists, nurses and social workers are the third most common designation. There does not, however, appear to be a clear pattern of Neo-Pagans in the healing professions in our data. Other professions could just as easily be grouped together to give a very different picture; for example, professions that use creative arts or that require the use of mathematics.

Marginal Religion: Mainstream Participants

Some scholars eschew the term *new religion* and instead suggest that religions, such as Neo-Paganism, be referred to as *marginal religions* or what Robert Ellwood (1979) calls *excursus religions*. The

TABLE 7: Occupation

Rank	Occupation	N	Nearest whole %
1	Student/Graduate student	192	16
2	Computer (mgr./prog./analyst)	118	10
3	Editor/Writer, etc.	91	8
4	Homemaker/Housewife/Mother	88	7
5	Teacher/Professor	87	7
6	Artist	52	4
7	Counselor/Therapist/Psychologist	47	4
8	Registered nurse	46	4
9	Administrator/Assistant	40	3
10	Business owner/Self-employed	38	3
11	Secretary	37	3
12	Sales	36	3
T13	Clerk	35	3
T13	Retired	35	3
15	Cook/Chef	25	2
16	Unemployed	24	2
17	Owner, Wiccan Supplies	23	2
18	Librarian	22	2
T19	Director (orgs.)	20	2
T19	Massage therapist	20	2
21	Customer service	19	2
T22	Accountant	18	2
T22	Social worker	18	2
24	Graphic artist/Designer	17	1
T25	Engineer	16	1
T25	Office administrator	16	1
T25	Technician	16	1

alternative terminology is used to deemphasize the age of the religion and instead focus on the religion's status as outside the mainstream. As shown in this chapter, Neo-Paganism, which has its origins in England, developed from several spiritual and intellectual traditions within the West, including a history of Masonic lodges, occult or magical practices, the romantic movement in art and literature, and an interest in folklore and indigenous cultures. The religion gained its first adherents in the United States among feminists, environmentalists, and those searching for alternative spiritual experiences during the late 1960s and early 1970s. In return, the religion has been transformed in the United States, influenced by the movements from which it drew adherents and by American individualism. The religion is continuing to draw new members, particularly among the young. Despite having its origins within several strands of Western culture and tradition, Neo-Paganism is a marginal religion, one that counters the style of worship, practices, and beliefs that are common in mainline churches and synagogues.

The image of participants in this new religion painted by our demographic data is of a group that is not outside the mainstream. Participants are highly educated, primarily white, and disproportionately female. A large proportion is composed of undergraduate or graduate students. Most Neo-Pagans are in stable relationships, and over 40 percent are parents. Neo-Pagans work in a variety of occupations, although they are most likely to be computer programmers or analysts. Half of all Neo-Pagans live in greater metropolitan and suburban areas, but the other half live in towns or rural settings. Neo-Paganism is a minority religion, but its adherents, as we have shown, are demographically mainstream.

2

MAGIC, MYSTICISM, AND POLITICS

Bumper stickers and pins sold by merchants at Neo-Pagan festivals declare, "The Goddess is alive and magic is afoot." Magic is central to Neo-Pagan spiritual practices and worldview. It is integrated into rituals, images of the Divine, and Neo-Pagan interpretations of daily life. Neo-Pagan magical practices and beliefs elicit both fear and cynicism by those outside the religion: fear that Neo-Pagans can use magic to harm others and cynicism that Neo-Pagans are fleeing from the pragmatics of daily life, particularly political involvement, into a fantasy world of magic. Although Neo-Pagan magical practices are in some ways unique, many of their beliefs and practices are part of a more general occult underground that permeates American society. Horoscopes in daily newspapers, the availability of tarot card readings, and belief in extra sensory perception are common phenomena. As Andrew Greeley asserts, mysticism has gone mainstream (1985).

To ascertain the degree to which Neo-Pagans' belief in the mystical is consistent with the beliefs of the larger American population, we include in our survey questions on paranormal beliefs and on views of the afterlife from the GSS. Although paranormal experiences are commonly reported in the United States, we find, not surprisingly, that Neo-Pagans are more likely to report having these experiences than other Americans. However, we also find that participation in a magical worldview does not result in Neo-Pagans fleeing from political involvement. A comparison of responses to questions from the GSS on political attitudes and activities indicates that Neo-Pagans are more politically active than the average American.

Neo-Pagans and Magical Beliefs

The fear that witches can and do harm their neighbors is historically common in many cultures. The spread of scientific rationalism is credited with the elimination of witch trials in the West.[1] A number of scholars suggest that the elite who controlled the courts ended the trials when they came to believe that scientific laws could not be superceded by magic, hence the accounts of the alleged witches' acts were apocryphal (Easlea 1980; Thomas 1971). Although the trials ended, the belief in witches who can harm their neighbors continues. Throughout the twentieth century there have been recurring news stories of individuals, usually women, accused by their neighbors of harming them through witchcraft (de Blécourt 1999). One such story tells of how Brandi Blackbear, a fifteen-year-old Wiccan high school student in Union Public Schools near Tulsa, Oklahoma, was suspended from school in October 2000 because the principal believed she used magic to harm one of her teachers (Fenwick 2000). Although the spread of scientific rationalism was expected to assign the belief in the efficacy of witchcraft and magic to folklore or to the superstitions of the uneducated and ill-informed, this has not occurred. Both the fear that witches are capable of magically harming others and the belief in the paranormal are commonplace in the United States, and not solely, or even primarily, among the uneducated.

Neo-Pagans claim magic is real and it works, although they are quick to add that they do not participate in magically harming others. Among Neo-Pagans, there is a strong ethic against using magic to harm others. The Wiccan Rede, which is known as the only rule all Witches must follow, states, "Do as thou will as long as thou harms none." Most Neo-Pagans, furthermore, believe in the rule of three-fold return—that is, the positive *or negative* magical energy you send out will return to you with three times the force. Ethical concerns about the practice of magic (such as whether helping one person injures another or casting a spell to save an ill person's life results in needlessly prolonging his or her suffering) are regularly raised in Neo-Pagan groups and journals and on the Internet.

Most magical workings are related to helping one's friends, associates, and family or the larger community. For example, magical workings are regularly performed to help someone find an apartment, job, or lover or to help the larger community by bringing rain during a drought or to protect the rain forest. The most popular form of magic is healing, whether the object is oneself, others, or the environment. Vivianne Crowley (2000) notes that by focusing on healing, Neo-Pagans can show not only their magical powers but also their willingness and ability to do benevolent acts. For most Neo-Pagans, magic includes creating changes through nonscientifically recognized methods, such as sending magical or healing energy or using the mind to will a change. Herbs, candles, chants, and amulets are also used in magical practices, although on the whole these aids are believed to help the magical practitioner in focusing her or his mental energies and not viewed as the actual cause of the magical changes.

Magic involves more than a set of spells: it is a worldview or manner of understanding reality. One respondent to our survey states, "Spiritually I am seeking ecstatic forms of awareness and other meaningful kinds of experience. This could be an intense, powerful ritual or just a deep interpersonal exchange among fellow Pagans or merely a satisfying meditation, perhaps on a scene of natural beauty. I, thus, hope to achieve a significant connection with the deepest levels of living and being. Magic-working and witchcraft are part and parcel of this for me" (Survey 1875).

Magic for Neo-Pagans, as the above quote suggests, involves both creating desired changes in the world and having mystical experiences. Robert Wuthnow defines mysticism as involving "meditation, introspection . . . intense transcendent experiences . . . an interest in noncognitive ways of knowing, such as experiencing nature or experiencing the body" (1978:84). The magical worldview of Neo-Pagans meets all these criteria. Neo-Pagan mysticism is not world rejecting. Earthly pleasures, including the body and sexuality, are to be celebrated, not avoided or ignored.

Neo-Pagans seek mystical experiences through rituals—drumming, dancing, chanting, and meditating—and in sweat lodges or through other techniques. By using these techniques, Neo-Pagans hope to have a direct experience of the Divine or of infinity. Some speak of being in the presence of the goddess or a particular goddess or god, while others speak of a powerful presence or sense of the infinite when in altered states of consciousness. At times they believe they are given messages from the Divine, including specific warnings about things to be aware of in the immediate future, things they need to change in their lives, or changes they should help bring about in the world, such as fighting to protect the environment. These messages may come while the participant is in a trance, taking part in a ritual, or during her or his daily routines. Unexpected or unplanned events, such as being delayed for an appointment due to one's car breaking down, may be seen as an indication that one is meant to be somewhere else or to be doing something else.

Within the magical worldview of Neo-Pagans, things do not happen by accident but are part of a larger web of interconnected reality. Phenomena that might be defined as serendipitous are normally viewed by Neo-Pagans as part of this web. Meeting friends who one did not know would be in a strange city is viewed as a magical occurrence, not just a happy coincidence. Daily life, therefore, becomes embedded with meaning. For some religious Christians, similar events might be viewed as divine providence. But Neo-Pagans go a step further, positing that people—through directing their wills or thoughts—can effect these seemingly coincidental occurrences. All people, according to Neo-Pagans, have the power to perform magic. But those, like themselves, who are magically trained are more likely to be successful. They point to phenomena, like someone thinking of another person only to have that person call, as a form of everyday magic in which we all have participated.

Some Neo-Pagans claim they are unsure how magic works but that they know that it does because they have experienced it. This claim is usually the result of a change attributed to participation in a magical ritual. For example, they have performed a magical working for someone's recovery, and the person beat the medical odds and improved or was healed more quickly than predicted by her or his doctors. For others, the magical component of the universe can be seen in things occurring serendipitously. Tanya Luhrmann (1989) contends that the training of Witches and other magical practitioners results in their learning to interpret daily events in a new, more magical fashion. Occurrence that in the past would have been interpreted as coincidences are reinterpreted as magical events.

Within sociological and anthropological literature, magic is traditionally viewed as distinct from religion, as the former is based on manipulation of deities, demons, spirits, or elements of the universe solely to achieve specific ends. Religion, to the contrary, is viewed as the worship of the Divine and an attempt to give larger meaning to reality in which prayers are requests for help, not demands (Durkheim 1965; Malinowski 1954). Magic as it is conceived by Neo-Pagans, however, is an element of their religious experience and is not separate from it. As an experiential religion, the mystical occurrences and the feeling of a direct connection with the Divine that are part of their magical acts are simultaneously an essential part of religion and an attempt to effect change. Síân Reid notes, "Although the ends are desired, it is nonetheless the process of becoming magical and performing magic that is of the greatest significance [for Neo-Pagans]" (1996:145).

Neo-Pagans claim that magic is either based on undiscovered scientific phenomena or will be explained within the new paradigm of quantum mechanics (H. Berger 1994; Luhrmann 1989). As one respondent to the The Pagan Census states, "I consider my beliefs to be spiritual/scientific. I'm not into a lot of ceremony or rituals but believe in the power of the mind and energy [and] that we have tapped very little of it" (Survey 1980). Neo-Pagans believe that rituals, candles, and other paraphernalia used in magic are props to help the mind focus its energy to perform magic (Starhawk 1982; Lurhmann 1989). Magic is viewed as an alternative or occult science. The occult, which literally means hidden knowledge, is a belief in the existence of knowledge that is presently outside the realm of traditional science but which, nonetheless, can be learned and used to create outcomes by the knowledgeable.

Many contemporary occult beliefs have their origins in the Renaissance (Shumaker 1972). Belief in horoscopes, laying on of hands, communication with the dead, premonitions, alternative forms of healing have all existed in the United States since the colonial period. European settlers brought these beliefs from their countries of origin (Beslaw 1992; Butler 1979). Interaction with Native Americans helped to infuse European occult beliefs and practices with some new elements (Cave 1992). Further waves of immigration and the forced migration of Africans during the era of slavery also brought new occult practices to the United States (Butler 1986; Patten 1992; Piersen 1992). Although many of these occult beliefs were at odds with the religious doctrines of mainline churches, individuals throughout American history both participated in occult practices and continued to attend their traditional churches.

The popularity of occult beliefs has waxed and waned throughout American history, but has never completely disappeared. During the first half of the twentieth century occult beliefs were less prominent than they are today. However, during the late eighteenth century through the nineteenth century, the importation of mesmerism and Swedenborgianism from Austria and Germany respectively helped to fuel an interest in occult. Both religions, which were founded by men with scientific backgrounds, held out the promise of providing a science of spiritual life (Webb 1974).

The notion of a scientific basis for mystical experiences and beliefs was further developed by Theosophy, which, as mentioned in the first chapter, influenced the development of Wicca in England. Spiritualists, who claimed to communicate with the dead, and Christian Science, which has faith healing as a central component of its religious tenets, were also influential in this era. These religions helped to create a cultural milieu in which magic, paranormal events, and belief in spirits became more acceptable. This milieu both helped to create the fertile ground in which Wicca could take hold when it was imported to the United States and contributed to the spread of occult beliefs and practices throughout the American population. It is this cultural milieu that helps to account for the similarity of occult or paranormal experiences between Neo-Pagans and the general American population. This similarity, while striking, should not be exaggerated. In comparing Neo-Pagans' paranormal experiences and their images of the afterlife, we find notable differences as well as similarities with the general American public.

Paranormal Experiences

To compare Neo-Pagans with the general American population, we include five questions on paranormal experiences from the GSS in The Pagan Census.[2] In this set of questions individuals are asked, "How often have you had any of the following experiences?"

1. Thought you were somewhere you had been before, but knew that it was impossible.
2. Felt as though you were in touch with someone when they were far away from you.
3. Saw events that happened at great distance as they were happening.
4. Felt as though you were really in touch with someone who had died.
5. Felt as though you were very close to a powerful, spiritual force that seemed to lift you out of yourself.

Respondents were provided with four alternative answers: never in my life, once or twice, several times, and often. A comparison of the responses received by the GSS and by us are presented in table 8. These data suggest that Neo-Pagans are more likely than the general American population to have had each of the five experiences described in the questions at least once and to have had these experiences more often. For example, on the first question only 6.2 percent of all Neo-Pagans claim they had not experienced being someplace before but knew it was impossible that they were there, as compared with 33.6 percent of the general American population. However, the majority of Americans (64.8 percent) did have this experience at least once. Similarly, the majority of Americans (61.2 percent) states that they have experienced being in touch with someone who was at a distance. Although Neo-Pagans are more likely than other Americans to say that they believe they saw events happen at a great distance as these events were happening (44.4 percent of Neo-Pagans as compared with 25.5 percent of the American public), it is an experience that happened at least once to a minority of both populations. A more pronounced difference exists between Neo-Pagans and the general American population in terms of the last two questions: being in touch with the dead and being close to a powerful force. The majority of Americans claims that they

TABLE 8: Comparison of Paranormal Experiences for Neo-Pagans and the General American Public

Thought You Were Somewhere You Had Been Before

Response	GNPP %	GSS %
Never	6.2	33.6
Once or Twice	22.1	30.7
Several Times	42.5	27.5
Often	28.1	6.6
No response	1.1	1.6
Total	100.0	100.0

Felt as Though You Were in Touch with Someone When They Were Far Away from You

Response	GNPP %	GSS %
Never	6.9	37.3
Once or twice	22.5	32.8
Several times	34.8	21.1
Often	34.7	7.3
No response	1.1	1.5
Total	100.0	100.0

Saw Events that Happened at a Great Distance as They Were Happening

Response	GNPP %	GSS %
Never	54.4	71.9
Once or twice	26.7	15.6
Several times	11.3	7.1
Often	6.4	2.8
No response	1.2	2.6
Total	100.0	100.0

Felt as Though You Were Really in Touch with Someone Who Had Died

Response	GNPP %	GSS %
Never	25.7	57.8
Once or twice	35.7	22.5
Several times	23.0	9.5
Often	14.6	4.4
No response	1.1	5.8
Total	100.0	100.0

Felt as Though You Were Very Close to a Powerful Spiritual Force

Response	GNPP %	GSS %
Never	14.4	63.8
Once or twice	24.1	16.7
Several times	28.2	8.0
Often	32.2	4.5
No response	1.1	7.0
Total	100.0	100.0

have never had these experiences, while only a few Neo-Pagans claim to have not had these experiences.

The overall greater frequency of reported paranormal experiences among Neo-Pagans can be explained by two factors. First, individuals who have had these experiences are more likely to be drawn to Neo-Paganism. It is common for Neo-Pagans to state that they "feel they are returning home" when they first learn about the religion. Finding a group that acknowledges and nurtures mystical and paranormal experiences is part of what Neo-Pagans mean when they experience a feeling of coming home. Second, magical training through covens, books, workshops, or informally through contact with other Neo-Pagans is aimed to enhance and increase paranormal experiences. Among Neo-Pagans there is an expectation that they and others around them will have these types of experiences regularly. Luhrmann (1989) defines this as learning to speak with a different rhythm, one in which there is a expectation by practitioners that they will have magical experiences.

Although Neo-Pagans are more likely to report having magical or paranormal experiences than the average American, what may be more interesting is the fact that reported paranormal experiences are so common in the general population. On one hand, as noted earlier, there is fear of the magical practices of Witches and Neo-Pagans. On the other hand, the paranormal experiences that these magical rituals help to elicit are becoming more common and accepted throughout American society.

Miracles

When asked if they believe in religious miracles, 64.4 percent of respondents to the GSS say they do (40 percent state that they definitely believe in miracles, the other 24.4 percent claim that it is probable). Only 9 percent state that they definitely do not believe in miracles.[3] Although the belief in miracles and the belief in magic are not completely equivalent, significant similarities exist. Robert Orsi's (1996) description of primarily women's devotion to Saint Jude, the saint of hopeless causes, shows a striking resemblance to magic. Saint Jude's devotees light candles, recite a set number of prayers, and carry pictures of the saint or place these pictures on their desks or in their homes. In speaking of their relationship with Saint Jude, they state that he is dependent on them to remember him, as they are dependent on him to hear their concerns and answer their wishes. The women speak of saying prayers, lighting candles, or meditating on Saint Jude's image in much the same language in which magic is spoken of by Neo-Pagans. There is an expectation by Saint Jude's devotees that if the prayers are completed, the candles lit, and the donations made to his shrine, their requests will be granted. Although in theory he can choose to ignore their pleas or find them unworthy, the language used to describe the women's relationship with the saint suggests that this is unimaginable. In casting a spell, Neo-Pagans often say, "As I will, so mote it be." Although the devotees of Saint Jude would never use these words, they do describe the devotees' expectations of having their wishes granted if they perform the right set of actions.

There are noteworthy differences between the concepts of magic and miracles. Those praying to Saint Jude, other saints, the Virgin Mary, or God are calling on a higher power to grant their wishes. The saints or the Virgin Mary is called on to intercede with God on the petitioners' behalf. Miracles are defined as outside any scientific explanation now or in the future. Magic as it is practiced by Neo-Pagans, to the contrary, is based on a notion of concentrating one's will or mental energies to enact a change. There is no need for an intermediary. Most Neo-Pagans believe that their methods ultimately will be or have been corroborated by science. For example, Dennis Carpenter, editor of the *Circle Sanctuary Newsletter*, states, "I would describe magic as the active cultivation of psi abilities. Similar to the beliefs of the parapsychologists identified by Krippner (1988)"[4] (1996:59). Parapsychology is one set of beliefs that are used by Neo-Pagans to explain magic. String theory, quantum mechanics, and other elements of the new physics are also viewed as offering a scientific explanation of the paranormal (H. Berger 1994).

Magic and miracles, although not the same, have striking similarities. In both there is a belief that the world is enchanted and that an alternative reality exists alongside the more mundane daily reality. Through uttering words, directing one's thoughts, or lighting candles, this alternative reality can be called upon to change the course of daily life. As research from the GSS suggests, belief in miracles, or at least openness to the possibility of their existing, is quite common among Americans.

The Afterlife

Most religions provide a way of interpreting and understanding death. Sociologists of religion note that the knowledge of our own death and the experience of the death of those we love and care for create a crisis of meaning. According to Peter Berger (1967), this crisis is due to death bringing into question the underlying assumption of there being an order and meaning to the universe and in everyday life. It is common for people to ask why they have been struck with a terminal illness or why their friend or child died at a young age. Being told the method through which the illness spreads, what is known about how it typically responds to treatment, or a statistical analysis of the probability of any one individual contracting this illness never fully answers the underlying question—that is, why me? Within the Judaic-Christian traditions the tenet that God has a plan that is ultimately unknowable helps to provide meaning for death, illness, and other disasters. The conviction that the dead have passed on to an afterlife provides solace to the living.

Neo-Pagans view death as part of the cycle of life. The yearly calendar marked by the eight sabbats focuses on the death and rebirth. Among groups that are inclusive of men and women, the mythology is based on the symbolic birth, maturation, and ultimate death of the horned god and the transformation of the goddess from maid to mother to crone. At Samhain the goddess takes on her crone aspect and becomes the bearer of death, and the god, now old, dies. In women-only groups the mythology focuses on Samhain as the time of the crone, the old wise woman who cuts the cord of life (Lozano and Foltz 1990). Death is viewed as both necessary for life and as a time of renewal. As Starhawk and M. Macha Nightmare note, "The heart of the Pagan understanding of death is the insight that birth, growth, death, and rebirth are a cycle that forms the underlying order of the universe. We can see that cycle manifest around us in every aspect of the natural world, from the decay of falling leaves that feed the roots of growing plants, to the moon's waning and waxing" (1997:58).

Neo-Paganism is not the only religion that views death as an essential element of life. This view, however, is radicalized within Neo-Pagan theology, or as it is also referred to, *thealogy*. Although the dead are mourned, death is celebrated, as it provides an opportunity for transformation and change. Melissa Raphael argues that this image of the goddess provides "a chaotic 'menstrual' cosmology in which the Goddess (as Cerridwen, Kali, Siris and others) generates, dissolves, and regenerates life within her churning womb/cauldron. Here the Goddess is the vortex from which all things are spun into existence and sucked back out of it" (1996:211). For Raphael the goddess as bearer of life and death becomes immune to human suffering and hence callous. She is not evil, as she does not intend harm, but nonetheless does harm some individuals in the name of ecological balance. Raphael believes it is a theological contradiction that Goddess Worshipers will ultimately need to confront. However, there is no problem for most Neo-Pagans who, like practitioners of other religions, feel no need for complete theological consistency. Furthermore, Neo-Pagans view the ambiguity of their symbols and myths as a positive—not negative—aspect of their religion.

The image of the dark goddess, combined with an emphasis on environmental and personal change and a notion of personal responsibility, establishes meaning in death for most Neo-Pagans. As Judy Harrow, a Wiccan high priestess states, "Much human suffering comes from the impersonal processes of change, which are inherent in Nature. . . . While the Crone's action, and our unthinking resistance, explain much of human suffering, they do not explain all of it. . . . Some human suffering and just about all eco-rape is caused by greed and malice" (1996:20).

The sadness of death, although acknowledged by Neo-Pagans, is further mitigated by the belief in reincarnation. In The Pagan Census 75.2 percent state that they believe in reincarnation; only 4.1 percent claim they do not believe in reincarnation (19.3 percent are unsure, and 1.2 percent do not answer this question). No question on reincarnation is included in the GSS, but according to market research completed in 1997 by Yankelovich Partners, 25 percent of Americans state they believe in reincarnation, an increase from 9 percent in 1976 (Wen 2001).

Starhawk and Nightmare describe reincarnation as "our essence, our Deep Self, is reborn, but our particular personality is wedded to a body, a gender, an ancestry, a life history. That personality will dissolve at death" (1997:99). Although this image of reincarnation is a common one among Neo-Pagans, it is not the only one. In their participant observation study of a Dianic coven with seven members, Wendy Lozano and Tanice Foltz (1990) note that most of these women do not literally accept the idea of reincarnation or the survival of the soul. In our survey two respondents describe the process of reincarnation of the body and its energies returning to nature but are not sure if the soul or essence of an individual survives. To quote one of these respondents: "Our bodies break apart and become part of mother earth. Our energy and substance becomes part of something else. I am open to the idea [that] the spirit may live on in some other form—but I've no idea or direct experience to confirm [it]. And I think it is enough to be part of the life cycle" (Survey 1770).

Neo-Pagans' belief in reincarnation is not inconsistent with a notion of an afterlife, as Neo-Pagans typically contend that after death, the soul or essence of the individual goes to a resting place, often called Summerland, prior to being reborn. In describing her difficulty answering questions on the afterlife, one respondent notes, "This is hard to fill out. I realize that I don't think there is any one 'afterlife'—but that our present lives are one of many conditions and adventures that the souls may go through, or may choose. Hence my selection of some seeming contradictions" (Survey 1753). Most Neo-Pagans, like most other Americans, believe in an afterlife. In our survey 79 percent of Neo-Pagans claim they believe in an afterlife, 4.1 percent state they do not believe in an afterlife, 15.5 percent are undecided, and 1.2 percent do not answer this question. The GSS reports that 72.2 percent of their respondents claim to believe in life after death, 17.1 percent say there is no life after death, 10.3 percent are undecided, and 0.4 percent do not answer this question.[5] To ascertain the degree to which the views of Neo-Pagans and of the general American public about the afterlife correspond, we ask questions, taken directly from the GSS, concerning nine images of the afterlife. Respondents are asked if they consider these images: very likely, somewhat likely, not too likely, or not likely at all. The GSS offers a fifth alterative: don't know.[6] Table 9 provides a comparison of the results.

Although obvious differences between Neo-Pagans and the general American public exist, there is also an overall similarity in responses. On the whole the particular images of the afterlife are more likely to be viewed as probable than others by both respondents to the GSS and respondents to The Pagan Census. As part of the larger culture, Neo-Pagans are influenced by the dominant images of the afterlife. Furthermore, many Neo-Pagans adhere to the notion that images individuals have of the afterlife influence what they will experience after death. Starhawk and Nightmare note, "Because the substance of the otherworld is malleable and fluid, it can be shaped and influenced by mind. So what we create, what we expect, becomes real" (1997:80). For many Neo-Pagans, if people believe in hell, heaven, or any other vision of the afterlife, their mental energies will make these images real. Hence, traditional images of the afterlife are filled with the mental energy of generations of believers. However, only those who believe in the image will make it part of their own reality after death.

While acknowledging the similarities, it is always important to note the marked differences between Neo-Pagans and the general American public's images of the afterlife. The notion that after death there is a life of peace and tranquility is held to be either very or somewhat likely by 91.4 percent of the general American population. Although a majority of Neo-Pagans, 68 percent, similarly believes this to be very or somewhat likely, the percentage is notably lower than among the general American population. Furthermore, more Neo-Pagans respond to the weaker "somewhat likely" than "very likely." In response to the afterlife being described as "a life of intense action," Neo-Pagans are split almost evenly (46 percent) between those who think this is likely and those who think it is not likely. The majority of GSS respondents (53.8 percent) believes this to be unlikely, and only 37.2 percent of the GSS sample believe this is likely. GSS respondents are more likely than Neo-Pagans to believe the afterlife is a paradise of pleasures and delights and a union with God.[7] As most of the images of the afterlife presented in the GSS are based on Christian theology, it is not surprising that Neo-Pagans are somewhat less likely to hold these images. Clearly, Neo-Pagans form a separate spiritual group, albeit influenced by the larger American culture.

It is surprising to us that one image, that of being reunited with loved ones, is supported more weakly by Neo-Pagans than the general American population. Most (79.9 percent) Neo-Pagans claim it is very likely or somewhat likely that the afterlife involves a reunion with loved ones as compared with the general American population in which 90 percent think such a reunion is likely. The image of Summerland, or the afterlife, which is held by many Neo-Pagans, is of a place in which the deceased meets again with those who were important in his or her previous life. It is a time to reconcile differences and consolidate relationships prior to all souls moving forward into new lives.

TABLE 9: Comparison of Images of Afterlife for Neo-Pagans and the General American Public

A Life of Peace and Tranquility

Response	GNPP %	GSS %
Very likely	24.5	64.2
Somewhat likely	43.5	27.2
Not too likely	17.1	3.7
Not at all likely	7.9	1.1
No response	7.0	3.8
Total	100.0	100.0

A Life of Intense Action

Response	GNPP %	GSS %
Very likely	11.2	11.7
Somewhat likely	34.8	25.5
Not too likely	33.9	36.2
Not at all likely	12.6	17.6
No response	7.3	9.0
Total	100.0	100.0

A Paradise of Pleasures and Delights

Response	GNPP %	GSS %
Very likely	9.8	35.2
Somewhat likely	32.0	28.2
Not too likely	33.7	20.0
Not at all likely	17.2	10.6
No response	7.2	6.0
Total	100.0	100.0

Reunion with Loved Ones

Response	GNPP %	GSS %
Very likely	43.1	70.1
Somewhat likely	36.8	19.9
Not too likely	8.3	3.9
Not at all likely	5.3	2.1
No response	6.4	4.0
Total	100.0	100.0

A Pale Shadowy Life, Hardly Life at All

Response	GNPP %	GSS %
Very likely	2.8	5.1
Somewhat likely	13.3	12.7
Not too likely	28.8	26.6
Not at all likely	48.0	47.7
No response	7.1	7.9
Total	100.0	100.0

A Spiritual Life Involving Our Mind but Not Our Body

Response	GNPP %	GSS %
Very likely	41.7	45.6
Somewhat likely	33.9	28.8
Not too likely	11.1	8.6
Not at all likely	7.0	10.6
No response	6.3	6.4
Total	100.0	100.0

TABLE 9 *(continued)*

A Life Like the One Here on Earth

Response	GNPP %	GSS %
Very likely	7.7	28.6
Somewhat likely	30.5	28.6
Not too likely	31.7	21.1
Not at all likely	22.7	16.6
No response	7.4	5.1
Total	100.0	100.0

A Place of Loving Intellectual Communion

Response	GNPP %	GSS %
Very likely	33.9	51.6
Somewhat likely	42.0	33.4
Not too likely	10.7	6.2
Not at all likely	6.6	2.9
No response	6.8	5.9
Total	100.0	100.0

Union with God (or Gods and Goddesses)

Response	GNPP %	GSS %
Very likely	49.5	78.4
Somewhat likely	31.6	15.5
Not too likely	7.4	1.8
Not at all likely	5.2	0.8
No response	6.3	3.5
Total	100.0	100.0

A Life without Many Things that Make Our Present Life Enjoyable

Response	GNPP %	GSS %
Very likely	11.5	20.6
Somewhat likely	20.2	24.7
Not too likely	28.1	26.8
Not at all likely	31.6	20.3
No response	8.5	7.6
Total	100.0	100.0

Neo-Pagans are clearly differentiated from the larger American society by their magical practices, mystical experiences, and images of the afterlife. They are more likely than mainstream Americans to report having paranormal experiences and report having more of them. Their images of the afterlife are not completely consistent with other Americans. However, it is a mistake to exaggerate this difference. The paranormal or occult experiences that Neo-Pagans report, such as out-of-body experiences, interactions with the dead, déjà vu, and premonitions, are part of a more general occult belief system that is becoming increasingly common and accepted throughout American culture. Neo-Pagans are a distinct spiritual and religious group, but one whose beliefs and practices have been influenced by one strain of American culture and history—that is, a belief in the occult and in the existence of an alternative reality.

Politics

In *Experimentation in American Religion*, Robert Wuthnow (1978) argues that there are two schools of thought within sociology about the relationship between mystics and political activity. The first and more popular, which was first put forth by Max Weber and his student, Ernst Troeltsch, view mysticism as antithetical to political activity. The second view, to the contrary, argues that mysticism can stimulate political action. Wuthnow, summarizing Weber and Troeltsch's argument, states that they provide six reasons mystics do not become politically involved.

1. Mystics seek salvation in contemplation and meditation and not in worldly activities.
2. The ethics of universal or cosmic love precludes mystics' involvement in the practical and partisan activities required by politics.
3. Mysticism is a private or personalistic form of religion, which is not conducive to political activity.
4. The emphasis on harmony results in mystics restricting their social relationship to others with the same worldview, a behavior that is counterproductive to politics.
5. Mystics are more interested in answers to transcendental questions than they are in meeting the challenges of daily life.
6. An emphasis on peace and the unity of all people results in mystics being unwilling to participate in political activity, which by its nature is contentious. (1978:79–81)

Those sociologists who disagree with Weber and Troeltsch's conclusions note two tendencies that they believe may increase mystics' involvement in politics. One, because mystics maintain that all authority rests with the individual, there is a tendency for moral relativism to develop. When this relativism comes in conflict with injustice and intolerance, mystics may be motivated to engage in political dissent. Two, there is a tendency toward liberalism among mystics, as all social arrangements are viewed as social constructs. Finding social forces restrictive, mystics may work to change those social realties (Wuthnow 1978).

Neo-Pagans have been viewed through both images of the relationship between mysticism and politics. The religion alternatively has been perceived as encouraging a withdrawal from political activity and as increasing participants' political participation. The concern that goddess worship will result in women's withdrawal from politics has been voiced by some feminists who claim that women's spirituality is a form of escapism that results in women worshiping the female divine instead of fighting for women's political rights. Cynthia Eller most recently presents this view in disputing the usefulness for feminism of the mythology of a prehistoric matriarchy— a mythology that is particularly important to women-only groups. She argues that "if this nostalgia enables those who experience it to imagine a different future and take steps to secure it, then it is functional. But nostalgia is rarely this functional, or rather, its function is usually escapist" (Eller 2000:183). Based on her interviews with one hundred Neo-Pagans throughout the United States, Margot Adler (1986) claims that most Neo-Pagans define themselves as apolitical and believe that while individual Neo-Pagans are free to express their political views, the religion is and should be separate from politics.

To the contrary, Graham Harvey (1997) argues that environmental activism is an outgrowth of Neo-Pagans' celebration of the earth as sacred. Although his study was conducted in the United Kingdom and Iceland, he also refers to the work of Starhawk and her group in the San Francisco Bay area, The Reclaiming Collective, which is noted for its political activism. Members of The Reclaiming Collective have participated in a number of protests for issues, including social justice, gay rights, women's rights, and environmental causes. Although Nancy Finley's (1991) study of 35 women who are involved in goddess worship is too small a sample to be conclusive, it does suggest that women's participation in goddess spirituality results in increased political participation. In his study of spiritual beliefs and activities among men and women in the San Francisco Bay area, Wuthnow (1978) finds that contemporary mysticism resulted in increased political participation. Our survey indicates that Neo-Pagans are politically active, but that they do not trust the political and social institutions in which they participate. Neo-Pagans' self-definition as apolitical in Adler's (1986) study may have more to do with their criticism of conventional social and political institutions than a reflection of their actual behavior.

Political Participation

Table 10 shows the extent of political participation of Neo-Pagans in traditional political activities, such as voting, campaigning, writing letters to legislators, and participating in protests. Because feminist scholars have questioned the effect of goddess worship on women's political participation, this table also provides a comparison of Neo-Pagan women's and men's political activities. As demonstrated in the table, although Neo-Pagan women are somewhat more politically active than Neo-Pagan men, both are politically active.

TABLE 10: Political Activity Divided by Gender

Registered to Vote

Response	GNPP %	Women %	Men %
No	11.4	9.4	15.3
Yes	87.8	90.6	83.8
No response	0.8	0.6	1.0

Voted in Last National Election

Response	GNPP %	Women %	Men %
No	16.2	15.1	18.6
Yes	70.9	72.1	68.4
No response	12.9	12.8	13.0

Voted in Last State Election

Response	GNPP %	Women %	Men %
No	27.4	27.6	27.1
Yes	58.8	58.6	59.2
No response	13.7	13.7	13.7

Voted in Last Local Election

Response	GNPP %	Women %	Men %
No	36.2	37.3	34.2
Yes	49.5	48.7	51.0
No response	14.3	14.0	14.8

Write Letters to Federal Legislators

Response	GNPP %	Women %	Men %
No	45.0	45.4	45.2
Yes	49.1	50.2	46.3
No response	5.9	4.4	8.5

Write Letters to State Legislators

Response	GNPP %	Women %	Men %
No	49.7	62.2	59.6
Yes	44.1	31.9	30.9
No response	6.2	5.9	9.4

Write Letters to Local Government

Response	GNPP %	Women %	Men %
No	61.2	62.2	59.6
Yes	31.6	31.9	30.9
No response	7.2	5.9	9.4

Participate in Grassroots Local Organizing

Response	GNPP %	Women %	Men %
No	67.5	69.3	64.8
Yes	24.8	24.4	24.7
No response	14.3	6.3	10.5

Participate in Town Meetings, Hearings, Forums, and Open Meetings

Response	GNPP %	Women %	Men %
No	67.4	70.0	62.3
Yes	24.9	23.5	27.8
No response	7.7	6.5	9.9

Participate in Special Events

Response	GNPP %	Women %	Men %
No	48.3	46.4	52.4
Yes	45.7	49.2	38.6
No response	6.0	4.4	9.0

TABLE 10 *(continued)*

Public Spokesperson for Causes of Personal Concern

Response	GNPP %	Women %	Men %
No	76.9	79.0	73.6
Yes	14.6	14.0	15.0
No response	8.5	7.0	11.4

Active Lobbier

Response	GNPP %	Women %	Men %
No	86.9	89.4	82.6
Yes	3.9	3.2	5.2
No response	9.1	7.5	12.1

Active in Campaigning

Response	GNPP %	Women %	Men %
No	83.1	84.4	81.2
Yes	8.2	8.4	7.3
No response	8.7	7.1	11.3

Hold/Have Held Public Office

Response	GNPP %	Women %	Men %
No	88.9	90.9	85.2
Yes	1.9	1.6	2.5
No response	9.2	7.6	12.3

A large percentage of Neo-Pagans are registered to vote and do vote, particularly in national elections. In The Pagan Census 70.9 percent state that they voted in the last national election, 58.8 percent in the last state election, and 49.5 percent in the last local election.

Neo-Pagan women are more likely to be registered to vote than men (90 percent of women and 84.8 percent of men were registered to vote). Neo-Pagan women are also more likely to vote in national elections but less likely to participate in state and local elections than men.

A large number of Neo-Pagans state they participate in some political activity beyond voting, although women are somewhat more likely to do so than men. The types of political activities that Neo-Pagans participate in differ somewhat by gender. Women are notably more likely to participate in special events, defined as marches and rallies, than are men (49.2 percent of women and 36.8 percent of men). However, both are remarkably more likely to participate in these activities than the general American population. The GSS asks respondents if in the last three or four years they attended any political meetings or rallies. Only 19 percent say they had, 80.4 percent say they had not, and 0.7 percent do not answer this question.[8] In comparison, 45.7 percent of Neo-Pagans say they participated in special events such as marches or rallies. In response to the GSS question asking if they would participate in a protest march or demonstration, about one-fifth of the GSS sample (20.8 percent) say that they definitely would, and another 23.3 percent say they would probably march or demonstrate. A larger percentage say they would not go on a protest march or demonstration, 27.9 percent say they would probably not, and 22.9 percent state they definitely would not. Three percent say they cannot choose, and 2.1 percent do not answer this question.[9] This question is hypothetical, and of course cannot measure what individuals would actually do when confronted with the possibility. Nonetheless, a notably smaller percentage of the general American population believe they would definitely go on a march or demonstration than the percentage of Neo-Pagans who claim that they have participated in this type of activity.

Although very few Neo-Pagans report holding public office, men are about twice as likely as women to report having held office. Only 4 percent of all Neo-Pagans report being active lobbiers, but men are more likely than women to report participating in this activity. Men are also more likely to report participating in town meetings than women. Women are slightly more likely to report being active in campaigns and to be spokespersons for causes than men. Women are also slightly more likely to report writing letters to their local, state, and federal legislators than men. Neo-Pagans, however, on the whole report being active letter writers. Although the aforementioned questions are not included in the GSS, it poses a similar question: "Have you done (other) work for one of the parties or candidates in most elections, some elections, only a few or have you never done such work?" The majority, 72.5 percent, says that they never did any such work; 2.6 percent says that they did such work in most elections—9.7 percent in some elections, 14.9 percent in only a few elections.[10]

Neo-Pagans report being politically active. The majority of Neo-Pagans reports being registered and voting, particularly in national elections. They also report being active in political marches and demonstrations and in writing letters to their legislators. To a lesser degree, Neo-Pagans report being active in other political activities, including holding office, working in grassroots organizations, and campaigning. Although the rates of participation reported by men and women vary somewhat, both Neo-Pagan men and women are politically active. Like those in Wuthnow's sample, Neo-Pagans' involvement in mysticism appears to stimulate, not deter, political involvement.

Political Attitudes

We use three sets of questions to determine Neo-Pagans' political attitudes: One set requests that respondents comment on whether they believe the United States government is spending too much, the right amount, too little, or if they do not know on a series of social programs. These questions, for comparative purposes, are taken directly from the GSS. Two, we ask the respondents to state their degree of agreement or disagreement with a series of questions related to issues of women's rights and gay and lesbian rights. Three, we ask respondents on a seven-point scale the degree to which they have confidence in a series of social institutions. As with the first set of questions, this set is taken from the GSS. The picture painted of Neo-Pagans from these statistics is of a group that is politically liberal but who has little trust in social institutions.

TABLE 11: Comparison of Neo-Pagans' and the General American
Public's Attitudes toward Government Spending

Space

Response	GNPP %	GSS %
Too much	35.6	47.6
Right amount	22.3	36.9
Too little	27.8	8.4
Don't know	11.1	6.8
No response	3.2	0.3
Total	100.0	100.0

Environment

Response	GNPP %	GSS %
Too much	1.3	9.3
Right amount	4.2	29.2
Too little	92.0	55.7
Don't know	0.8	4.5
No response	1.7	0.6
Total	100.0	100.0

Health

Response	GNPP %	GSS %
Too much	6.9	7.5
Right amount	9.9	17.1
Too little	73.4	71.5
Don't know	7.2	3.3
No response	2.5	0.6
Total	100.0	100.0

TABLE 11 *(continued)*

Big Cities

Response	GNPP %	GSS %
Too much	8.9	11.5
Right amount	12.4	21.9
Too little	54.0	53.7
Don't know	21.8	12.0
No response	2.9	0.9
Total	100.0	100.0

Crime

Response	GNPP %	GSS %
Too much	14.7	4.9
Right amount	15.2	20.4
Too little	49.8	70.5
Don't know	17.0	3.6
No response	3.3	0.6
Total	100.0	100.0

Drug Addiction

Response	GNPP %	GSS %
Too much	19.1	7.9
Right amount	13.9	27.2
Too little	49.7	59.6
Don't know	14.2	4.5
No response	3.2	0.8
Total	100.0	100.0

African Americans

Response	GNPP %	GSS %
Too much	13.1	15.5
Right amount	21.4	39.4
Too little	36.2	35.5
Don't know	25.8	9.1
No response	3.4	0.5
Total	100.0	100.0

Military

Response	GNPP %	GSS %
Too much	79.7	41.3
Right amount	12.4	44.2
Too little	3.3	10.3
Don't know	2.9	3.8
No response	1.8	0.4
Total	100.0	100.0

Foreign Aid

Response	GNPP %	GSS %
Too much	65.6	69.5
Right amount	14.1	20.7
Too little	4.2	4.9
Don't know	13.5	4.6
No response	2.6	0.3
Total	100.0	100.0

TABLE 11 *(continued)*

Welfare

Response	GNPP %	GSS %
Too much	38.4	53.6
Right amount	19.6	24.8
Too little	21.3	16.3
Don't know	16.9	5.0
No response	3.8	0.3
Total	100.0	100.0

Highways

Response	GNPP %	GSS %
Too much	15.3	9.1
Right amount	33.7	48.0
Too little	26.8	37.9
Don't know	21.3	5.0
No response	2.9	0.0
Total	100.0	100.0

Social Security

Response	GNPP %	GSS %
Too much	14.4	7.1
Right amount	29.1	43.1
Too little	29.5	43.6
Don't know	23.9	6.2
No response	3.1	0.0
Total	100.0	100.0

Mass Transportation

Response	GNPP %	GSS %
Too much	4.8	9.6
Right amount	17.9	44.2
Too little	58.7	34.8
Don't know	16.0	11.4
No response	2.6	0.0
Total	100.0	100.0

Parks

Response	GNPP %	GSS %
Too much	2.2	6.3
Right amount	27.4	57.8
Too little	54.1	30.2
Don't know	13.5	5.7
No response	2.7	0.0
Total	100.0	100.0

The Arts*

Response	GNPP %
Too much	8.2
Right amount	26.3
Too little	49.5
Don't know	13.3
No response	2.7
Total	100.0

*No GSS data for this question in 1993.

TABLE 11 *(continued)*

AIDS*

Response	GNPP %
Too much	4.6
Right amount	16.5
Too little	66.3
Don't know	9.9
No response	2.7
Total	100.0

*No GSS data for this question in 1993.

The Homeless*

Response	GNPP %
Too much	5.4
Right amount	11.5
Too little	70.0
Don't know	10.3
No response	2.7
Total	100.0

*No GSS data for this question in 1993.

Education

Response	GNPP %	GSS %
Too much	4.2	4.8
Right amount	10.3	22.1
Too little	77.8	69.7
Don't know	5.0	1.8
No response	2.6	1.6
Total	100.0	100.0

Table 11 compares GSS and The Pagan Census responses on government spending for social programs. The data indicate that Neo-Pagans' views diverge from and are more liberal than the general American public. Some differences between Neo-Pagans and the general American public are worth highlighting. The vast majority, 92 percent of Neo-Pagans, reports that we are not spending a sufficient amount on the environment as compared with 55.7 percent of the general American population. Those drawn to Neo-Paganism may come from part of the American public that is already sensitive to environmental issues. The large disparity between the responses of Neo-Pagans and the general American public supports Harvey's (1997) claim that participation in Neo-Paganism strengthens individuals' commitment to environmental issues.

Other areas in which a substantial percentage of Neo-Pagans indicate that more money should be spent on a social issue than the general American population does, in rank order, are: mass transit, parks and recreation, crime, and drug addiction. Investment in mass transit and parks and recreation is consistent with concern for the environment. The concern for crime may be explained by the fact that about half of our respondents live in a greater metropolitan area. Neo-Pagans on the whole are interested in and concerned about health issues, including those of addiction.

The GSS question on the arts is phrased slightly differently from the one we use.[11] It asks if the respondent thinks that we should spend much more, spend more, spend the same as now, spend less, or spend much less money on the arts. Very few GSS respondents believe that we should spend more on the arts—specifically, 10 percent state more money should be spent, and 2.2 percent indicate that much more money should be spent on the arts. In our study almost half, 49.5 percent, believe we are spending too little on the arts. A larger percentage of Neo-Pagans believe we are spending too much on the military than do other Americans. On the whole Neo-Pagans' answers to questions about government spending are politically liberal.

An examination of table 12, which compares Neo-Pagan women's and men's responses to whether or not we are spending too much or too little on social programs, indicates that on the whole women

TABLE 12: Comparison of Women's and Men's Attitudes toward Government Spending

Space

Response	GNPP %	Women %	Men %
Too much	35.6	41.0	25.4
Right amount	22.3	21.6	24.3
Too little	27.8	21.2	40.0
Don't know	11.1	12.9	7.2
No response	3.2	3.3	3.1

Environment

Response	GNPP %	Women %	Men %
Too much	1.3	0.6	2.7
Right amount	4.2	3.4	5.6
Too little	92.0	93.6	89.1
Don't know	0.8	0.7	1.0
No response	1.7	1.7	1.6

Health

Response	GNPP %	Women %	Men %
Too much	6.9	5.8	8.9
Right amount	9.9	7.5	14.5
Too little	73.4	76.9	66.9
Don't know	7.2	7.4	7.2
No response	2.5	2.5	2.4

Big Cities

Response	GNPP %	Women %	Men %
Too much	8.9	5.8	15.0
Right Amount	12.4	11.5	14.4
Too little	54.0	55.9	50.1
Don't know	21.8	23.9	17.9
No response	2.9	3.0	2.5

Crime

Response	GNPP %	Women %	Men %
Too much	14.7	11.3	20.9
Right Amount	15.2	12.9	19.4
Too little	49.8	53.1	43.9
Don't know	17.0	19.3	12.9
No response	3.3	3.4	3.0

Drug Addiction

Response	GNPP %	Women %	Men %
Too much	19.1	15.4	25.8
Right Amount	13.9	13.0	15.5
Too little	49.7	52.4	44.6
Don't know	14.2	15.8	11.3
No response	3.2	3.4	2.7

TABLE 12 *(continued)*

African Americans

Response	GNPP %	Women %	Men %
Too much	13.1	9.8	19.6
Right amount	21.4	19.4	25.3
Too little	36.2	39.2	30.6
Don't know	25.8	27.9	21.5
No response	3.4	3.6	3.0

Military

Response	GNPP %	Women %	Men %
Too much	79.7	83.2	72.9
Right amount	12.4	9.4	18.2
Too little	3.3	2.2	5.1
Don't know	2.9	3.3	2.3
No response	1.8	1.8	1.6

Foreign Aid

Response	GNPP %	Women %	Men %
Too much	65.6	66.5	64.5
Right amount	14.1	12.6	17.1
Too little	4.2	3.3	5.5
Don't know	13.5	14.8	10.7
No response	2.6	2.8	2.1

Welfare

Response	GNPP %	Women %	Men %
Too much	38.4	35.6	44.4
Right amount	19.6	19.9	19.2
Too little	21.3	21.7	20.2
Don't know	16.9	18.7	13.4
No response	3.8	4.1	2.8

Highways

Response	GNPP %	Women %	Men %
Too much	15.3	15.8	14.4
Right amount	33.7	31.9	37.4
Too little	26.8	25.4	29.7
Don't know	21.3	23.9	16.0
No response	2.9	3.0	2.5

Social Security

Response	GNPP %	Women %	Men %
Too much	14.4	12.7	18.2
Right amount	29.1	28.0	30.5
Too little	29.5	29.3	29.9
Don't know	23.9	26.7	18.8
No response	3.1	3.3	2.5

TABLE 12 *(continued)*

Mass Transportation

Response	GNPP %	Women %	Men %
Too much	4.8	4.7	5.2
Right amount	17.9	17.7	18.4
Too little	58.7	56.2	63.1
Don't know	16.0	18.7	11.0
No response	2.6	2.7	2.3

Parks

Response	GNPP %	Women %	Men %
Too much	2.2	2.2	2.3
Right amount	27.4	27.9	26.6
Too little	54.1	51.5	58.6
Don't know	13.5	15.6	9.9
No response	2.7	2.7	2.7

The Arts

Response	GNPP %	Women %	Men %
Too much	8.2	7.5	9.7
Right amount	26.3	26.5	26.4
Too little	49.5	49.1	49.9
Don't know	13.3	14.0	11.6
No response	2.7	2.9	2.4

AIDS

Response	GNPP %	Women %	Men %
Too much	4.6	3.4	6.9
Right amount	16.5	16.7	16.0
Too little	66.3	67.1	64.7
Don't know	9.9	10.1	9.6
No response	2.7	2.7	2.8

The Homeless

Response	GNPP %	Women %	Men %
Too much	5.4	4.0	8.2
Right amount	11.5	10.6	13.4
Too little	70.0	71.8	66.4
Don't know	10.3	10.6	9.6
No response	2.7	3.0	2.4

Education

Response	GNPP %	Women %	Men %
Too much	4.2	4.0	4.8
Right amount	10.3	9.7	11.6
Too little	77.8	78.4	76.4
Don't know	5.0	5.3	4.7
No response	2.6	2.6	2.5

hold more liberal views than men. For example, on the issue of welfare, 44.4 percent of the men and 35.6 percent of the women think we are spending too much. A larger percentage of women believe that more money should be spent on the environment, health, big cities, crime, the problems faced by African Americans, education, and drug addiction than Neo-Pagan men do. However, a larger percentage of men support more money being spent on the infrastructure, specifically bridges and highways, and parks and recreation. A larger percentage of women than men state that we are spending too much on the military, space exploration, and foreign aid.

On the whole Neo-Pagans support gender and sexual orientation equity, although women's support tends to be stronger than men's, as shown in table 13. For example, on the issue of whether or not there should be an Equal Rights Amendment (ERA) to the United States Constitution, 90 percent of Neo-Pagan women say there should be an amendment, with 68.1 percent feeling strongly about the issue. This response can be compared with Neo-Pagan men, among whom 84 percent state they are in support of the amendment, and 54.1 percent say they feel strongly about the issue. Only 7.9 percent of the men oppose the ERA; the rest either have no opinion or do not answer this question. When Neo-Pagans are compared with the general American public, however, it is clear that Neo-Pagan men are more supportive of the ERA than the average American. The GSS asks if their respondents "strongly favored, somewhat favored, somewhat opposed, or strongly opposed this (ERA) amendment." The GSS findings, which are not divided by gender, indicate that 67.1 percent favor the ERA, with only 21.6 percent strongly favoring the amendment. Twenty-five percent of the population opposes the ERA.[12]

On the more radical issue of preferential hiring of women to redress previous discrimination, more women oppose this proposition than support it. In total, 52.7 percent are opposed, although the largest percentage (20.5 percent) are qualified in their opposition. In comparison, 47.1 percent of Neo-Pagan women support preferential hiring, with the largest percentage (21.1 percent) giving qualified agreement. The majority (63.7 percent) of Neo-Pagan men opposes the idea of preferential hiring.

The GSS asks whether the respondents agree with a similar proposition: "Because of past discrimination, employers should make special efforts to hire and promote qualified women." They find that the majority (54.9 percent) of Americans supports this proposition, although only 17 percent do so strongly.[13] The question as it is worded by the GSS does not speak of preferential hiring but instead speaks of special efforts. The less radical nature of the GSS's proposal may

TABLE 13: Comparison of Women's and Men's Views on Gender and Sexual Preference Equality

There Should Be an Equal Rights Amendment

Response	GNPP %	Women %	Men %
Strongly disagree	1.6	0.8	3.0
Disagree	1.2	0.7	2.4
Qualified disagree	2.1	1.8	2.5
No opinion	5.3	4.7	6.8
Qualified agree	7.8	6.5	10.3
Agree	16.9	15.4	19.6
Strongly agree	63.4	68.1	54.1
No response	1.7	1.9	1.3

Women Should Not Be Included in the Draft

Response	GNPP %	Women %	Men %
Strongly disagree	22.9	17.1	33.8
Disagree	20.5	17.9	25.1
Qualified disagree	17.6	20.8	11.6
No opinion	10.4	11.5	8.6
Qualified agree	9.3	11.0	6.2
Agree	7.0	8.3	4.9
Strongly agree	9.6	10.6	7.8
No response	2.5	2.7	1.9

TABLE 13 *(continued)*

Same-Sex Marriage Should Be Legal

Response	GNPP %	Women %	Men %
Strongly disagree	1.7	0.9	3.4
Disagree	0.9	0.7	1.6
Qualified disagree	0.9	0.8	1.1
No opinion	6.3	4.8	9.5
Qualified agree	5.3	4.7	6.5
Agree	24.1	22.9	26.4
Strongly agree	59.9	64.5	50.4
No response	0.8	0.6	1.1

There Should Be Preferential Hiring for Women

Response	GNPP %	Women %	Men %
Strongly disagree	14.4	9.1	24.4
Disagree	17.8	16.9	19.5
Qualified disagree	20.5	21.1	19.8
No opinion	7.5	7.2	8.2
Qualified agree	20.8	23.9	14.3
Agree	7.5	9.2	4.5
Strongly agree	10.1	11.2	8.1
No response	1.3	1.3	1.3

Women in the Military Forces Should Be Included in Combat Positions

Response	GNPP %	Women %	Men %
Strongly disagree	4.2	3.7	5.2
Disagree	2.7	2.6	2.9
Qualified disagree	5.7	5.9	5.5

Women in the Military Forces (continued)

Response	GNPP %	Women %	Men %
No opinion	8.6	9.4	7.1
Qualified agree	22.9	25.6	17.8
Agree	29.2	29.9	27.9
Strongly agree	24.9	21.1	31.9
No response	1.7	1.8	1.6

Nondiscrimination on the Basis of Sexual Preference

Response	GNPP %	Women %	Men %
Strongly disagree	0.9	0.8	1.3
Disagree	0.8	0.4	1.7
Qualified disagree	1.1	0.8	1.7
No opinion	2.3	1.2	4.4
Qualified agree	5.1	4.5	6.2
Agree	21.6	19.6	25.9
Strongly agree	66.9	71.8	57.2
No response	1.2	0.9	1.6

Homosexuals Should Be Excluded from the Military

Response	GNPP %	Women %	Men %
Strongly disagree	67.3	71.4	58.9
Disagree	18.9	17.7	21.2
Qualified disagree	4.8	3.9	6.6
No opinion	3.8	2.4	6.6
Qualified agree	1.5	1.1	2.3
Agree	0.9	0.7	0.9
Strongly agree	1.9	1.6	2.7
No response	1.0	1.1	0.7

explain why their responses are more positive than ours. Nonetheless, the response by Neo-Pagans surprises us, as we anticipated stronger support from a group among whom a large number self-define as feminists. The anarchistic and individualistic tendencies in the movement might work against notions of preferential hiring. Furthermore, feminism is not monolithic. There are serious philosophical divisions among feminists. Which branch or branches of feminism Neo-Pagans support is unclear. Unfortunately, we do not have statistics on the national average of those who support preferential hiring. We suspect that if we did, Neo-Pagans would be more supportive of the proposition than the average American.

Most Neo-Pagans support the notion that women should be included in a military draft. Neo-Pagan men support this proposition more strongly than women do: 70.5 percent of the men and 33.8 percent of the women strongly feel that women should be included in a military draft. This response can be compared with the women: 55.8 percent support women being included in the draft, with the largest percentage (20.8 percent) giving it qualified support. The GSS includes the question, "If we should return to a military draft at this time, should young women be drafted as well as young men, or not?"[14] They find the population almost evenly divided on the question, with 45.7 percent favoring and 48.5 percent opposing women being included in the draft. Neo-Pagan men's strong support for this proposition may come from a notion that if they are obliged to be part of the pool of potential draftees, then women should also share this burden.

A pervasive image of Neo-Pagans is that they are pacifists. Chas Clifton (2000), in examining the media coverage of the Fort Hood incident in Texas, finds that the media promulgated a pacifist image of Neo-Pagans.[15] He contends that this image originates from the writings of some well-known Neo-Pagans who are pacifists, most notably Starhawk, the most widely read American Witch. To the contrary, he argues that although there are some Neo-Pagans who are pacifists and view pacifism as part of their religious beliefs, they do not speak for all Neo-Pagans.

Our survey asks respondents to state the degree to which they agree or disagree with the statement "Compulsory military service is incompatible with Pagan religious beliefs." Forty-five percent agree to some degree with this proposition, with 17.7 percent doing so strongly, 21.1 percent have no opinion, and 2.4 percent did not respond. Thirty-one and a half percent disagree to some degree with this statement. Only 7 percent disagree strongly. We find a gender division in the responses to this statement. Nearly half (48.5 percent) of women agree, with 18.4 percent doing so strongly. Among men, 41.2 percent disagree, with 11 percent doing so strongly. A notable percentage of both women and men have no opinion on this issue (22.5 percent of women and 18.2 percent of men). Our statistics support Clifton's claim that not all Neo-Pagans are pacifists or opposed to military service for Neo-Pagans.

Neo-Pagan women are more likely to oppose compulsory military service than Neo-Pagan men are. One woman respondent to our survey states, "I think it should be illegal for anyone to be drafted into a military, and it should be illegal for anyone to raise or join one, man or woman, black or white, straight or gay. . . . All opinions I have written reflect only my personal beliefs and *not* my interpretation of 'Pagan Religious Beliefs'" (Survey 2101). However, a substantial proportion of Neo-Pagan women and a larger proportion of Neo-Pagan men do not view compulsory military service as antithetical to Neo-Paganism. Covenant of the Goddess (2000), a national umbrella organization that conducted a survey of Neo-Pagans on the Internet, finds that 13 percent of all Neo-Pagans are now or have been in the military. Women compose 32 percent of those who are or have been members of the armed services.

Our data show that Neo-Pagans strongly support gay rights, although women do so more strongly and in somewhat larger numbers than men do. The GSS asks their respondents the degree to which they agree or disagree with the proposal, "Homosexual couples should have the right to marry one another." The overwhelming majority of Americans, 67.2 percent, of which 43.4 feel strongly, opposes homosexual marriages. Only 11.4 percent of Americans support this proposition.[16] In comparison, 89.3 percent of all Neo-Pagans support same-sex marriages, with 60 percent feeling strongly about this issue. Neo-Pagan women are even more supportive than Neo-Pagan men are: 92.2 percent of women support same-sex marriages,

TABLE 14: Political Affiliation Divided by Gender

Party	GNPP %	Women %	Men %
Not Registered	5.1	4.2	6.8
Democrat	42.9	45.2	38.3
Republican	6.6	5.8	8.5
Independent	27.9	28.6	26.7
Green	4.4	4.5	4.2
Liberal	0.2	0.3	0.0
NYS Choice	0.1	0.0	0.3
Libertarian	2.1	1.5	0.3
Anarchist	0.2	0.1	0.3
Socialist	0.3	0.3	0.3
Nonpartisan	0.3	0.4	0.2
Bipartisan	0.1	0.0	0.1
Uncommitted	0.2	0.3	0.0
Reform	0.1	0.0	0.1
Not a U.S. citizen	1.3	1.3	1.2
No response	9.2	7.4	9.9

with 64.5 percent feeling strongly about this issue. Same-sex marriage is supported by 83.3 percent of men, with 50.4 percent feeling strongly about the issue. When asked if nondiscrimination on the basis of sexual preference should be part of any civil right legislation, 95.9 percent of Neo-Pagan women and 89.4 percent of men support this proposition. When asked if "homosexuals should be excluded from the military," 93.1 percent of Neo-Pagan women and 87.4 percent of men disagree with this proposal. Scholars of the Neo-Pagan movement all note the religion's celebration of sexual diversity. Neo-Pagans' responses to questions about gay and lesbian rights are a reflection of that aspect of their religion.

Table 14 indicates that more Neo-Pagans are registered as Democrats than for any other party. Women are somewhat more likely to be Democrats than men are. Independent is the second most likely category for both women and men. Very few Neo-Pagans are registered Republicans. The GSS results indicate that 35.8 percent of their sample are Democrats, 32.5 percent Independent, and 31.1 percent Republican, while the others either self-describe as in another party or do not answer the question.[17] Neo-Pagans' more liberal political position is more in line with the Democrats than with the Republicans. Furthermore, the religious rights, vocal support, and apparent control of the Republican Party might be an anathema to many Neo-Pagans.

Confidence in Social Institutions

Although Neo-Pagans are politically active, they are on the whole more skeptical of social institutions than the general American public, as shown in table 15.

There is one possible exception—the press—in which Neo-Pagans and the general American public have approximately the same low level of confidence. Although Neo-Pagan men and women differ somewhat in their support of different social institutions, their overall support for social institutions in general is on par.

Neo-Pagans' lack of enthusiasm for social institutions is consistent with their criticism of contemporary society. As noted in the first chapter, although many Neo-Pagans recognize that their religion is new, they also adhere to a belief that they are "returning" to older spiritual beliefs and practices. Many Neo-Pagans view their spirituality as offering an alternative image of the relationship of people to one another and to the earth—an image in which people respect each other and treat Mother Earth with respect. This image is of less bureaucratic societies that are based on concern and sharing, and which eschew hierarchical institutionalized power. For Neo-Pagans this image serves as an alternative to what they believe are the problems of contemporary life. Although as our data show, Neo-Pagans use the political system to work for social change, ultimately they have little faith in the bureaucracies and social institutions they use.

Religion and Politics in Late Modernity

In reconciling his findings that contemporary mystics are politically active with Weber and Troeltsch's model of the relationship between mysticism and politics, Wuthnow (1978) contends that Weber and Troeltsch are not wrong. He argues that their model is correct within

TABLE 15: Comparison of Neo-Pagans' and the General American Public's Confidence in Social Institutions

Banks and Financial Institutions

Response	GNPP %	GSS %
1 – Complete confidence	1.5	13.5
2	4.5	19.7
3	10.1	20.9
4	19.3	24.0
5	20.1	8.4
6	22.2	6.9
7 – No confidence	19.4	6.6
No response	2.8	0.0

Major Companies

Response	GNPP %	GSS %
1 – Complete confidence	1.2	11.7
2	3.7	17.2
3	6.7	23.0
4	16.4	32.1
5	17.9	12.4
6	24.5	3.6
7 – No confidence	26.7	0.0
No response	3.1	0.0

Organized Religion

Response	GNPP %	GSS %
1 – Complete confidence	1.9	17.9
2	1.7	17.2
3	2.6	17.7

Organized Religion *(continued)*

Response	GNPP %	GSS %
4	8.4	20.0
5	12.7	10.6
6	23.9	8.8
7 – No confidence	45.8	7.8
No response	2.9	0.0

Education

Response	GNPP %	GSS %
1 – Complete confidence	1.6	8.9
2	4.7	17.1
3	15.9	19.5
4	23.7	20.8
5	21.9	17.1
6	16.7	11.7
7 – No confidence	12.6	4.9
No response	2.8	0.0

Executive Branch of Government

Response	GNPP %	GSS %
1 – Complete confidence	1.2	7.5
2	7.4	14.5
3	10.6	14.5
4	16.4	22.8
5	15.4	14.9
6	19.7	13.2
7 – No confidence	25.8	12.6
No response	3.5	0.0

TABLE 15 *(continued)*

Organized Labor

Response	GNPP %	GSS %
1 – Complete confidence	1.4	6.5
2	3.8	9.7
3	9.0	14.2
4	22.9	25.4
5	19.6	17.2
6	18.3	13.8
7 – No confidence	20.5	13.2
No response	4.5	0.0

The Press

Response	GNPP %	GSS %
1 – Complete confidence	1.3	1.3
2	4.3	4.2
3	11.1	16.1
4	20.9	24.6
5	19.9	15.0
6	18.8	14.6
7 – No confidence	20.8	7.0
No response	2.9	0.0

Medicine

Response	GNPP %	GSS %
1 – Complete confidence	1.2	18.0
2	8.2	29.3
3	16.8	20.1
4	18.2	14.0

Medicine (continued)

Response	GNPP %	GSS %
5	19.7	8.9
6	18.6	5.7
7 – No confidence	14.3	4.0
No response	3.0	0.0

Television

Response	GNPP %	GSS %
1 – Complete confidence	1.1	7.4
2	2.5	10.8
3	5.6	13.8
4	15.1	28.4
5	16.2	15.7
6	24.5	13.8
7 – No confidence	32.0	10.2
No response	3.0	0.0

Supreme Court

Response	GNPP %	GSS %
1 – Complete confidence	1.7	11.4
2	10.5	23.1
3	14.9	20.3
4	20.7	19.4
5	18.7	11.1
6	16.4	8.1
7 – No confidence	13.3	6.6
No response	3.7	0.0

TABLE 15 *(continued)*

Scientific Community

Response	GNPP %	GSS %
1 – Complete confidence	2.5	14.3
2	15.8	27.4
3	21.3	22.4
4	24.3	19.7
5	15.6	7.0
6	10.4	6.3
7 – No confidence	6.9	2.9
No response	3.1	0.0

Congress

Response	GNPP %	GSS %
1 – Complete confidence	0.8	4.6
2	1.1	12.3
3	4.8	21.2
4	14.1	30.0
5	18.0	19.1
6	25.4	12.8
7 – No confidence	31.7	0.0
No response	4.1	0.0

some social formations but not in others, particularly those of what he calls mass society. He characterizes mass society as having "accessible political channels but relatively low institutional differentiation," at least in some segments of society. According to Wuthnow, the lack of institutional differentiation among members of the counterculture in the 1960s resulted in the blurring of the boundaries between mysticism and politics.

Other scholars also note that the late 1960s signaled a change in the political and spiritual environments. Wade Roof (1993), in his study of baby boomers, notes that members of the generation, whether politically to the left or right, came to choose a spiritual expression that often had less to do with family histories or alliance and more to do with their own personal quests for self-transformation. Often there was a layering of religious beliefs, which was combined with a form of political activism that centered on subjective understandings of social goals. Ellwood (1994:9) contends "the religious and political sides of the Sixties should not be set against each other so much as seen as bands of a single spectrum." Both, he argues were involved with transcendental questions of community and meaning.

Ellwood views the late 1960s as a watershed for cultural, social, and political changes, which he defines as the transition from modernity to postmodernity. Other scholars label the changes noted by Ellwood as a transition to late modernity, not postmodernity (see, for example, Giddens 1987, 1990). Whether referred to as postmodernity or late modernity, these scholars all point to similar social changes, notably the breakdown of grand narratives, which resulted in the questioning of universal truths, particularly those of science and politics. Skepticism toward universal truths resulted in a belief in relative or personal truths. There was a growth of pluralism—in politics, in religion, in views of reality. The notion of a unified self or personality gave way to a concept of multiple Promethean selves. Religions too changed, to a more decentralized and personalized religious expression. James Beckford defines the religions that personify this new era as embracing "diversity of discourse and the abandonment of unitary meaning systems; cross-references between and pastiches of, different religious traditions; collapse of the boundary between high and popular forms of religion; and an accent on playfulness or cynicism" (1992:20). Beckford further notes that within these religions there is a new sense of politics that makes it part of an individual's spirituality.

Neo-Paganism, as noted in chapter 1, is defined as a religion of postmodernity or late modernity. It is a religion, in other words, that fits the criteria set forth by Beckford and as such incorporates a new sense of politics into its spiritual expression. Adler, after noting that many Neo-Pagans consider themselves apolitical, observes that by another definition of politics they could be considered very political. "Most feminists, most militant ecologists, and most people who had gone through the sixties understood 'politics' to be something akin to the 'decisions that affect our daily lives'" (1986:405–6). These people, according to Adler, often say that Neo-Paganism is intensely political. Helen Berger (1999a), relying on the work of Anthony Giddens (1991), labels Neo-Pagans' political attitudes as life politics—that is, the politics based on choices made in daily life, such as the decision to recycle or to fight racism, sexism, or homophobia in one's personal life, workplace, or community. These choices, particularly when part of a social movement, in which others are also intent on working for change in their personal milieu, eventually help to form and change social life. As the slogan of the second wave of the women's movement declares, "The personal is political."

Giddens defines life politics as distinct although not in opposition to what he labels emancipatory politics—that is, the politics of fighting for personal and civil rights through the courts, elections, and protests. Our data on Neo-Pagans suggest that within this group life politics and emancipatory politics have become integrated. As one of our respondents notes, "I understand 'politics' can be divisive, offensive etc, but my spiritual feelings and beliefs are completely (or *very* closely) integrated into my daily life and how I feel about the political world. If people really try to live a pagan life that seems inconsistent (to me) with mentally supporting world domination by capital" (Survey 1905). Although not all Neo-Pagans would agree with the political worldview of this respondent, what is clear is that Neo-Pagans are politically active in traditional venues—they vote, work on campaigns, run for election, and participate in letter-writing campaigns and protests. The mystical experiences of Neo-Pagans clearly do not result in their withdrawing from the world but instead focus the participants' attention on issues of diversity, environmental responsibility, and respect for multiple truths. At the same time that Neo-Pagans participate in political activities, however, they remain skeptical of the institutions they are working to change. They simultaneously participate in and question traditional politics.

3

SPIRITUAL PATHS, FORMS OF PRACTICE, AND REGIONAL VARIATIONS

> Pagan is a term that denotes a variety of spiritual paths and traditions
> that spring from history and mythology and differ from the major
> monotheistic religions. No "policy" statement can encompass all
> groups and beliefs except that we stand together to be allowed true
> religious freedom, acceptance, and recognition. (Survey 1779)

The image of diversity of religious practice is a central belief among
Neo-Pagans, as is the notion that different spiritual paths have different histories and mythologies. Although sharing many similarities,
Neo-Pagans differentiate themselves from one another by the spiritual path, or tradition, they belong to and whether they choose to
practice alone, with one partner, or in a group. Geographic differences, for Neo-Pagans as for all Americans, are also often viewed as
being reflected in differences in attitudes and practices.

As noted in chapter 1, Neo-Pagans pride themselves on the amorphous boundaries of their religion. The terms *spiritual path,* or *tradition,* instead of *sect,* is normally used by Neo-Pagans to denote
differences of spiritual and magical practice and mythology among
practitioners, as the term *spiritual path* permits the possibility of
some individuals having unique paths that differ from all others.
Throughout this chapter we will refer to different forms of Neo-
Paganism as sects, although the term as noted by Michael York
(1995) is imperfect for describing Neo-Paganism. By using this term,

we do not mean to imply that these different forms of Neo-Pagan-ism completely fit the definition of sect as presented by Max Weber, Ernst Troeltsch (1960), and other scholars who have since attempted to refine this term. However, no other term is as useful for our pur-poses. *Spiritual path* remains too vague, as it connotes both individ-ual practices and those of groups. In using the term *sect,* we want merely to denote that we are speaking about different branches or forms of Neo-Paganism.

In this chapter we will be comparing and contrasting six sects: Wiccans, Pagans, Goddess Worshipers, Druids, Shamans, and Uni-tarian Universalist (UU) Neo-Pagans. As over half of our respon-dents state that they practice as solitaries, we will also look at the distinctions and similarities among those who practice alone, with one partner, or in groups. A comprehensive comparison of Neo-Pagan sects' histories, mythologies, and ritual practices is beyond the data available in our survey. Instead, our intention in this chapter is to compare and contrast Neo-Pagan sects, forms of practice, and geographic differences in terms of their demographics, political activities, and spiritual beliefs as reflected in the questions that were discussed in the last chapter. The object of this comparison is to pro-vide an overview of the similarities and differences that exist among sects within the parameters set by our survey.

In our survey we provide twenty designations for different forms of Neo-Paganism, plus a twenty-first ("other") with room for respon-dents to write in an alternative label. From these designations we have chosen to compare six sects based on two criteria: the number of respondents who claim the sect as their primary spiritual path and the extent to which the sect's practices make it particularly distinct. As we know that some Neo-Pagans consider their personal spiritual path influenced by more than one sect, we request that they rank order those spiritual paths that have influenced their spirituality. Some individuals list more than one spiritual path as primary. This is particularly true for the designation *Wiccan* and *Pagan*, in which three hundred people choose both as a primary designation. As one respondent notes, "Witch is a subset of Pagans with a certain stylistic aesthetic [differences] and [unique] beliefs" (Survey 2193). In interpreting these data, we decided that it is more important to include all those that self-defined within a particular spiritual path than to have mutually exclusive categories. The overlap in the data is an indication of the degree of fluidity of the categories within this religion. The degree of overlap, however, should not be exaggerated, as in most instances individuals list only one category as primary.

The three most popular sects are Wiccans, Pagans, and Goddess Worshipers, with respectively 1,332 (54.7 percent), 1,120 (53.6 percent), and 929 (44.5 percent) people selecting each as their primary (or one of their primary) spiritual path(s). The term *Neo-Pagan* is used by far fewer individuals than *Pagan* is. *Goddess Worshiper* would be included even if it were not the third most popular sect, as it distinguishes itself from other forms of Neo-Paganism by focusing on the goddess to the exclusion of the gods or god force. Goddess spirituality, with its links to feminism, has, furthermore, become the focus of a number of studies (Eller 1993; Griffin 2000). In his book on contemporary Paganism in England, Graham Harvey (1997) examines five sects that he believes most clearly reflect the diversity within the Neo-Pagan movement: Druids, Witches, Heathens, Goddess Spirituality, and Shamans. Heathens, or Odinists, are not as large or influential a part of the Neo-Pagan movement in the United States as they are in Europe. Odinists were discussed in the first chapter as one of the minority voices within American Neo-Paganism. Druids, Shamans, and Goddess Spirituality, however, do create distinct forms of Neo-Paganism in the United States, which we will explore in this chapter. We also include Neo-Pagans who are part of the Unitarian Universalist Association (UUA). These Neo-Pagans distinguish themselves by having joined an old and established religious organization and integrating their religious practices with those of non-Neo-Pagan congregants.

Wiccans, Pagans, and Goddess Worshipers

Demographically and politically, Wiccans, Pagans, and those who practice Goddess Spirituality are quite similar. Members of all three sects have comparable levels of education, with the largest percentage of their members having a college degree or at least some college. Approximately the same percentage of all three sects' members are married or in what they define as a committed relationship. If one adds together those who are legally married, ritually married, or

TABLE 16: Comparison of Marital Status for Goddess Worshipers, Pagans, and Wiccans

Status	GNPP %	Goddess %	Pagan %	Wiccan %
Never married	26.1	23.3	25.8	25.1
Married legally	33.3	32.1	32.9	34.3
Married ritually	4.8	5.9	4.9	5.1
Live with lover	13.8	14.5	14.3	13.4
Divorced	15.2	15.4	14.9	14.9
Widow/er	1.0	1.4	1.0	1.1
Separated	2.4	3.4	2.9	2.8
Group marriage	0.4	0.3	0.4	0.4
Other	1.7	2.2	1.9	1.9
No response	1.2	1.5	1.0	1.1

living with their lover, approximately half (52.5 percent) of each sect's members are in committed relationships (see table 16).

There is a higher proportion of women to men among Goddess Worshipers than among the other two groups. Within Goddess Spirituality 74.4 percent are women, 24.6 percent are men, and 1.2 percent do not answer this question. This response can be compared with Wiccans and Pagans, which respectively are composed of 68 percent and 67 percent women. It is to be expected that Goddess Worshipers have a larger proportion of women than other sects do. Women are the majority, however, in all three sects. Male respondents compose almost one quarter of those who claim Goddess Worship as their primary spiritual path. For at least some men, worshiping the goddess is an aspect of getting in touch with their feminine side, which is most typically defined as the nurturing or caring part of their personalities. Goddess Worshipers also distinguish themselves from the other two sects by having a higher proportion of members who are lesbians (see table 17). The existence of one wing of the Goddess Spirituality movement that embraces radical feminist separatism provides an explanation for this difference.

All three groups have the same median income of between $30,000 and $40,000. This is true even though Goddess Worshipers have a larger percentage of women members. As noted in chapter 1, women within Neo-Paganism, as women in the general society, tend to earn less than men. Why this is not the case for those who participate in Goddess Worship is unclear. Women within Goddess Spirituality have basically the same educational level as other Neo-Pagan women. Although there are some minor differences, the majority of members of all three sects defines their residential area as either urban or suburban.

As measured by the GSS questions on government spending and level of confidence in social institutions, the political attitudes of Wiccans and Pagans are on the whole similar. Goddess Worshipers distinguish themselves as being somewhat more liberal in their responses to questions about government spending in the areas of drug addiction, conditions of African Americans, AIDS research and prevention, homelessness, and education. In each of these areas members of Goddess Worshipers believe even more money should be spent than do Wiccans and Pagans, although the differences are not large. Goddess Worshipers also advocate more money being spent in the area of foreign aid than Wiccans or Pagans, although again, this difference is small. Over 80 percent of all three sects believe too much money is being spent on the military; however, a higher percentage (84.1 percent) of Goddess Worshipers hold this belief.

TABLE 17: Comparison of Sexual Orientation for Goddess Worshipers, Pagans, and Wiccans

Orientation	GNPP %	Goddess %	Pagan %	Wiccan %
Heterosexual	67.8	63.4	66.3	68.0
Lesbian	4.8	7.1	4.6	5.3
Gay Men	4.5	3.2	4.1	4.5
Bisexual	19.0	22.2	21.2	18.9
Other	1.9	2.0	2.2	1.5
No response	1.9	2.0	1.5	1.7

All three groups support gender and sexual preference equity. Goddess Worshipers, however, feel stronger about these issues than do Wiccans and Pagans. Ninety percent of Goddess Worshipers support the ERA, with 68.9 percent doing so strongly. This figure can be compared with that of the Wiccans, in which 85.1 percent support the ERA, 65.4 percent strongly, and Pagans in which 88.6 percent support the ERA, with 64.8 percent supporting it strongly. Goddess Worshipers are almost equally divided between those who support preferential hiring to address previous discrimination and those who oppose it—45.7 percent support the proposal and 44.9 percent oppose it. Like Neo-Pagans in general, a larger number of Pagans and Wiccans oppose preferential hiring than support it. Over 95 percent of Goddess Worshipers and just fewer than 95 percent of Wiccans and Pagans believe that nondiscrimination based on sexual preference should be part of any civil rights legislation. Although Goddess Worshipers like Wiccans and Pagans support women being included in the draft and women being put in combat positions, their support is somewhat weaker. This response can be understood within the context of their previously stated belief that less money should be given to the military.

The more liberal views of Goddess Worshipers can, in part be explained by the larger percentage of women among their membership. As noted in chapter 2, Neo-Pagan women have somewhat more liberal views than Neo-Pagan men do. In comparing men and women Goddess Worshipers, we find that although these women tend to be more liberal than these men are, both are slightly more liberal than their counterparts within the larger Neo-Pagan movement. For example, 91.4 percent of women, and 88.6 percent of men Goddess Worshipers support the ERA. These percentages can be compared with the general Neo-Pagan population in which 90 percent of women and 84 percent of men support the ERA. On the more volatile issue of preferential hiring, we find that 49.7 percent of women and 32 percent of men Goddess Worshipers support this proposition, with 14 percent of women giving strong support. As among Neo-Pagans in general, there is a gender divide among Goddess Worshipers on this issue. Nonetheless, men Goddess Worshipers give stronger support for preferential hiring than Neo-Pagan men in general do. Similarly, in their responses to other questions on gender and gay and lesbian issues, there is a gender difference among Goddess Worshipers just as there is in the larger Neo-Pagan population. However, Goddess Worshiper men consistently give slightly stronger support for these issues than men do in the general Neo-Pagan population.

Similar to the general Neo-Pagan population, members of all three sects are registered to vote, do vote, and are politically active. Most (87 percent) of all three sects are registered to vote, and 70.9 percent of Wiccans, 70.4 percent of Pagans, and 69.4 percent of Goddess Worshipers state that they did vote in the last national election. With modest variations, all three sects follow the same general party allegiances as the larger Neo-Pagan population. Among Wiccans, 44.5 percent report that they are registered Democrats, 26.6 percent are Independents, 5.6 percent are Republicans, and 4.3 percent are members of the Green Party. Pagans report that 40.5 percent of their members are registered Democrats, 27.9 percent are Independents, 6.3 percent are Republicans, and 4.9 percent are members of the Green Party. Forty-five percent of Goddess Worshipers are registered Democrats, 25.5 percent are Independents, 4.7 percent are Republicans, and 5.1 percent are members of the Green Party. Goddess Worshipers are more likely to be members of the Green Party than they are to be members of the Republican Party. They are the least likely to be registered as Republicans of the three sects, although on the whole very few Neo-Pagans are registered Republicans.

Wiccans, Pagans, and Goddess Worshipers, like the general Neo-Pagan population, are involved in political activities. Goddess Worshipers have a higher percentage of their membership that claim to have participated in events such as marches and rallies than either of the other two sects. Approximately half (49.8 percent) of Goddess Worshipers and 51.5 percent of women Goddess Worshipers have participated in marches or rallies, as compared with 46.8 percent of Wiccans and 46.3 percent of Pagans. The participation of Goddess Worshipers in these political activities helps to dispel the notion that Goddess Worship results in women becoming apolitical. As noted in the last chapter, some scholars suggest that mysticism in general and

Neo-Paganism in particular result in participants becoming removed from political activity. Based on her participant observation study of women who joined the women's spirituality movement, Cynthia Eller (1993) contends that these women come from the more cultural and less political wing of the women's movement. She notes that almost from the outset of the second wave of feminism there has been a tension between the cultural and political wings of the movement. Looking specifically at those individuals who define themselves as Goddess Worshipers, our data indicate that this group is politically active, in some regards more so than the general Neo-Pagan population. Our data does not permit us to say whether members of Goddess Spirituality were politically active prior to joining or if their participation in Goddess Spirituality resulted in their political activity. It is clear, however, that those who self-define as Goddess Worshipers are highly political in the traditional sense of politics— that is, writing letters, attending marches, and acting as spokespersons for causes. It is plausible that participation in the goddess movement has resulted in participants becoming more politically involved because the rituals, mythology, and other members of the community encourage them to focus on inequality, particularly around issues of gender and sexual orientation and on environmental concerns.

As measured by the GSS questions on paranormal experiences, there are no differences in the kind or number of paranormal experiences reported among Wiccans, Pagans, Goddess Worshipers, and members of the larger Neo-Pagan community. As noted in the previous chapter, Neo-Pagans in general are more likely to report having these types of experiences than the general American public. There are also no notable differences among the three sects in their response to the GSS questions on the afterlife. Both the GSS questions on paranormal experiences and on the afterlife are included in our survey to enable us to compare Neo-Pagans with the general American public. These questions do not provide a basis for comparing theological issues or differences in practice that may exist among sects. Nonetheless, it is interesting that no differences appear among these three sects in their responses to questions about paranormal experiences and the afterlife. At least as compared with the general population, Neo-Pagan sects appear quite similar to one another.

Druids, Shamans, and UU Neo-Pagans each provide an interesting alternative form of Neo-Paganism. Druids are most clearly a sect, with their own mythology, ritual calendar, and some unique or different ritual practices. Shamans share a set of ritual practices that have been culled from a variety of cultures. UU Pagans may come from many different sects or forms of Paganism. What they share in common is attempting to integrate their Neo-Pagan practices with participation in a more traditional church that meets on Sunday mornings and has a majority of congregants who are not Neo-Pagans. In the first section of this chapter we compared and contrasted the three largest sects of Neo-Paganism. In this section we will examine Druids, Shamans, and UU Pagans separately against the background of the general Neo-Pagan movement.

Druids

> The archetypal Druid is a bearded man in a white robe greeting the rising sun at Stonehenge or talking on equal terms with a venerable oak tree. (Harvey 1997:19)

The image of Druids painted by Harvey grows out of academic and literary portrayals of the ancient Celtic pagan religion in which Druids were the priests and political leaders of their community. Contemporary Druids in the United States, while claiming historic links to the ancient religion, do not view themselves as direct descendants of the ancient Celts. They do, nonetheless, share some things with the archetype presented by Harvey.

Unlike the more popular sects of Neo-Paganism, a higher proportion of those self-defining as Druids in our survey are men (49.7 percent men, 48.2 percent women, with 2 percent not answering this question). In our survey Druids distinguish themselves from the larger Neo-Pagan community as having a larger proportion of members who are heterosexual. Almost three-quarters of Druids (73.6 percent) claim to be heterosexual. A very small proportion is composed of lesbians (1.5 percent) or gay men (3 percent), and a smaller proportion than exist among the larger Neo-Pagan community claim to be bisexual (16.2 percent). The median income of Druids, which is between $20,000 and $30,000, is lower than the average for Neo-Pagan. Given the higher proportion of men in this group, this finding is surprising, particularly because the educational level of Druids is about the same as other Neo-Pagans.

Margot Adler (1986) and Graham Harvey (1997) note that not all Druids self-define as Neo-Pagans. As our survey is titled The Pagan Census, it is fair to presume that all those Druids who answered our survey sufficiently self-identify with Neo-Paganism to include themselves within this description. Druidism as practiced in the United States shares with other forms of Neo-Paganism the commemoration of the eight yearly sabbats, a celebration of the "old ways" or old religion, a veneration of multiple gods and goddesses. The two solstices, in the spring and fall, are the most important of the sabbats for Druids. Within Druid groups, known as groves, there are normally three roles, that of the leader, known as the druid; the poet, storyteller, or holder of old wisdom, known as the bard; and the ovate, who can foretell the future and is believed to be in communion with the spirits of the earth. The oak tree is sacred for contemporary Druids as it was for the historic Druids. Most Druids prefer to hold their rituals outdoors among oak trees and on the whole prefer to wear white robes when participating in rituals (Harvey 1997).

Adler (1986) attributes the founding of at least one branch of Druidism in the United States, the Reformed Druids of North America (RDNA), to a student protest against the requirement to attend chapel in the early 1960s at Carlton College in Minnesota. What began as a lark in which students created rituals and what some of its founders defined as a philosophy conducive to any religion, turned into a self-consciously created new religion after Carlton College revoked its rule requiring students to attend chapel. The religion gained adherents and grew beyond the bounds of Carlton College with groves forming in other parts of the United States. Adler (1986) notes that Druids maintain a sense of humor about their religious practice. This aspect is shared with many other sects of Neo-Paganism in the United States. Participants may make fun of their own rituals, practices, and beliefs and simultaneously take them quite seriously. Tanya Luhrmann (1989) and Margot Adler (1986) both view this playfulness as a form of what Johan Huizinga

(1950) calls deep-play—that is, play that has as one of its aspects the questioning and restructuring of social arrangements.

Not all groves of the RDNA are self-defined as Neo-Pagan, but those who formed into the New Reformed Druids of North America (NRDNA) are. One member of the NRDNA, Isaac Bonewits, best known for his first book *Real Magic* (1989), which is based on his undergraduate thesis, formed a new Neo-Pagan organization, Ár nDraíocht Féin, of which he is the Arch-Druid. Bonewits openly acknowledges that the organization is hierarchical. Training, which is highly structured and involves demarcated levels of attainment, is required of all who want to become leaders within the religion. In

TABLE 18: Political Party Affiliations for the General Neo-Pagan Population and Druids

Party	GNPP %	Druid %
Not Registered	5.1	7.1
Democrat	42.9	31.0
Republican	6.6	4.6
Independent	27.9	35.5
Green	4.4	3.6
Liberal	0.2	0.0
NYS Choice	0.1	0.0
Libertarian	2.1	5.1
Anarchist	0.2	0.0
Socialist	0.3	0.0
Nonpartisan	0.3	0.0
Bipartisan	0.1	0.0
Uncommitted	0.2	0.0
Reform	0.1	0.0
Not a U.S. citizen	1.4	1.5
No response	8.4	11.7

1986 Adler reported that this movement had approximately two hundred members.

Druids are similar to the general Neo-Pagan population, although there are some notable political differences. Fewer Druids are registered to vote and do vote in national elections than members of the general Neo-Pagan population. Among Druids, 83.8 percent claim they are registered to vote as compared with 87.8 percent of Neo-Pagans. As shown in table 18, notably fewer Druids are registered as Democrats, and slightly fewer are registered as Republicans than the general Neo-Pagan population. A larger percentage of the Druids are registered Independents. On the whole Druids are about as politically active as other members of the Neo-Pagan community. In some areas of political activity Druids are less active, while in other areas they are more active, although these differences tend to be small. For example, Druids are less likely to state that they have written letters to local legislatures—28.9 percent of Druids claim to have done this in the previous year as compared with 31.6 percent of Neo-Pagans. Druids are more likely than the general Neo-Pagan population to note that they have participated in grassroots organizing—29.4 percent of Druids state they have participated in this activity in the previous year as compared with 24.8 percent of Neo-Pagans.

Druids' political views as reflected in their responses to the GSS questions about government spending on social issues indicates that this group is very similar to the general Neo-Pagan population. There are two notable differences, however. One, a much larger proportion of Druids (43.7 percent) than the general Neo-Pagan population (27.8 percent) believe that we are spending too little on space exploration. Two, although not as pronounced as space exploration, a larger percentage of Druids (70.6 percent) than Neo-Pagans (66.3 percent) state that they think we were spending too little on AIDS research.

On the whole Druids have slightly less confidence in social institutions than the general Neo-Pagan population as gauged by their responses to the GSS questions. Organized religion, however, is one social institution in which Druids have slightly higher confidence than other Neo-Pagans. This confidence may be accounted for by

TABLE 19: **Paranormal Experiences for the General Neo-Pagan Population and Druids**

Thought You Were Somewhere You Had Been Before

Response	GNPP %	Druid %
Never	6.2	4.1
Once or twice	22.1	16.2
Several times	42.5	43.7
Often	28.1	36.0
No response	1.1	0.0

Felt as Though You Were in Touch with Someone When They Were Far Away from You

Response	GNPP %	Druid %
Never	6.9	7.1
Once or twice	22.5	19.3
Several times	34.8	36.5
Often	34.7	37.1
No response	1.1	0.0

Saw Events that Happened at a Great Distance as They Were Happening

Response	GNPP %	Druid %
Never	54.4	46.2
Once or twice	26.7	28.9
Several times	11.3	12.7
Often	6.4	11.7
No response	1.2	0.5

TABLE 19 *(continued)*

Felt as Though You Were Really in Touch with Someone Who Had Died

Response	GNPP %	Druid %
Never	25.7	21.3
Once or twice	35.7	34.0
Several times	23.0	25.4
Often	14.6	19.3
No response	1.1	0.0

Felt as Though You Were Very Close to a Powerful, Spiritual Force

Response	GNPP %	Druid %
Never	14.4	14.2
Once or twice	24.1	22.3
Several times	28.2	28.4
Often	32.2	34.5
No response	1.1	0.5

the fact that Druids on the whole are more hierarchically organized than other Neo-Pagans. Druids give slightly weaker support to issues of gender and sexual orientation equality than other Neo-Pagans, although the views are on the whole quite similar. As noted in the last chapter, men on the whole tend to have somewhat weaker support of gender and sexual orientation equality issues than women do. The higher proportion of men within this sect accounts for the differences between the general Neo-Pagan community and Druids.

Table 19 indicates that Druids on the whole claim to have more paranormal experiences than the general Neo-Pagan population does, at least as indicated by their responses to the GSS questions. Fewer Druids claim to never have had any of these experiences, and more Druids claim to have had these experiences more often than other Neo-Pagans. As all Neo-Pagans emphasize mystical and magical experiences, it is unclear why Druids have these experiences at a higher rate than other Neo-Pagans.

Shamans

We received 363 responses from individuals who listed their primary spiritual path as Shamanism. Of this number, 60.6 percent indicate that they are women, 38.3 percent indicate that they are men, and 1.1 percent do not answer the question. The term *shaman* was originally applied to the spiritual practice of peoples of the Siberian Tungus. Anthropologists later expanded the definition to include spiritual practices among indigenous peoples that involved initiation and spirit quests. According to Harvey, shamans' initiations "typically include teaching by an experienced Shaman, a vision-quest or withdrawal to a remote place to fast and hold a vigil until spirit-guides or power-animals manifest themselves. Serious illness (e.g. epilepsy or smallpox) or spontaneous trance may mark an individual out as a likely candidate for initiation" (1997:108–9). After initiation, the shaman is expected to go into the spirit world both to gain insight and to do battle against illness and spiritual attacks.

Harvey refers to the shamanism practiced by Westerners as Neo-Shamanism. He contends that Neo-Shamans, unlike shamans of traditional societies, are not integrated into a larger community. Unlike traditional shamans, Neo-Shamans do not experience real danger. Instead, they are introduced to a series of techniques for getting into altered states, such as drumming, dancing, or meditation culled from a number of different indigenous cultures, through workshops or books such as Michael Harner's *The Way of the Shaman* (1982). Elements of shamanistic practices have been incorporated into Neo-Pagan magical practices. Scott Cunningham (1988) describes one form of Neo-Paganism, Wicca, as a shamanic religion because of its incorporation of shamanic techniques for gaining altered states of consciousness. Although aspects of shamanism have been integrated into almost all sects of Neo-Paganism, Shaman does form a distinct self-identification from other forms of Neo-Paganism in the contemporary United States.

Harvey notes that Western Shamanism is individualistic. Certainly the image of the Shaman is of a solitary practitioner. Our statistical data, however, indicate that while Shamans are slightly less likely to practice in groups than the general Neo-Pagan population, the difference is small. Among Shamans, 28.4 percent practice in groups as compared with 32.2 percent of the general Neo-Pagan population, 10.2 percent of Shamans and 9.2 percent of the general Neo-Pagan population practice with a partner, and 52.9 percent of shamans and 50.9 percent of the general Neo-Pagan population practice as solitaries.

Demographically, Shamans are quite similar to the general Neo-Pagan population. They earn the same median income, have about the same educational level, and have approximately the same number of homosexual and bisexual members. Shamans are slightly more likely to live in rural areas than other Neo-Pagans are. Among Shamans, 8 percent live in a secluded rural area, and 13.5 percent live in a rural community. This statistic can be compared with the general Neo-Pagan community, among whom 5.6 percent live in a secluded rural area, and 10.1 percent live in a rural community. Politically, Shamans are quite similar to the general Neo-Pagan population. Approximately the same number of Shamans is registered to vote as the rest of the Neo-Pagan population. A slightly higher percentage of Shamans is registered as Democrats than the general Neo-Pagan community—46.6 percent of Shamans and 42.9 percent of the general Neo-Pagan community are Democrats. Approximately the same percentage of Shamans and the general Neo-Pagan population vote in national elections.

Shamans on the whole are politically more active than the general Neo-Pagan population. Shamans, for instance, are more likely to write their legislators (58.3 percent of Shamans versus 49.1 percent of Neo-Pagans write to their federal legislators), participate in grassroots organizations (29.5 percent of Shamans versus 24.8 percent of Neo-Pagan), attend town meetings (27.5 percent of Shamans versus 25 percent of Neo-Pagans), are public spokespersons (17.1 percent of Shamans versus 14.6 percent of Neo-Pagans), and attend rallies and marches (48.5 percent of Shamans versus 45.7 percent of Neo-Pagans). Shamans, like other Neo-Pagans, support gender and sexual-preference equality. On the whole, Shamans support more money being spent on social programs than other Neo-Pagans, although the difference is quite small. Like the general Neo-Pagan population, Shamans tend to have little trust in social institutions. However, they are somewhat less confident in science than other Neo-Pagans are, as demonstrated in table 20.

TABLE 20: Degree of Confidence in the Scientific Community by the General Neo-Pagan Population and Shamans

Response	GNPP %	Shaman %
1 – Complete Confidence	2.5	2.5
2	15.8	12.1
3	21.3	17.9
4	24.3	26.4
5	15.6	18.5
6	10.4	11.8
7 – No confidence	6.9	8.3
No response	3.1	2.5

The lack of confidence in science may be related to the greater degree to which Shamans report having paranormal experiences such as déjà vu, being in touch with those people or events that are at a distance, having an out-of-body experience, or being in touch with the dead. As seen in table 21, Shamans are more likely than the general Neo-Pagan population to have these types of experiences. As Shamanism emphasizes, possibly even more so than other sects of Neo-Paganism, the use of a series of techniques to get in touch with the "other world," it is not surprising that more members of this group claim to have had these experiences. However, the image of Shamans as extreme individualists who are disengaged from worldly matters is not substantiated by our data.

Unitarian Universalist Pagans

Unitarian Universalist (UU) Pagans may come from a wide range of spiritual paths, but they share their integration of Neo-Paganism with their participation in a UU church or association. By joining a UU church, these Neo-Pagans have chosen to become part of a more conventional religious tradition, although one that is itself somewhat on the margins of mainstream religions. Unitarian Universalism, which grew out of the liberal Christian tradition, today boasts members who are secular humanists, Jews, and Buddhists, as well Christians and Neo-Pagans.

TABLE 21: Paranormal Experiences for the General Neo-Pagan Population and Shamans

Thought You Were Somewhere You Had Been Before

Response	GNPP %	Shaman %
Never	6.2	2.8
Once or twice	22.1	16.0
Several times	42.5	44.4
Often	28.1	35.5
No response	1.1	1.4

Felt as Though You Were in Touch with Someone When They Were Far Away From You

Response	GNPP %	Shaman %
Never	6.9	2.2
Once or twice	22.5	18.5
Several times	34.8	33.6
Often	34.7	44.9
No response	1.1	0.8

Saw Events that Happened at Great Distance as They Were Happening

Response	GNPP %	Shaman %
Never	54.4	41.3
Once or twice	26.7	30.6
Several times	11.3	14.0
Often	6.4	12.7
No response	1.2	1.4

Felt as Though You Were Really in Touch with Someone Who Had Died

Response	GNPP %	Shaman %
Never	25.7	14.3
Once or twice	35.7	35.3
Several times	23.0	30.6
Often	14.6	19.0
No response	1.1	0.8

Felt as Though You Were Very Close to a Powerful, Spiritual Force

Response	GNPP %	Shaman %
Never	14.4	7.9
Once or twice	24.1	12.9
Several times	28.2	29.2
Often	32.2	49.0
No response	1.1	0.8

The influx of Neo-Pagans into the UUA began in the 1970s and 1980s, during the period in which the association was increasing the spiritual component of their liturgy as a way of courting unchurched baby boomers. During this period, baby boomers were turning toward a new spirituality that was distinct from traditional religious expression (Meyer 1994; Lee 1995). At the same time, long-term members of the UUA, particularly women, were becoming interested in Goddess Spirituality as an element of their support for feminism. Workshops developed around *Cakes for the Queen of Heaven* (Ranck 1995) of interested UU women and in some instances men (H. Berger 1999a). The result was, as one minister who later became president of the UUA states, "to put it in symbolic terms, Ashtar, the Goddess, has been issued invitation where formerly only Lord Jehovah dared to tread" (as quoted in York 1995:129). It is within this context that the Covenant of the Unitarian Universalist Pagans (CUUPS) was formed in 1987. There are presently about 600 CUUPS members. However, many Neo-Pagans who have joined the

UUA have not joined CUUPS, either because they are not inter-ested in paying the dues, do not feel the organization will be of help to them, or simply have not gotten around to filling out the paper-work. There are many more Neo-Pagans, therefore, within the UUA than there are CUUPS members or chapters.

In our survey 193 individuals self-identify as Unitarian Univer-salists. We do not differentiate between those who are CUUPS members and those who are not. Although the self-identified UUs in our survey are in many ways similar to the larger Neo-Pagan com-munity, they differentiate themselves in several meaningful ways. As seen in table 22, a larger percentage of UU Pagans are legally mar-ried than the general Neo-Pagan population. This is true, although there is no real difference in the percentage of individuals who are heterosexual. Among those who self-identify as UU Pagans, 67.4 percent report that they are heterosexual as compared with the gen-eral Neo-Pagan population in which 67.8 percent report their sexual preference as heterosexual. There is a slightly higher percentage of men to women among UU Neo-Pagans than in the general Neo-Pagan community. Among UU Neo-Pagans, 62.7 percent are women,

TABLE 22: Comparison of Marital Status for the General Neo-Pagan Population and UU Neo-Pagans

Status	GNPP %	UU %
Never married	26.1	20.7
Married legally	33.3	39.4
Married ritually	4.8	3.6
Live with lover	13.8	11.9
Divorced	15.2	17.6
Widow/er	1.0	1.0
Separated	2.4	3.6
Group marriage	0.4	0.5
Other	1.7	0.5
No response	1.2	1.0

35 percent are men, as compared with the general Neo-Pagan population in which 64.8 percent are women, and 33.9 percent are men, with the remaining percentage of both groups not answering this question. UU Neo-Pagans are also somewhat better educated than the general Neo-Pagan population, as seen in table 23, although the

TABLE 23: Comparison of Education Level for the General Neo-Pagan Population and UU Neo-Pagans

Level	GNPP %	UU %
Less than high school	2.4	1.6
High school diploma	5.4	3.6
Some college	25.4	20.2
College diploma	25.6	31.6
Professional or technical school	11.6	7.3
Postgraduate work	11.4	13.5
Postgraduate degree	15.9	22.3
Other	1.6	0.0
No response	0.6	0.0

TABLE 24: Comparison of Residential Area of the General Neo-Pagan Population and UU Neo-Pagans

Area	GNPP %	UU %
Secluded rural	5.6	6.2
Large town	13.6	16.1
Rural community	10.1	10.9
Suburb	23.0	21.2
Small town	14.9	15.0
Metropolitan area	27.6	24.4
Other	3.8	4.7
No response	1.3	1.6

median income for both groups is the same. A smaller percentage of UU Neo-Pagans live in urban and suburban communities, and a greater percentage live in large towns than the general Neo-Pagan population, as seen in table 24.

Politically, UU Neo-Pagans are more active than the general Neo-Pagan population. Among UU Neo-Pagans, 91.2 percent are registered to vote, and 78.8 percent state they did vote in the last national election. This response can be compared with the general Neo-Pagan population in which 87.4 percent are registered to vote, and 70.9 percent did vote in the last national election. Table 25 indicates that for almost every form of political activity, UU Neo-Pagans are more active than the general Neo-Pagan population, including running for political office.

TABLE 25: Comparison of Political Activity for the General Neo-Pagan Population and UU Neo-Pagans

Registered to Vote

Response	GNPP %	UU %
No	11.4	8.3
Yes	87.8	91.2
No response	0.8	0.5

Voted in Last National Election

Response	GNPP %	UU %
No	16.3	16.5
Yes	70.1	78.5
No response	13.6	5.7

Writes Letter to Federal Legislators

Response	GNPP %	UU %
No	45.0	36.3
Yes	49.1	59.1
No response	5.9	4.7

Writes Letter to State Legislators

Response	GNPP %	UU %
No	49.7	42.5
Yes	44.1	52.8
No response	6.2	4.7

Writes Letter to Local Government

Response	GNPP %	UU %
No	61.2	63.2
Yes	31.6	29.5
No response	7.2	7.3

Participates in Grassroots Local Organizing

Response	GNPP %	UU %
No	67.5	60.6
Yes	24.8	33.2
No response	7.7	6.2

Participates in Town Meetings, Hearings, Forums, and Open Meetings

Response	GNPP %	UU %
No	67.4	59.6
Yes	25.0	33.7
No response	7.7	6.7

Participates in Special Events

Response	GNPP %	UU %
No	48.3	42.5
Yes	45.7	53.4
No response	6.0	4.1

TABLE 25 *(continued)*

Public Spokesperson for Causes of Personal Concern

Response	GNPP %	UU %
No	76.9	76.2
Yes	14.6	15.5
No response	8.5	8.3

Active Lobbier

Response	GNPP %	UU %
No	86.9	87.0
Yes	4.0	4.1
No response	9.1	8.8

Active in Campaigning

Response	GNPP %	UU %
No	83.1	82.9
Yes	8.2	9.3
No response	8.7	7.8

Hold/Have Held Public Office

Response	GNPP %	UU %
No	88.9	86.5
Yes	1.9	4.1
No response	9.2	9.3

In general, UUs are noted for their participation in liberal causes. In a survey of their readership, in which they received 748 responses, *The World,* a journal published by the UUA for their membership, finds that in the previous twelve months their members participated in the following activities:

Voted in an election	86 percent
Signed a petition	70 percent
Attended a public meeting	50 percent
Wrote or visited an elected official	37 percent
Addressed a public meeting	17 percent
Held or ran for office	6 percent
Attended rally/speech	30 percent (UUA 1992:33)

Although the questions we asked in The Pagan Census are not exactly the same as those asked by *The World,* it is, nonetheless, possible to compare the political activities of UU Neo-Pagans and other UU members. As seen in comparing the two sets of data, there are some areas in which UU Neo-Pagans appear to exceed and other areas in which they are less active than other UUs. For example, UU Neo-Pagans have a lower voting rate and are less likely to run for public office than other UUs. However, they are more likely to write a letter to an elected official than other UUs and to attend a demonstration or march than other UUs are to attend a rally or speech.

In comparing UU Neo-Pagans and the Neo-Pagan population's responses to the GSS questions concerning government spending on social issues, we find that on the whole the two groups' responses are quite similar. UU Neo-Pagans are more likely than other Neo-Pagans to believe that we are spending too little money on mass transit, although the majority of both groups believes we are spending too little in this area.[1] A smaller proportion of UU Neo-Pagans than the general Neo-Pagan population believes we are spending too little on big cities, crime, and drug addiction.[2] In their responses to questions about gender and sexual preference issues, UU Neo-Pagans do not notably differentiate themselves from the general Neo-Pagan population. On the whole, UU Neo-Pagans in their responses to the GSS questions show somewhat greater confidence in social institutions than the general Neo-Pagan population.

Although UU Neo-Pagans share similar political views with other Neo-Pagans, they tend to be somewhat more politically active. The greater political activity of UU Neo-Pagans can be explained by an elective affinity between politically active Neo-Pagans and Unitarian Universalism. It is also possible, however, that participating in churches in which other congregants are politically active results in Neo-Pagans becoming even more politically active.

More UU Neo-Pagans are uncertain about reincarnation than the general Neo-Pagan population. Approximately one-third (31.1 percent) UU Neo-Pagans report that they are not sure, 8.3 percent state they do not believe in reincarnation, and 59.6 percent state they do believe in reincarnation. This statistic can be compared with the general Neo-Pagan population in which 75.3 percent state they believe in reincarnation, 4.1 percent say they do not believe in rein-carnation, and 19.3 percent are unsure. In response to the GSS questions concerning paranormal experiences, UU Neo-Pagans on the whole report having fewer of these experiences than the general Neo-Pagan population, as can shown in table 26.

Although the differences are small, UU Neo-Pagans on the whole appear somewhat more mainstream than other Neo-Pagans. For example, UU Neo-Pagans are more likely to be legally married, they are more likely to be members of one of the two major parties, and they state that they have fewer paranormal experiences than other Neo-Pagans. Politically, UU Neo-Pagans are on the whole more active than the general Neo-Pagan population. The UUA may be drawing to its churches those Neo-Pagans who are more conserva-tive in their life-style and more politically active than Neo-Pagans who choose to practice within the coven system, in groups, with a partner, or as solitaries. As joining a church is outside the main-stream of Neo-Paganism, it seems likely that those who choose to do so may in some respects be different from the larger Neo-Pagan community. Those Neo-Pagans who join a UU church may also find that over time their life-style, spiritual, and political views are influ-enced by the larger congregation.

Forms of Practice

Traditionally, Wicca in particular but Neo-Paganism in general was taught and practiced in groups. The publication of books such as *The Spiral Dance* by Starhawk (1979) and *Women's Book of Mysteries*

TABLE 26: Comparison of the General Neo-Pagan Population's and UU Neo-Pagans' Paranormal Experiences

Thought You Were Somewhere You Had Been Before

Response	GNPP %	UU %
Never	6.2	6.2
Once or twice	22.1	24.9
Several times	42.5	48.2
Often	28.1	19.2
No response	1.1	1.6

Felt as Though You Were in Touch with Someone When They Were Far Away from You

Response	GNPP %	UU %
Never	6.9	7.8
Once or twice	22.5	34.2
Several times	34.8	32.6
Often	34.7	23.8
No response	1.1	1.6

Saw Events that Happened at Great Distance as They Were Happening

Response	GNPP %	UU %
Never	54.4	63.2
Once or twice	26.7	22.3
Several times	11.3	6.7
Often	6.4	6.2
No response	1.2	1.6

TABLE 26 (continued)

Felt as Though You Were Really in Touch with Someone Who Had Died

Response	GNPP %	UU %
Never	25.7	31.1
Once or twice	35.7	38.3
Several times	23.0	14.0
Often	14.6	14.5

Felt as Though You Were Very Close to a Powerful, Spiritual Force

Response	GNPP %	UU %
Never	14.4	13.5
Once or twice	24.1	24.9
Several times	28.2	34.2
Often	32.2	24.9
No response	1.1	2.6

by Zsuzsanna Budapest (1986) helped to spread information about ritual and magical practices beyond the confines of the coven. The availability of such books made it possible for individuals, based completely on their readings, to either form covens, practice with one other person—most commonly their significant other—or to practice alone. Scott Cunningham, possibly more than anyone else with his book *Wicca: A Guide for the Solitary Practitioner* (1988) contributed to the growth of individuals practicing alone. In the introduction to his second book for solitary practitioners, Cunningham writes, "This book has been written with a single premise: that Wicca is an open religion. All can come before the altar and worship the Goddess and God, whether alone or in the company of others; initiated or not" (Cunningham 1993:xiii). Particularly within Wicca, the largest sect of Neo-Pagans, there is a debate about whether or not solitary practitioners, especially those who have no coven training, are equally well trained and proficient in spiritual and ritual matters. As one respondent to our survey states, "I have read much debate about the authenticity of self-initiated Wiccans, solitaries in particular. While I'm sure those in favor of coven-initiation-only have valid reasons for this, there are those of us who have no access and no hope of access to a coven. I would still be adrift spiritually were it not for the books of Scott Cunningham and Z Budapest. They informed me it was possible to be a Witch alone and told me how to go about accomplishing that goal" (Survey 1061). Although our survey does ask if the respondent practices in a group, with a single partner, or alone, it does not ask individuals their opinions about solitary practitioners. Some individuals, like the respondent above, write about the issues surrounding solitary practice in the free-response area. Most of those who write about solitary practitioners are either now or have been at some time a solo practitioner. In almost all cases they write to support the equal inclusion of solitary practitioners within the Neo-Pagan community. Like respondent 1061, most who take the time to write about the issue feel that those who are self-initiated Wiccans or self-trained Neo-Pagans are given less respect within the Neo-Pagan and particularly within the Wiccan community than those who are coven trained. Within Wiccan covens it is the high priestess or both the high priestess and high priest, or in some cases those considered the elders of the coven, who determine when an initiate is ready to be awarded their first, second, or third degree (H. Berger 2000). Those who have not been trained in the coven system are normally self-initiated.

Some individuals begin and remain solitaries throughout their lives, while others may be solitary practitioners for a short period of time until they find an appropriate group. Some who have been members of covens in the past subsequently choose to practice alone. Often this choice is based on the feeling that there is too much infighting within the coven. One respondent observes, "I find many covens are just as cliquish as some organized religions. I work as a solitary because I have not found a coven I'm comfortable with, and at this time I am hesitant to seek out others due to the rather dogmatic reactions I have been faced with (i.e., "our way or else") This disappoints me" (Survey 1503). We do not distinguish between those who are solo practitioners for a short time, a long period, or since they first became Neo-Pagans. Our survey focused on respondents' present form of spiritual practice.

Neo-Pagans normally speak about practicing or working magic or rituals and of working in a group, alone, or with one other person. They do not usually speak about participating in worship, although at rituals the goddess or goddesses and gods are venerated. The focus for Neo-Pagans is on the ritual activity and the magical or mystical experience it elicits. We, therefore, refer throughout this text to three forms of practice or work—groups, spiritual partners and solitaries—and not of worship.

Demographics

Demographically, individuals, regardless of their form of practice, have approximately the same ratio of women to men. As demonstrated in table 27, a larger percentage of those who work with a partner are legally married than those who work either in groups or as solitaries. Combining those individuals who are ritually married or living with their lover and those who are legally married, 63.3 percent of those working with a partner are in a relationship. Solitaries are the least likely to be in a committed relationship and the least

TABLE 27: Marital Status for the Three Forms of Spiritual Practice

Status	GNPP %	Group %	SP %	SO %	NR %
Never married	26.1	21.5	16.1	31.4	22.0
Married legally	33.3	37.0	43.0	30.5	25.2
Married ritually	4.8	5.9	7.3	3.4	6.3
Live with lover	13.8	12.2	13.0	14.6	16.4
Divorced	15.2	16.2	12.4	14.2	21.4
Widow/er	1.0	1.5	1.0	0.7	0.6
Separated	2.4	2.4	1.0	2.3	5.0
Group marriage	0.4	0.4	1.6	0.1	1.3
Other	1.7	1.5	3.1	1.8	0.6
No response	1.2	1.3	1.6	1.1	1.3

Note: The three forms of spiritual practice are group, spiritual partner (SP), and solitaire (SO).

TABLE 28: Age Ranges for the Three Forms of Spiritual Practice

Age	GNPP %	Group %	SP %	SO %	NR %
8–9	0.2	0.1	0.0	0.1	0.0
10–19	3.4	1.8	3.6	4.1	2.5
20–29	27.9	20.9	31.0	32.3	24.0
30–39	32.9	37.3	28.0	30.8	34.1
40–49	23.3	24.9	27.3	21.3	25.8
50–59	7.5	9.2	3.0	7.1	7.0
60–69	1.9	2.6	1.5	2.1	1.8
70–79	0.3	0.2	0.0	0.3	0.0
No response	2.7	2.4	3.1	2.5	5.0

likely to be married. Nonetheless, almost half (48.5 percent) are legally married, ritually married, or living with their lover.

As shown in table 28, more solitaries are between that ages of twenty and twenty-nine than are those who work in groups. However, those working with a spiritual partner have approximately the same percentage of members who are in their twenties as solitaries. The lower rate of committed relationships among solitaries can in part be explained by their relative youthfulness; however, it does not explain the differences between solitaries and those working with a partner. Our data suggest that although not all those working with a spiritual partner are working with their spouse or significant other, many are.

As table 29 demonstrates, a larger percentage of solitaries and those working with a partner are heterosexual than are those who are in groups. A greater percentage of lesbians, gay men, and bisexuals work in groups than either alone or with one partner. The reason fewer homosexual and bisexual individuals work alone or with one other person is unclear. It might be, however, that those individuals who have found their sexual preference discriminated against in other situations are drawn to groups because of the open acceptance of all forms of sexuality within Neo-Paganism.

TABLE 29: Sexual Preferences for the Three Forms of Spiritual Practice

Preference	GNPP %	Group %	SP %	SO %	NR %
Heterosexual	67.8	66.1	70.5	70.0	56.6
Lesbian	4.8	6.1	4.7	4.0	5.0
Gay Men	4.5	5.2	1.0	4.5	6.3
Bisexual	19.0	19.9	18.1	18.1	22.0
Other	1.9	1.6	3.6	1.4	4.4
No response	1.9	1.0	2.1	1.9	5.7

Those who are solitaries are more likely to define the type of community they live in as secluded rural, rural, or a small town than members of the other two forms of practice are. Most solitaries, however, like most members of the Neo-Pagan community, live in urban or suburban communities. As shown in table 30, those who work in groups tend to have the highest educational achievement of the three categories of practice. This discrepancy can be explained in part by the age difference between those who practice in groups and other Neo-Pagans. Those in their twenties and early thirties are most likely not to have completed their education and to have listed their occupation as student.

Age and sexual preference appear to be the strongest indicators of the type of spiritual practice in which an individual participates. Although approximately a third of all those practicing with a partner or alone are forty or older, the larger proportion of younger adults in these two forms of practice suggests that the religion may be in the process of change. Traditionally, entrance into Neo-Paganism has been through groups; however, our data suggest that for a substantial subsection of Neo-Pagans, solitary practice may be their first step into the Neo-Pagan community. Although some of these individuals will ultimately join a group, some will remain solitaries. As the form and content of training in groups often differs from that available on the Internet or through books, the large number of primarily young adults practicing as solitaries may ultimately result in the focus of the religion changing or with the religion bifurcating.

Table 30: Education Levels for the Three Forms of Spiritual Practice

Level	GNPP %	Group %	SP %	SO %	NR %
Less than high school	2.4	2.4	1.6	2.8	0.6
High school diploma	5.4	3.6	8.3	6.2	4.4
Some college	25.4	21.8	26.4	27.3	26.4
College diploma	25.6	27.3	22.3	24.6	28.3
Professional or technical school	11.6	9.8	13.5	12.3	12.6
Postgraduate work	11.4	11.9	7.3	11.8	11.9
Postgraduate degree	15.9	21.8	15.0	12.8	13.2
Other	1.6	1.0	4.1	1.4	1.9
No response	0.6	0.3	1.6	0.7	0.6

Politics

On the whole, solitaries are less politically active and less liberal than members of groups and to a lesser degree than those who practice with a partner. Among those who practice in groups, 91.2 percent are registered to vote, although only 76.5 percent report that they did vote in the last national election. This statistic can be compared with solitaries in which 86.2 percent are registered to vote and 66.8 percent did vote in the last national election, and to those who practice with a partner in which 87 percent are registered to vote and 77.2 percent report voting in the last national election. Just over 50 percent (50.1 percent) of those who practice in groups, 42 percent of those who work with a partner, and 38.3 percent of those who are solitaries are registered as Democrats. Among those working in groups, 5.6 percent are registered as Republicans. These figures can be compared with those who are working with a partner, among whom 5.2 percent are registered Republicans, and solitaries, among whom 7.8 percent are registered Republicans. Solitaries are the most likely of the three forms of practice to report being Independents, with 31.2 percent of their numbers selecting this designation. Among those who work in groups, 27.9 percent report being Independents, and among those who work with a partner, 28 percent are Independents. Among both those who work in groups and those who work with a partner, the same percentage of individuals are members of the Green Party as are members of the Republican Party. Solitaries have a slightly lower rate of participation in the Green Party, with 3.7 percent of solitaries claiming membership in this party.

In our survey those who practice in groups are more politically active in almost every indicator of political activity. The two exceptions to this occurrence are grassroots organizing and running for public office in which those who work with a partner report that they are slightly more active than those who work in groups in these two areas. Solitaries in all instances are the least politically active of the three forms of spiritual practice. The differences, particularly between the solitaries and those who practice in groups, may be an indication of the influence of covens or groups on increasing political activity, or of generational differences, or of a predisposition of those who choose to work alone to avoid public activities such as politics. Solitaries, however, appear to be more politically active than the general American public, at least as far as a comparison is possible based on the statistics of the general American public discussed in the last chapter.

All three forms of spiritual practice support gender and sexual-preference equity. Although there are some variations in responses, overall, those who practice in groups tend to be more supportive of gender and sexual-preference issues. When combining those who strongly agree, agree, and agree with qualification, 89 percent of those who practice in groups, 88.1 percent of those who practice with a partner, and 87 percent of solitaries support the ERA. Those who practice in groups are most likely to give strong support to the ERA. Combining the three degrees of disagreement, 61.8 percent of group participants and solitaries, and 60.6 percent of those who practice with a partner do not support excluding women from the draft. Those who work with a partner are the most strongly opposed to this proposition. Among those who practice in groups, 92.7 percent support to some degree same-sex marriages, with 63.7 percent supporting this proposition strongly. These figures can be compared with those who practice with a partner, in which 85.5 percent support gay marriages, with 52.9 percent doing so strongly and solitaries, among whom 87.7 percent support gay marriages, with 58 percent doing so strongly. The majority of members of all three forms of spiritual practice opposes preferential hiring. Combining all three categories of disagreement, 53.2 percent of both group participants and solitaries, and 55 percent of those who practice with a partner oppose preferential hiring. More members of groups than the other two forms of spiritual practice oppose with qualifications preferential hiring. Slightly over three-quarters of individuals in all three forms of spiritual practice support, to some degree, women in combat positions. Over 90 percent of members of all three forms of spiritual practice agree that there should be legislation making discrimination on the basis of sexual preference illegal. However, a larger percentage of those in groups both support this proposition and are more likely to support it strongly than the other two forms of practice. Similarly, members of all three groups oppose gays being excluded from the military, but those who practice in groups are more likely to oppose this proposition and are more likely to strongly oppose it.

Although there are variations among the three forms of practice about whether the government is spending the correct amount, too much, or too little on social programs, there does not appear to be a distinct pattern of responses among the three forms of spiritual practice. Members of all three categories have about equal lack of trust in social institutions. It is interesting that solitaries appear to have the least trust, and those in groups to have the most trust in organized religion, although the difference is very small. Those in groups, furthermore, have much less trust in organized religion than does the general American public.

Paranormal Experiences
Regardless of their form of practice, Neo-Pagans on the whole have the same types of paranormal experiences. Less than 7 percent of individuals, regardless of their form of practice, have never thought they were somewhere before but knew it was impossible. Similarly, less than 10 percent of our respondents, regardless of their form of practice, claim they never felt they were in touch with someone when they were away from that individual. A less common phenomenon,

regardless of form of practice, is seeing events at a great distance as they are occurring. Over 50 percent of both groups participants and solitaries, and slightly less than 50 percent of those practicing with a partner claim they never had this experience. Approximately 25 percent of individuals, regardless of their form of practice, claim to never have felt they were in touch with someone who is dead. And about 15 percent of those in each form of practice never have felt they were close to a powerful, spiritual force that seemed to lift the individual out of herself or himself. Individuals who practice with a partner on the whole are more likely to claim that they more often have paranormal experiences than members of either of the other two forms of spiritual practice.

Our items investigating paranormal experiences are limited to those that appear in the GSS. It is possible that if another set of questions were asked, significant differences among the three forms of practice would appear. Nonetheless, the parallelism of frequency of different types of paranormal experience among all three forms of spiritual practice suggests that what are normative forms of paranormal experience and of training to elicit these experiences is consistent throughout the Neo-Pagan community. Coven or group training does not result in individuals having more or less frequent paranormal experiences than those whose training is from books, workshops, and chats on the Internet.

Regional Differences

> I am from the Midwest—I'd love to know geographic differences. I find it very difficult to find adequate teachers anywhere nearby. (Survey 1615)

The United States is known for its regional diversity. Some areas are noted as being more culturally and politically progressive and others more conservative. We find that although in both the GSS and in our survey regional differences do exist, these differences do not follow the same pattern in the two surveys. For example, in both surveys regional differences in educational levels are evident, but not in the same regions. Similarly, there are regional differences in the frequency of paranormal events reported in both surveys; however, again, these are not in the same region. On the whole, regional differences among

Neo-Pagans are less dramatic than those among the general American population, suggesting that Neo-Pagans are drawn from a similar strata of American society regardless of geographic area.

Demographics

Demographically, there are some notable differences among Neo-Pagans. Although Neo-Pagans—regardless of the region in which they live—are in stable relationships, there is some variation among regions in terms of the number who are legally married, as shown in table 31. In both the East South Central and the West South Central areas, 43.1 percent of the Neo-Pagan population are legally married. Compared with the West North Central region, 28.2 percent are legally married, and compared with the Pacific and Mid-Atlantic regions, 29.1 percent are legally married. These discrepancies cannot be explained by age differences. Although there is some small variation in the ages of Neo-Pagans by regions, such variations do not correspond to more Neo-Pagans in their forties, or thirties and forties, living in areas with the highest marital rates. Our statistics suggest that although on the whole Neo-Pagans are sexually experimental, those who live in more culturally conservative areas of the United States are more likely to be legally married than those who live in more liberal regions.

The majority of Neo-Pagans, regardless of region, reports that they are heterosexual. Nonetheless, there is some variation among regions. The Pacific region has the lowest rate of heterosexuals, with only 58.1 percent claiming this sexual orientation. The other regions range from 76.7 percent of Neo-Pagans in the West South Central area identifying as heterosexual compared with 61.5 percent in the West North Central area. In the Pacific region a high proportion of individuals (22.3 percent) self-define as bisexual, although other regions have a proportion of bisexuals as high or even higher; for instance, 26.5 percent of Neo-Pagans in the West North Central region and 23.1 percent of those in the Mountain region self-define as bisexual. The Pacific region, however, most clearly differentiates itself by having the highest percentage of women (9.9 percent) who state they are lesbians and a high percent of men (5.3 percent) that self-identify as gay. The Mid-Atlantic region has a larger percentage of gay men (8.8 percent) but has fewer lesbians and bisexuals than

TABLE 31: Comparison of Marital Status by Region

Status	ENC %	ESC %	MA %	MO %	NE %	PA %	SA %	WNC %	WSC %
Never married	20.9	19.6	37.0	21.2	30.6	24.7	29.8	24.4	16.3
Married legally	38.5	43.5	29.1	37.8	32.1	29.1	34.3	28.2	43.1
Married ritually	4.5	10.9	3.5	0.6	5.7	6.6	3.6	7.7	3.4
Live with lover	12.0	6.5	17.7	12.8	12.5	14.6	14.5	10.2	11.2
Divorced	17.9	10.9	7.5	18.6	14.3	16.6	12.9	23.1	17.2
Widow/er	0.7	4.3	0.0	0.0	0.0	2.2	0.6	1.3	1.7
Separated	2.1	0.0	3.5	1.9	2.6	2.4	2.4	0.0	2.6
Group marriage	0.7	0.0	0.4	0.6	0.0	0.2	0.6	1.3	0.0
Other	2.1	2.1	0.8	1.9	0.4	2.6	0.6	3.8	2.6
No response	0.7	2.1	0.4	4.5	1.8	0.9	0.6	0.0	1.7

Note: Regions designated are East North Central (ENC), East South Central (ESC), Middle Atlantic (MA), Mountain (MO), New England (NE), Pacific (PA), South Atlantic (SA), West North Central (WNC), West South Central (WSC). The states included and percentage of Neo-Pagans in each region is listed on pages 30–31.

the Pacific region. Although regional differences in sexual orientation are interesting to note, these differences on the whole are small.

As table 32 indicates, regional variations of educational levels among Neo-Pagans are small. This observation is surprising when we compare our results to the findings of the GSS in table 33, which shows significant regional differences in educational level among the general American public. Furthermore, regardless of region, Neo-Pagans on average have a higher educational level than their neighbors do. As noted in chapter 1, those drawn to Neo-Paganism tend to be better educated than the average American. Regional differences that affect educational levels for the general American public do not appear to affect Neo-Pagans. This variation suggests that Neo-Pagans are disproportionately drawn from the more educated sections of U.S. society regardless of regional education level. Neither our finding nor those of the GSS are based on the length of time individuals have lived in a region. As we do not ask our respondents how long they have lived in a particular region, we cannot determine if our respondents are more geographically mobile than other Americans. Greater mobility might help explain some of the educational differences that exist between Neo-Pagans and their neighbors; however, Americans on the whole are geographically mobile.

As shown in table 34, whether individuals practice in a group, with one partner, or alone varies by region. These differences, however, cannot be explained simply by regional density. Although the East South Central region, which has the lowest proportion of Neo-Pagans of all the regions in the United States, also has the largest proportion of solo practitioners, other areas with high rates of solitaries, such as New England, have a large proportion of Neo-Pagans. Those areas with high rates of solitary practitioners tend to have a larger proportion of younger adherents. Although for some individuals the decision to work alone may be the result of their inability to find an appropriate group, for others it is a choice. One respondent to The Pagan Census states, "Personally I prefer the focus and energy of a solitary. Too many circles have I joined for holidays when you join the group in perfect love and perfect trust and another in the group is off or angry or unfocused—It breaks the energy and you will have a hard time regaining it" (Survey 2664).

TABLE 32: Comparison of Education Level by Region

Level	ENC %	ESC %	MA %	MO %	NE %	PA %	SA %	WNC %	WSC %
Less than high school	1.7	2.2	2.8	1.9	2.3	0.9	3.9	2.6	2.6
High school diploma	6.5	6.5	6.7	3.8	4.9	2.4	6.3	6.4	8.6
Some college	28.2	30.4	24.8	26.3	19.2	24.9	26.8	29.5	30.2
College diploma	24.7	34.8	28.7	17.9	29.4	26.0	26.8	23.1	18.9
Professional or technical school	9.9	13.0	9.8	17.9	9.8	12.4	10.5	14.1	12.9
Postgraduate work	10.7	4.3	7.9	10.3	14.7	13.2	13.3	7.7	10.3
Postgraduate degree	16.5	6.5	16.1	20.5	18.1	17.4	11.7	11.5	13.8
Other	1.0	0.0	1.9	0.6	1.5	1.9	0.6	3.8	2.6
No response	0.7	2.2	1.2	0.6	0.0	0.7	0.0	1.3	0.0

TABLE 33: Comparison of Education Level of the General American Public by Region

Level	ENC %	ESC %	MA %	MO %	NE %	PA %	SA %	WNC %	WSC %
Less than high school	17.1	38.8	21.3	10.5	11.7	13.8	21.0	11.0	14.7
High school diploma	57.2	42.6	47.8	61.6	45.0	52.0	49.3	55.1	60.7
Junior college	5.7	7.0	5.2	7.0	3.3	7.1	6.9	6.8	4.0
Bachelor's degree	14.4	7.0	16.1	11.6	28.3	19.7	15.6	21.2	12.7
Graduate degree	5.7	4.7	9.6	9.6	11.7	7.5	7.2	5.9	8.0

TABLE 34: The Three Forms of Spiritual Practice by Region

Form	GNPP %	ENC %	ESC %	MA %	MO %	NE %	PA %	SA %	WNC %	WSC %
Group	32.2	30.6	21.7	36.2	30.8	26.0	31.8	40.1	29.5	25.0
Spiritual partner	9.2	11.0	10.9	10.6	12.8	7.5	8.2	5.7	11.5	15.5
Solitary	50.9	53.6	63.0	46.9	47.4	57.7	50.6	46.4	51.3	52.6
No response	7.6	4.8	4.3	6.3	9.0	8.7	9.5	7.8	7.7	6.9

Paranormal Experiences

In chapter 2 we note that Neo-Pagans report having more paranormal experiences than other Americans do. The same is true for every region of the United States. Although there are regional variations among Neo-Pagans, the differences tend to be much smaller than the regional differences found in the GSS as evidenced by comparing tables 35 and 36. Furthermore, the regions of greater or fewer paranormal experiences shown in the GSS are different from those in our survey. In response to the question of how often Neo-Pagans felt they were somewhere before but knew it was impossible, all respondents to The Pagan Census who answered this question in the East South Central region claim they had this experience at least once. The vast majority of Neo-Pagans in all regions report having this experience several times or often. These statistics can be compared with the results from the GSS in which the Mountain region reports having the smallest percentage (18.3 percent) who never had this experience and the West North Central region the largest percentage (45.3 percent) that never had this experience. Comparatively, Neo-Pagans in the West North Central region rank seventh and those in the Mountain region rank sixth among all regions for inhabitants who have never had this experience.

Neo-Pagans in the East South Central region again are the most likely to at least once have felt in touch with someone who is at a distance. Only 2.2 percent of Neo-Pagans in this region state that they never had this experience. The East North Central area has the largest percentage (8.6 percent) who never had this experience. The difference between the regions in which the fewest and the most Neo-Pagans have not had this experience is quite small. The results from the GSS show a wider range among the regions. In the GSS the South Atlantic region has the largest percentage of the population having had this experience at least once. In this region only 28.2 percent claim they never had this experience. The West North Central region again has the lowest rate of paranormal experiences, with 42 percent who has not had this experience.

The regional difference among GSS respondents decreases for the question of whether the individual has perceived events at a great distance. The West South Central region, the area in which

TABLE 35: Paranormal Experiences by Region

Thought You Were Somewhere You Had Been Before

Response	Total %	ENC %	ESC %	MA %	MO %	NE %	PA %	SA %	WNC %	WSC %
Never	6.2	6.2	0.0	8.3	4.5	7.2	7.1	4.8	3.8	3.4
Once or twice	22.1	21.6	17.4	26.4	23.7	20.4	23.6	20.8	23.1	17.2
Several times	42.5	45.7	45.7	37.4	44.2	44.5	41.9	41.0	42.3	46.6
Often	28.1	25.8	37.0	27.6	26.9	26.4	26.5	32.5	29.5	30.2
No response	1.1	0.7	0.0	0.4	0.6	1.5	0.9	1.0	1.3	7.6

Felt as Though You Were in Touch with Someone When They Were Far Away from You

Response	Total %	ENC %	ESC %	MA %	MO %	NE %	PA %	SA %	WNC %	WSC %
Never	6.9	8.6	2.2	5.9	7.1	7.9	7.5	6.3	5.1	3.4
Once or twice	22.5	20.6	28.3	26.0	23.1	24.5	20.5	22.3	24.4	20.7
Several times	34.8	34.7	39.1	36.2	34.0	32.5	35.3	38.3	32.1	32.8
Often	34.7	34.7	30.4	31.5	35.3	32.8	36.0	32.2	37.2	41.4
No response	1.1	1.4	0.0	0.4	0.6	2.3	0.7	0.9	1.3	1.7

TABLE 35 (continued)

Saw Events that Happened at Great Distance as They Were Happening

Response	Total %	ENC %	ESC %	MA %	MO %	NE %	PA %	SA %	WNC %	WSC %
Never	54.4	55.7	52.2	59.4	52.6	56.2	56.5	50.6	46.2	43.1
Once or twice	26.7	28.5	26.1	18.1	30.1	24.5	26.9	29.2	32.1	31.9
Several times	11.3	8.2	17.4	12.2	10.9	12.5	10.6	13.9	10.3	14.7
Often	6.4	6.9	4.3	9.1	5.8	4.2	5.3	5.4	7.7	8.6
No response	1.2	0.7	0.0	1.2	0.6	2.6	0.7	1.0	3.8	1.7

Felt as Though You Were Really in Touch with Someone Who Had Died

Response	Total %	ENC %	ESC %	MA %	MO %	NE %	PA %	SA %	WNC %	WSC %
Never	25.7	23.7	19.6	27.2	28.8	26.8	21.6	28.0	20.5	28.4
Once or twice	35.7	35.4	52.2	31.1	35.9	38.1	37.7	32.8	30.8	37.1
Several times	23.0	23.0	19.6	12.2	20.5	20.4	25.2	23.8	28.2	20.7
Often	14.6	17.5	8.7	9.1	14.1	12.5	15.0	14.2	19.2	12.1
No response	1.1	0.3	0.0	1.2	0.6	2.3	0.4	1.2	1.3	1.7

Felt as Though You Were Very Close to a Powerful, Spiritual Force

Response	Total %	ENC %	ESC %	MA %	MO %	NE %	PA %	SA %	WNC %	WSC %
Never	14.4	15.8	8.7	17.3	15.4	16.2	13.5	13.0	11.5	13.8
Once or twice	24.1	23.0	19.6	21.3	20.5	28.3	21.0	27.7	28.2	29.3
Several times	28.2	27.8	41.3	27.6	25.6	29.4	31.6	25.3	17.9	28.4
Often	32.2	32.6	3.4	33.1	37.8	24.2	33.3	32.5	41.0	26.7
No response	1.1	0.7	0.0	0.8	0.6	1.9	0.7	1.5	1.3	1.7

TABLE 36: Americans' Paranormal Experiences by Region

Thought You Were Somewhere You Had Been Before

Response	Total %	ENC %	ESC %	MA %	MO %	NE %	PA %	SA %	WNC %	WSC %
Never	32.7	30.8	37.1	28.0	18.3	35.0	25.0	38.6	45.3	35.6
Once or twice	32.3	33.8	37.1	37.7	39.4	23.8	30.2	29.7	26.3	31.1
Several times	28.4	29.3	22.9	29.5	32.7	31.2	35.5	25.9	24.1	24.2
Often	9.3	6.2	2.9	4.8	9.6	10.0	9.3	5.8	4.4	9.1
No response	0.0	0.0	0.0	0.0	0.0	0.0	0.0	0.0	0.0	0.0

TABLE 36 (continued)

Felt as Though You Were in Touch with Someone When They Were Far Away from You

Response	Total %	ENC %	ESC %	MA %	MO %	NE %	PA %	SA %	WNC %	WSC %
Never	35.2	32.3	40.0	39.3	29.5	38.8	33.7	28.2	42.0	41.2
Once or twice	35.4	39.2	40.0	33.0	38.1	28.8	34.9	37.8	30.4	30.5
Several times	21.5	20.4	19.0	20.9	21.0	27.5	20.9	25.5	18.8	19.1
Often	8.0	8.1	1.0	6.8	11.4	5.0	10.5	8.5	8.7	9.2
No response	0.0	0.0	0.0	0.0	0.0	0.0	0.0	0.0	0.0	0.0

Saw Events that Happened at Great Distance as They Were Happening

Response	Total %	ENC %	ESC %	MA %	MO %	NE %	PA %	SA %	WNC %	WSC %
Never	71.7	71.5	77.5	69.2	74.3	77.5	70.6	70.2	79.0	63.1
Once or twice	17.2	20.7	12.7	16.4	15.2	15.0	17.1	17.1	12.3	23.8
Several times	7.6	5.9	6.9	10.9	9.5	6.2	7.6	7.8	5.8	7.7
Often	3.4	2.0	2.9	3.5	1.0	1.2	4.7	5.0	2.9	5.4
No response	0.0	0.0	0.0	0.0	0.0	0.0	0.0	0.0	0.0	0.0

Felt as Though You Were Really in Touch with Someone Who Had Died

Response	Total %	ENC %	ESC %	MA %	MO %	NE %	PA %	SA %	WNC %	WSC %
Never	60.1	60.7	58.1	50.6	54.3	63.8	66.1	56.2	65.2	56.8
Once or twice	24.2	25.6	26.7	25.1	31.4	20.0	20.1	23.5	19.6	26.5
Several times	10.1	9.9	13.3	9.4	9.5	13.8	7.5	11.2	10.1	9.1
Often	5.6	3.8	1.9	4.9	4.8	2.5	6.3	9.2	5.1	7.6
No response	0.0	0.0	0.0	0.0	0.0	0.0	0.0	0.0	0.0	0.0

Felt as Though You Were Very Close to a Powerful, Spiritual Force

Response	Total %	ENC %	ESC %	MA %	MO %	NE %	PA %	SA %	WNC %	WSC %
Never	68.5	73.9	67.3	72.0	62.9	80.0	60.7	62.5	71.0	70.2
Once or twice	18.3	15.3	17.3	14.0	18.1	12.5	25.4	21.6	18.1	19.8
Several times	8.6	6.5	10.6	8.0	15.2	5.0	7.5	12.0	6.5	6.1
Often	4.5	4.2	4.8	6.0	3.8	2.5	6.4	3.9	4.3	3.8
No response	0.0	0.0	0.0	0.0	0.0	0.0	0.0	0.0	0.0	0.0

the most individuals had this experience at least once, report 63.1 percent who never had this experience. These responses can be compared with the region with the fewest individuals who have had this experience—the West North Central region—in which 79 percent state they never had this experience. In comparison, the regional difference among respondents to The Pagan Census who never had this experience is greater than for previous questions on the paranormal. The percentages vary among Neo-Pagans from 43.1 percent in the West South Central region to 59.4 percent in the Mid-Atlantic region.

GSS responses to the question of how often an individual has experienced being in touch with the dead ranges from a low of 54.3 percent in the Mountain region to a high of 66.1 percent in the Pacific region who have never had this experience. The range of difference is smaller for respondents to The Pagan Census, in which 19.6 percent in the East South Central region and 28.8 percent in the Mountain region never had this experience. Similarly, there is a smaller range of responses in our survey than the in the GSS to the question of how often the respondents felt they were close to a powerful, spiritual force that seemed to lift them outside of themselves. Responses to The Pagan Census range from 8.7 percent in the East South Central region to 17.3 percent in the Mid-Atlantic region of respondents who had never had this experience. This percentage range can be compared with the responses to the GSS, in which the Pacific region has the fewest respondents (60.7 percent) who never had this experience and New England has the most respondents (80 percent) who had never had this experience.

If one looks only at the regions in which there are the highest or lowest incidences of individuals having at least one paranormal experience, it appears in general that individuals in the southern United States have a higher rate of paranormal experiences. This observation is misleading, as in the GSS and even more so in The Pagan Census there are usually several regions with similar scores. In general there is no regional pattern of where paranormal experiences are more common or less common, with the possible exception of the West North Central region, in which respondents to the GSS consistently had fewer paranormal experiences.

Neo-Pagans' paranormal experiences are tied to their spiritual orientation and not the region in which they reside. There is a greater consistency of levels of paranormal experience among Neo-Pagan respondents to our survey than among respondents to the GSS. Furthermore, there is no relationship between the regions in which Neo-Pagans have fewer or more paranormal experiences and regional rates of these experiences among the general American public. Neo-Pagans are encouraged by their religion to have and to acknowledge paranormal experiences. Those who self-define as members of this religion appear more likely to identify with other Neo-Pagans throughout the country in defining their paranormal experiences than they are to identify with their neighbors.

Politics

Based on the indicators used in our survey, there are very few regional differences in political activity or attitudes among Neo-Pagans. Although some small variations exist among regions on issues of government spending and levels of confidence, none of the differences are noteworthy. New England and Pacific regions stand out, however, in their support of preferential hiring. In most regions considerably more Neo-Pagans disapprove of preferential hiring than approve of it. However, in the Pacific region 45 percent agree to some degree, and 44 percent disagree to some degree with the proposition that "to redress previous discrimination there should be preferential hiring of women at all levels of employment." In New England 44 percent agree to some degree, and 47 percent disagree to some degree with this statement. The Pacific region, in which 69.5 percent of respondents are women, has a slightly higher proportion of women to men than other regions. As women are somewhat more likely than men to support preferential hiring, some of the difference can be explained by the disproportionate number of women in this region.

Across the nation Neo-Pagans participate at about the same rate of political activity, such as writing to legislators, grassroots organizing, and participating in political campaigns. When asked about special events, such as participating in marches and demonstrations, however, there are marked regional differences. Neo-Pagans in culturally more conservative regions are less likely to participate in marches or demonstrations of any kind. In only one region, the Pacific, is there a majority (52.1 percent) of Neo-Pagans who state they have participated in this type of activity. Two regions, East North Central and New England, have more individuals who say they have participated in these activities than those who state that they have not. In the East North Central region 47.1 percent of the respondents claim that they have participated in these types of activities, and 46.7 percent state they have not. Similarly, in New England 46.3 percent of respondents indicate they have participated in these activities, and 45.7 percent state they have not. The Mid-Atlantic region has almost as many respondents (45.6 percent) who claim they have participated in these activities as those who have not (49.6 percent). These four regions stand out from the other five regions in which between 21.6 percent and 30.8 percent of the respondents claim to have participated in these activities.

Responses to our questions about gay and lesbian rights receives very high support among Neo-Pagans throughout the country. It is possible that if we had asked more controversial questions, such as the one about preferential hiring, we would find some notable differences. We unfortunately do not ask our respondents if they are out of the broom closet, so to speak, about their spiritual practices with their neighbors, friends, families, and work associates. We suspect that such a question would reveal important regional differences. As one respondent to The Pagan Census remarks, "There are already Wiccans on both the Church Council of Greater Seattle and the Washington State Interfaith Council (W.S.I.C.). One of our Wiccan representatives to the W.S.I.C. has recently been elected vice president (No, I'm not kidding!)" (Survey 3049). Although in some parts of the country Neo-Pagans are welcome on interfaith councils, in others Neo-Pagans fear that they will suffer discrimination if they are open about their religious affiliation.

Dissimilarities and Similarities

This chapter explores differences and similarities among six sects of Neo-Paganism, three forms of spiritual practice, and regions based on responses to questions on demographics, politics, and paranormal experiences. Overall, there is a great deal of similarity among the groups with some notable exceptions. Goddess Worshipers have a higher proportion of women and Druids a higher proportion of men. Heterosexual Neo-Pagans in more conservative areas of the country are more likely to be legally married than they are to be living together or ritually married. Those involved in covens or groups, UU Neo-Pagans, and Shamans are more politically active than other Neo-Pagans. Solitaries are the least politically active and least concerned with issues of gender and sexual-preference equality. This occurrence may be related in part to a larger proportion of these individuals being in their twenties and thirties. Regional political attitudes among Neo-Pagans are quite similar, but those living in more conservative regions are less likely to participate in rallies or demonstrations. As Neo-Pagans in general tend to be more politically active and liberal than the general American population, Neo-Pagans—regardless of sect, form of practice, or region of residence—distinguish themselves from the general American public by being more politically active and more liberal.

In subsequent chapters we explore the extent to which participation in different sects, forms of worship, and region of residence influence individuals' views on the creation of clergy, greater organizational structure, and the involvement of children in Neo-Paganism. Issues of specific differences in ritual practice—for example, how the goddess or goddess and gods are called into a circle (if indeed a circle is cast), what particular incantations are used, and specific ways of thinking about the divine—are outside the scope of our data. It would be interesting in future research to have data on these specific questions, as such information would help to determine the degree to which Neo-Pagan spiritual paths form distinct practices.

4

Families, Children, and Sexuality

> There are at least 3 newer covens & groups who have started up [in the area] in the last few years and show great promise. There is emphasis on families (heterosexual & gay/lesbian as well) and these groups support the Pagan community. (Survey 2125)

As this quote suggests, there is a desire among some Neo-Pagans for more family-friendly spiritual groups—groups that facilitate raising children and are open to alternative family forms. Neo-Pagans are sexually open and experimental. Gay and lesbian couples as well as group or open marriages are welcomed and acknowledged within the Neo-Pagan community. The openness of sexuality is viewed as part of Neo-Pagans' world-affirming theology, or thealogy. Although open sexuality in all forms is celebrated, its appropriateness when expressed around children or between teacher and student has been questioned. In this chapter we explore responses to questions concerning family forms, the sharing of spiritual paths with romantic partners and children, the appropriateness of sexual relations between teachers and students, and issues surrounding the inclusion other people's children in Neo-Pagan circles.

Sexuality, Polyamoury, and Teachers and Students

"Paganism is the only sex-positive religion that I know of" (Survey 1989). The celebration of consensual sexuality is viewed as an element of what Neo-Pagans define as their earth-based life-affirming spirituality. Starhawk asserts, "When the sacred is immanent, the body is sacred. . . . All of our bodily processes, especially the deep, pleasure-giving force of our sexuality are sacred processes. A psychology of liberation is not one of repression, nor does earth-based spirituality call us to asceticism" (1987:22). The sexual openness of Neo-Paganism has resulted in an acceptance of homosexual, bisexual, and transgendered individuals into the community and in experimentation with family forms. It also has resulted over time in some problems and raised some issues, such as the appropriateness of sexual relations between spiritual teachers and seekers, and the means by which children can be introduced to a positive view of sexuality without being prematurely sexualized or traumatized. Because Neo-Pagans view sexuality as a magical and positive force but are also aware that sexuality can be exploitative, they often are confronted with discerning in everyday life when sexual expressions cease being life affirming and, hence, not a positive or magical act.

Susan Palmer (1994) describes new religious movements as cocoons in which alternative family forms and gender roles can be and are explored. The sexual openness of Neo-Pagans has resulted in the growth within Neo-Paganism of interest in polyamorous relationships—that is, relationships in which the members of the couple are free to explore sexual relations with others outside of their marriage or primary relationship, or in which a group marriage occurs. Group marriages are never legal but are customarily ritual marriages; i.e., three or more individuals participate in a handfasting—the Neo-Pagan religious ritual for marriage. Handfastings can be performed as a legal marriage if a heterosexual couple has obtained a marriage license, and the officiating high priestess or high priest is a licensed cleric in the state in which the wedding occurs. However, handfastings are also performed for heterosexual couples who want to be ritually but not legally married, for homosexual couples, or for members of group marriages. These handfastings are performed as spiritual, but not legal, unions that are usually considered binding for a year and a day but may be for longer periods of time.

Group marriages may involve all members of the same sex or may be gender-mixed marriages. Tanice Foltz (1996) provides an ethnographic description of an anticipated group marriage of three women. Two of the women had a long-term relationship, bought a home together, and legally changed their last names to share a new one. Initially, there was an attempt to form into a group marriage with a third significantly younger woman, but ultimately the original couple separated, with one of the women leaving with the younger woman. Sarah Pike (2001:35) mentions a workshop titled "The Path of Polyamoury" and the handfasting of one man to two women at a festival she attended. She further notes that workshops on open marriages are common at festivals.

The idea of group marriages is prevalent within the Neo-Pagan community, but only 0.4 percent of our sample claim to live in this type of family. There is no geographical pattern of region for these individuals. Our data do not permit us to discuss the stability of group marriages compared with other relationships, nor whether they are more common among gays, lesbians, heterosexuals, or bisexuals. Our statistics do suggest that there is greater theoretical interest in group marriages than in actual participation in this family form. We do not ask how many couples who are legally or ritually married or living together have sexually open relationships. We suspect there would be many more individuals in this category than there are in group marriages. Although occurrence is not common, the image of group marriages as one acceptable family form among Neo-Pagans is prevalent, as witnessed by the ethnographic accounts.

To determine the extent of support for group marriages, we ask respondents to indicate the extent to which they agree with the statement "Polygamy should be legal in the U.S." We anticipated strong agreement with this statement, in part because Neo-Pagans pride themselves on a general laissez-faire attitude. Most Neo-Pagans (51 percent) do agree with this statement, but by a smaller margin than we imagined. Twenty-four percent indicate they have no opinion about this issue, and 23.1 percent disagree, with 8.3 percent strongly disagreeing. Variation among sects in response to this question is small. The strongest support for polygamy is expressed by Shamans, among whom 57.6 percent agree to some degree and 21.2 percent strongly agree with polygamy being legalized in the United States. The weakest support is expressed among Goddess Worshipers, among whom 48 percent support this proposition to some degree and 16 percent do so strongly.

Women are less likely to support legalization of group marriage than are men—44.1 percent of women support the legalization of polygamy, with 12 percent strongly supporting it. These responses can be compared with the men's, among whom 63.8 percent support legalization of group marriage, with 25.3 percent doing so strongly. Although the differences between men's and women's responses are noteworthy, more women support the legalization of polygamy than oppose it. Only 23 percent of Neo-Pagan women are in opposition. A majority (24 percent) of the rest has no opinion, and a small minority (2 percent) does not answer this question. Women Goddess Worshipers are less likely than other Neo-Pagan women to support polygamy. Of women Goddess Worshipers, 41.1 percent to some degree support the legalization of polygamy, 26.8 percent have no opinion, and 30.1 percent are opposed to its legalization. Linda Jencson (1998) contends in her ethnographic research that group marriages among one woman and two men are short-lived. She concludes that group marriages are more beneficial to men than to women. The lower statistical support of group marriage among women Neo-Pagans may reflect Jencson's sentiment among Neo-Pagans. However, even among women Goddess Worshipers, the group that gives the least support for group marriages, more support than opposition is expressed for the legalization of polygamy. More ethnographic research is needed on alternative family forms, particularly on group marriages and polyamorous relationships among Neo-Pagans, to explore these gender differences and to determine why, on the one hand, this type of relationship is relatively rare and, on the other hand, it is so popular as an image.

As table 37 demonstrates, support for legalization of polygamy varies by region. Neo-Pagans in the East South Central and Mountain regions are most likely to support legalization of polygamy, with nearly 61 percent of this population agreeing to some degree with the proposition. Less than 50 percent of Neo-Pagans in the East North Central, South Atlantic, New England and Mid-Atlantic regions support legalization of polygamy. In all other regions the majority of Neo-Pagans supports polygamy.

We do not ask our respondents their opinion of group marriages. It would be difficult in a survey form to explore the complexity of

TABLE 37: Regional Attitudes toward the Legalization of Polygamy among Neo-Pagans

Response	Total %	ENC %	ESC %	MA %	MO %	NE %	PA %	SA %	WNC %	WSC %
Strongly disagree	8.3	8.2	10.9	9.8	5.8	11.7	6.6	9.0	5.1	6.0
Disagree	8.2	7.6	6.5	9.8	4.5	10.9	5.7	12.0	3.8	6.0
Qualified disagree	6.5	7.9	2.2	6.7	4.5	7.9	7.3	4.8	3.8	6.0
No opinion	24.0	28.2	19.6	22.8	24.4	20.4	23.4	25.6	30.8	19.8
Qualified agree	16.6	18.2	17.4	19.3	16.7	12.8	18.3	15.4	14.1	15.5
Agree	17.7	14.8	28.3	12.6	19.2	21.5	18.1	16.9	25.6	19.8
Strongly agree	16.7	14.4	15.2	17.3	25.0	12.1	18.5	13.9	15.4	25.0
No response	2.0	0.7	0.0	1.6	0.0	2.6	2.0	2.4^	1.3	1.7

this question. The laissez-faire attitude of Neo-Pagans probably would result in their supporting each individual's choice to enter or not enter this type of relationship. However, whether they believe that such relationships are good for these individuals or if the interviewee would be willing to enter into one is something probably best discovered through ethnographic research.

Teachers and Students

The issue of whether or not it is ethical for teachers of Neo-Pagan traditions to have sexual relations with their students became an important issue among Neo-Pagans after Gavin and Yvonne Frost, two leaders within the Neo-Pagan community, suggested in their book, *The Witch's Bible* (1975), that sex be used in initiation rites and in rites of passage to adulthood for boys and girls. There was an outcry within the Neo-Pagan community against the practices the Frosts' recommended. One respondent to our survey maintains, "I resent the Frosts (Gavin & Yvonne) being accepted to Pagan gatherings and they have the nerve to call themselves Pagans. They exploit women and children and they are the worst experience for any person at any level of incest recovery" (Survey 2240). Covenant of the Goddess and other organizations within the Neo-Pagan community went on record opposing the practices recommended by the Frosts. In the second edition of their book, the Frosts removed the offending paragraphs. Nonetheless, the uproar around the Frosts' publication resulted in Neo-Pagans focusing on the issue of potential sexual exploitation within their community. One respondent suggests, "*Sex as an act of love* that is *mutual* & *respectful* is never unethical—sex as an act of exploitation or pseudo-love or as the desire/volition of just one of the two people involved *is* unethical. Sex between teacher & student often—but *not always*—falls into the latter category because of the issue of power/authority that is likely to arise in student/teacher relationships. With today's cultural overlays & patterns in this area, *great* caution would be my policy as either student or teacher" (Survey 2222). We ask survey respondents to state the degree to which they agree or disagree with the statement "Sex between a spiritual teacher and a student is unethical." As shown in table 38, approximately half (49.2 percent) of the Neo-Pagan respondents agree to some degree with this proposition, and 16.9 percent do so strongly. Although this figure is slightly less than half, 15.4 percent of Neo-Pagans have no opinion on this issue, and 32.9 percent disagree with the proposition to some degree. More Neo-Pagans disapprove of spiritual teachers and students having sexual relations than approve of this behavior.

Neo-Pagan women are more likely to disapprove of sex between spiritual teachers and their students than men. Table 38 indicates that 55.3 percent of Neo-Pagan women agree that it is unethical for spiritual teachers to have sex with their students, with 19.6 percent holding this position strongly and 21.1 percent doing so with reservations. This statistic can be compared with Neo-Pagan men, among whom only 37.6 percent agree with this proposition, 11.7 percent strongly and 16.5 percent with reservations. The differences in their responses to this question may be explained by Neo-Pagan women being more aware of and concerned with the issues of sexual exploitation than men are, particularly in relationships that are not equal in power, as is suggested by respondent 2222. Although most men within the Neo-Pagan movement would be expected to know about these issues, since they are discussed by some of the major writers on Neo-Paganism, raised at Neo-Pagan gatherings, and discussed in Neo-Pagan chat rooms, the men's responses suggest that

TABLE 38: Women's and Men's Attitudes toward Student/Teacher Sexual Relations

Response	GNPP %	Female %	Male %	No Gender Listed %
Strongly disagree	4.6	3.5	6.6	3.6
Disagree	9.2	7.2	13.3	3.6
Qualified disagree	19.1	16.6	23.7	21.4
No opinion	15.4	14.8	16.4	17.9
Qualified agree	19.6	21.1	16.5	25.0
Agree	12.7	14.6	9.5	0.0
Strongly agree	16.9	19.6	11.7	21.4
No response	2.4	2.4	2.3	7.1

they are not as concerned as the women are. Men may also tend to focus more on the other issue raised by respondent 2222—that is, the concern that nonexploitative, sexual relationships between teacher and students be seen as valid. Spiritual teachers and students often are about the same age and are both self-supporting adults, making the practice of teacher-student sexual relations appear more acceptable. Nonetheless, in a religion, which prides itself on being feminist or celebrating gender equality, women are more concerned about feminist issues than men are. Men express less apparent concern about sexual exploitation, and as discussed in chapter 2, indicate weaker support for issues of gender equity.

The majority of Wiccans, Goddess Worshipers, UU Neo-Pagans, and Druids to some degree disapproves of sexual relations between spiritual teachers and students. UU Neo-Pagans report the strongest opposition, with 58.1 percent stating that they agree it is unethical for spiritual teachers and their students to have sexual relationships. Only 29.8 percent of UU Neo-Pagans state that they disagree to some degree, with 20.7 percent doing so with qualification. Goddess Worshipers, a group with the highest proportion of women, has a lower rate of disapproval of spiritual teachers having sex with their students than UU Neo-Pagans do, even though, as noted above, women on the whole are more disapproving of this behavior. Among Goddess Worshipers, 51.8 percent believe and 18.3 percent believe strongly that it is unethical for spiritual teachers to have sex with their students. Thirty-two percent disagree with this proposition, 17.2 percent with qualification. Among women Goddess Worshipers, 59.6 percent disapprove, with 14.7 percent disapproving strongly to the proposal that teacher-student sexual relations are acceptable. Less than one-third (30.9 percent) of women Goddess Worshipers view spiritual teachers and their students having sexual relations as ethical; the remainder either report having no opinion or do not answer this question.

Pagans and Druids are the two sects in which there is less than 50 percent disapproval of spiritual teachers and students having sexual relations. In both cases just fewer than 50 percent agree with the proposition that it is unethical for spiritual teachers to have sex with their students. Among Pagans, 47.2 percent and among

Shamans, 46.6 percent agree to some degree with the proposition. Just over 34 percent of members of each of these sects disagree to some degree with the proposition. The remainder of each sect either has no opinion or do not answer this question. Shamans' response to both the question of whether polygamy should be legal and to the issue of spiritual teachers having sex with their students indicates that this sect appears to be consistently less in favor of either legal or social sanctions for sexual behavior.

Those individuals working in groups are the most likely both to be confronted with the issue of spiritual teachers and students having sexual relationships and to disapprove of this behavior. The differences among the three forms of practice are not large, but are, nonetheless, noteworthy. Among those working in groups, 54.1 percent agree that teacher-student sexual relations are unethical—20.2 percent agree strongly, and another 20.2 percent with qualifications. The weakest disapproval comes from solitaries, among whom 47.1 percent to some degree find it unethical for spiritual teachers to have sex with their students. In this cohort 18.3 percent have no opinion on this issue, which can be compared with group participants in which 12.3 percent have no opinion and those working with a spiritual partner, in which 14 percent have no opinion. Among those working with a single partner, 48.7 percent disapprove of spiritual teachers and students having sexual relations. These statistics suggest that those individuals who are most likely to be in a group in which students and teachers might have sexual relationships are also the ones who are most likely to view the behavior as unethical.

Table 39 indicates that the East South Central region contains the lowest proportion of individuals supporting the proposition that it is unethical for spiritual teachers and students to have sexual relationships. Those in the Mountain and South Atlantic regions have the highest disapproval rate. Although notable differences among the regions exist, there is no clear pattern for areas with the highest and lowest levels of approval.

A tension exists between two ideals within the Neo-Pagan community—that of sexual freedom and the freedom from being exploited in any manner, particularly by other Neo-Pagans. Shamans appear most likely to be concerned with the issue of sexual freedom. UU

TABLE 39: Regional Attitudes toward Student/Teacher Sexual Relations

Response	GNPP %	ENC %	ESC %	MA %	MO %	NE %	PA %	SA %	WNC %	WSC %
Strongly disagree	4.6	2.7	4.3	7.5	4.5	3.0	6.0	3.3	9.0	5.2
Disagree	9.2	7.9	6.5	11.4	12.2	8.7	9.9	7.8	2.6	8.6
Qualified disagree	19.1	17.2	17.4	15.7	17.9	19.2	21.6	20.8	15.4	18.1
No opinion	15.4	19.2	30.4	15.4	10.3	18.1	11.0	14.8	25.6	16.4
Qualified agree	19.6	21.3	15.2	20.1	20.5	21.1	21.2	17.2	19.2	18.1
Agree	12.7	12.4	10.9	13.8	9.6	11.7	12.6	15.7	7.7	12.1
Strongly agree	16.9	17.2	15.2	12.6	22.4	14.7	14.8	19.2	17.9	20.7
No response	2.4	2.1	0.0	3.5	2.6	3.4	2.9	1.0	2.6	0.9

Neo-Pagans, Goddess Worshipers, and Neo-Pagan women in general are more concerned with the issue of potential sexual exploitation. Despite regional differences, there does not appear to be a clear pattern. Nonetheless, issues such as spiritual teachers and students having sexual relationships help to highlight tensions between laissez-faire ideals of Neo-Pagans and concern for social equity.

Children and Parents

The birth of children to Neo-Pagans has brought to light other tensions within the religion, specifically whether Neo-Paganism is a spiritual path chosen by adults or a religion in which children are raised (H. Berger 1999a, 1999b). Among our respondents, 41.1 percent report that they are parents, 58.6 percent are childless, and 0.2 percent do not answer this question. A slightly higher percentage of female than male respondents report that they are parents (42.3 percent of women and 39.9 percent of men). Approximately 8 percent of both male and female respondents are grandparents. The relatively large proportion of Neo-Pagans who are parents, particularly those of minor children, has resulted in traditional forms of spiritual practice and training being brought into question. One respondent comments, "It seems like an important need of many of 'us' to find a 'church' or meeting place—to be more visible, accessible, a part of the community. . . . Also emphasis on raising children, especially boys, in a spiritual way, teaching them our craft & reverence for women & nature" (Survey 1459).

All new religious movements, if they are to survive past the first generation of adherents, must address the issue of children born to followers (Palmer and Hardman 1999). For Neo-Pagans, there is a particular issue of the appropriateness of including children in their spiritual path. A deep respect for individual freedom among Neo-Pagans has resulted in some Neo-Pagans arguing that training children in the religion limits their personal choice. Another survey respondent declares, "I will encourage [them to follow in my spiritual path] only if my children are interested. Religion and spiritual orientation is very personal" (Survey 2128). Although most Neo-Pagans adhere to the idea that each individual must find his or her own spiritual path and generally profess the belief that all spiritual paths are valid, there is frequently a caveat that only those other faiths that are also tolerant of religious freedom, are environmentally concerned, and sympathetic to issues of gender equality can be supported. Furthermore, most Neo-Pagans indicate that they choose their religion because they feel it to be a positive, life-affirming spiritual path and they want their children to also have the benefits of the same spiritual wisdom. One respondent observes, "I chose to be Wiccan. I hope my children will choose a Pagan Path, not because it is what I want, but because it is what right for them" (Survey 1160). Amber K, a well-known and published Witch, more broadly describes what she views as the issue of involving children specifically in Wicca, although similar statements can and have been made about Neo-Paganism in general. "Part of the parenting equation for Wiccans is the question: 'Should I raise my kids Wiccan or leave them alone to choose their own spirituality?'" In answer to her own question, she says, "As parents, we have the responsibility to teach our children the best that we can and expose them to beliefs and activities that will help them grow into strong loving, and wise women and men. When they become adults they will have the option to choose another religion or lifestyle. . . . If Wicca works for you then give your child the gift of Wicca" (1998:279–80).

Our survey finds that the majority of respondents (70 percent) who are parents claims they encourage their children to follow a Neo-Pagan spiritual path. Although a majority of both mothers and fathers states that they encourage their children to become Neo-Pagans, mothers are more likely to consciously raise their children as Neo-Pagans than fathers (77.4 percent of mothers and 54.8 percent of fathers encourage their children to follow the parental spiritual path). Part of the difference between mothers' and fathers' religious child-rearing behavior can be explained by the larger percentage of mothers who have primary custody and of fathers who are noncustodial parents. Of the 188 Neo-Pagan women who are single parents of minor children, 67.6 percent report having primary custody, 23.9 percent have joint custody, and only 8.5 percent are not a custodial parent. In contrast, 76 Neo-Pagan men are single parents of minor children, of which only 13.2 percent have primary custody and the rest are evenly divided between those who have joint custody and those who are noncustodial parents. Although part of the difference between mothers and fathers can be explained by differences in custody arrangements, the majority of Neo-Pagan parents with minor children does not include single parents: 65.7 percent of mothers and 74.1 percent of fathers report that they are not single parents. This statistic suggests that other factors are involved. Research on American families concludes that mothers, even when employed full time and in marriages that are considered egalitarian, continue to make most of the decisions about children's upbringing (Hochschild 1990; Huber and Spitze 1983).

A great deal of similarities and some notable differences exist among the sects. Druids are the least likely to have children, with only 38 percent of our sample identifying themselves as parents. Of those who are parents, a smaller proportion (64.9 percent) encourage their children to become Druids than other sects' members do. Druids are slightly more likely to be single parents, with 34.6 percent stating they are single parents. A slightly larger percentage of Druids than other sects have either primary custody (53.6 percent) or joint custody (28.6 percent). The larger proportion of men may explain the difference in the proportion of Druids that encourage their children to follow in their spiritual path, although it should be noted that within this group those who do have children are among the least likely to be noncustodial parents.

UU Neo-Pagans are the most likely to both have children and to encourage them to follow in their spiritual path. A majority of UU Neo-Pagans is parents (52.3 percent), and of these, 77.7 percent encourage their children to follow in their spiritual path. UU Neo-Pagans are the least likely to be single parents. Of those who are single parents (37.5 percent), most (44 percent) have joint custody, 36 percent have primary custody, and only 20 percent are noncustodial parents. These statistics further support the contention, developed in chapter 3, that UU Neo-Pagans have a somewhat more conventional life-style than other Neo-Pagans. The greater proportion of UU Neo-Pagans who are parents, furthermore, supports the notion that one of the appeals of the UUA for Neo-Pagans is that it provides a more traditional venue in which to raise children. UU Neo-Pagans have successfully fought for the inclusion of earth-based religions as one of the sources of inspiration for Unitarian Universalism and for the incorporation of Neo-Pagan concepts in the religious education program (H. Berger 1999a). As the UUA and its religious education program incorporate inspiration and aspects of many of the world religions, UU Neo-Pagan parents can simultaneously introduce their children to Neo-Pagan rituals and beliefs and those of other religious traditions. For these parents there may be less of a dilemma of bringing their children into their spiritual path, because through their participation in a UU church, they provide their children with a view into other religious traditions. Although the majority of Neo-Pagans who claim Unitarian Universalism as their primary path are parents, 47.7 percent of UU Pagans are not parents. The appeal of the UUA for Neo-Pagans, therefore, is not limited to those concerned with religious education for their children.

The other four sects—Wiccans, Pagans, Goddess Worshipers, and Shamans—do not notably distinguish themselves from the general Neo-Pagan community. Between 40.4 percent and 42.9 percent of members of each of these sects are parents. Of these four sects, Shaman parents are the most likely to encourage their children to follow in the parental spiritual path, followed by Goddess Worshipers, although in all cases over 70 percent of parents encourage their children to follow in the parental spiritual path. As noted in chapter three, the image of the Shaman is of a preclusive individualist who is chosen to follow his or her path by a life-altering event. However, within the American context Shamanism has become a form of religion that can be passed on to children. For Goddess Worshipers, particularly in women-only groups, the desire to have their children, including their sons, involved in their religion provides a particular challenge. Some Dianic groups forbid all except infant males from participating in rituals or attending gatherings. We have no data on how the growth of children in these groups has affected their policy of women-only rituals. It will be interesting to see if the needs of mothers to include their male progeny in their spiritual path results in changes in policies regarding male attendance. If this policy change is to occur, it might result in radical changes in the religious practices of these groups as boys become men and participate in the rituals.

The percentage of respondents who are parents and the percentage of parents that encourage their children to practice Neo-Paganism vary somewhat by region. In four regions—the New England,

South Atlantic, Mountain, and West North Central—over 70 percent of custodial parents that answer the question encourage their children to follow in the parental spiritual path. In the East South Central region only thirteen respondents answer the question. There appears to be no relationship between those regions in which parents are more likely to encourage their children to follow in their spiritual path and regions in which a larger proportion of respondents have primary or joint custody. Regional differences alone seem to account for the different rates of parents involving children in Neo-Paganism. Although some areas have a higher rate of children's involvement, except for the East South Central region, the majority of Neo-Pagan parents encourages their children to follow Neo-Paganism.

A growing number of books aid parents in teaching Neo-Paganism, or in some cases more specifically, Wicca, to the their children (see, for example, Serith 1994; O'Gaea 1993; Starhawk, Baker, and Hill 1998). Anne Hill, one of the authors of a recent book on Neo-Pagan child rearing, states her reason for writing *Circle Round: Raising Children in Goddess Traditions:* "I was overwhelmed [with work and family responsibilities] . . . and had to create a religious celebration that would convey the essence of Samhain to my children in a meaningful way. Leaning against the stove, I screamed inside, why isn't there just a book I could open? I fantasized about this book" (Starhawk, Baker, and Hill 1998:3). The increasing number of Neo-Pagans who are parents has also resulted in books on coven formation and maintenance, including chapters that explore issues surrounding the inclusion of children in their spiritual circles (see, for example, Harrow 1999 and K 1998). For parents who practice in groups and for those groups, children present a challenge to traditional coven work. Neo-Paganism as it first developed is a religion for adults. Rituals and religious practice require meditating and focusing on imagery of the Divine. Although children can easily be included in aspects of the rituals, such as chanting, dancing, thinking about things one wants to change in the world or for oneself, the usual focus of rituals is getting into an altered state of mind where an individual becomes one with the Divine or the Infinite. Judy Harrow (1999) notes that children can be a disruption to adults' abilities to concentrate and the presence of children may limit the topics of inquiry that can be explored in circle. Some topics, Harrow believes, specifically those that deal with sacred sex, may be considered inappropriate for children by some parents or other coven members.

Amber K (1998) argues that it is the responsibility of the Pagan community to pass their knowledge on to their children. She fears that if the spiritual void is not filled, the children will be drawn into other religions. Judy Harrow (1999), however, is more ambivalent. She draws a line between children being taught the basic principles of Neo-Paganism that are age appropriate, but outside the coven setting and coven training, which she views as training for the priestesshood or priesthood of Neo-Paganism. Harrow views Neo-Pagans as the laity and Wiccans as those who are coven trained for the clergy. Her view of the distinction between Neo-Pagans and Wiccans, although shared by others, is not universally accepted within the Neo-Pagan community. Within Wicca, all those who are initiated are considered priestesses or priests; no Wiccan is part of the laity. It is a religion in which all are clergy and in which each individual has ultimate authority in religious matters. Although some Wiccans view themselves as being clergy for the larger Neo-Pagan community, not all do. Furthermore, many Neo-Pagans define themselves as following a different spiritual path than that of Wicca and hence do not consider Wiccans their clergy.

As her book focuses on covens and not on raising Neo-Pagan children, Harrow does not speak of how children should be given religious or spiritual training. She provides an interview with one Witch, Lady Theos, now a grandmother, who organized a Moonday school—the equivalent of Sunday school for Christians—for her own and other Wiccan children. Lady Theos feels that the Moonday school she organized and ran was ultimately not a good thing, although none of the children were harmed by it. She never explains why she has come to feel that the children would have been better served if they were permitted to find Neo-Paganism on their own in adulthood.

Giving children religious education in Neo-Paganism may have some logistical problems. In some regions there are not enough children in one area to form a school, or there may not be enough support to provide teachers for these schools. Most books on training children in Neo-Paganism focus on rituals that are organized at home by the parents, to celebrate the sabbats and the esabat, and daily rituals to commemorate the deities. These books also encourage parents to train their children in simple magic, and as they become older to teach them ways to get into altered mental states. There is little emphasis in the literature on involving Neo-Pagan children from one family with those from other families, although this does occur at festivals, where children accompany their parents. Of those who report attending one or more festivals in the previous year, 42.1 percent are parents. We do not ask whether or not they brought their children with them to the festival(s); however, it is common for children to join their parents at festival events, some of which provide daycare or encourage parents to share childcare. Children often participate in simple rituals and in some magical workings while they are attending the festivals (Orion 1995; H. Berger 1999a; Pike 2001).

Although we find that the majority of coven members is childless (58.6 percent), 72.5 percent of those who have children encourage them to follow in the parental spiritual path. Our survey does not ask how coven members deal with the issue of child rearing or how other coven members respond to having children participate in some or all coven events. The respondent quoted at the beginning of this chapter reports that there is the growth of more family-friendly covens in her community. Ethnographic research similarly notes the development of family-oriented groups (H. Berger 1999a, 1999b). Further quantitative research is needed to determine the percentage of Neo-Pagan groups that are oriented in part or whole to incorporating children into their circles as compared with those groups that self-define as for adults only.

Solitary practitioners are the least likely to report having children, with only 37.2 percent stating that they are parents. Those solitary practitioners who do have children are the least likely of the three forms of worship to involve their children in the parental spiritual practices, although even in this group the majority, 64.7 percent, does report involving their children in Neo-Paganism. Those working with one partner are the most likely to both have and involve their children in their spiritual path. Among this cohort the majority

(52.9 percent) includes parents, 75.5 percent of which encourage their children to participate in their religion.

Our data do not permit us to say why those who work with a partner are more likely to have and to encourage their children to practice Neo-Paganism. One possible explanation is that parents find that the intensity and obligations of belonging to a coven inconsistent with participation in parenting. Also, some groups may not welcome children or be willing to accommodate parents who need to skip coven meetings and classes to care for their children. Judy Harrow presents the opinion that "covens are not tiny congregations; they are more like non-residential monasteries. The training appropriate for entering a religious order is given at maturity, and only to those who have a specific calling. Seminary is not the same thing as Sunday school" (1999:83).

Because some covens or groups are training groups that teach magical and spiritual techniques, participants are required to regularly attend. Other covens believe it is important for group cohesion for members to be present at most of the celebrations and magical workings. In either case parents who cannot or choose not to bring their children and have difficulty finding alternative childcare may need to leave the group. Some parents may decide to practice with one another or with another partner when their children are young, as it permits more flexibility for arranging rituals. For those parents who practice with their romantic partner, the religious rituals may occur at home, therefore enabling the parents to involve children in the rituals and magical practices.

Although the majority of Neo-Pagan parents reports raising their children in the religion, there are few structures within the Neo-Pagan community to help them in the process. Books, journal articles, chats on the Internet, and child-centered events within some communities serve as the only resources for parents training their children.

Romantic Partners, Spiritual Partners

Given the high rate at which Neo-Pagan parents state that they encourage their children to follow in their spiritual path, it is surprising that only slightly over one-third (36 percent) of Neo-Pagans report that their romantic partner shares their spiritual orientation. An additional 29.4 percent say that their romantic partners are either sympathetic (15.8 percent) or tolerant (13.6 percent) of their spiritual orientation. Only 1.6 percent report that they experience hostility toward their spiritual orientation from their romantic partners. This question was not answered by 29.9 percent of our respondents and the rest claim they are unaware of their partners' feelings about their spiritual orientation. Those not answering this question include both those who do not have a romantic partner and those who simply choose not to answer the question. Of those who answer this question, a slight majority (51.4 percent) does share their spiritual orientation with their romantic partners, and 42.2 percent report having romantic partners who are either tolerant (19.5 percent) or sympathetic (22.5 percent) toward Neo-Paganism. Using as a base only those who answer the question, these statistics are consistent with those for children's involvement in their parents' spiritual paths.

The rate of interfaith marriage is high among Neo-Pagans. In comparison, only 18 percent of Catholics, 11.8 percent of Jews, and 7.4 percent of Protestants are married to someone of another faith (Shehan and Kammeyer 1997). One respondent to The Pagan Census suggests that she "would like to see a Pagan singles resource directory" (Survey 1113). Unlike other religions in which church attendance often results in unattached individuals meeting others of the same faith to date, and possibly to marry, covens are small groups that do not provide a large circle of potential mates. For those practicing as solitaries, the problem is exacerbated. Festivals and large Neo-Pagan circles celebrating sabbats provide places for single Neo-Pagans or those interested in polyamorous relationships to meet. Neo-Pagan romantic partners also meet through the Neo-Pagan network of people who know one another from festivals, workshops, attendance at large sabbat celebrations, or from having trained with the same original coven. However, many Neo-Pagans meet their romantic partners outside Neo-Pagan networks.

The higher interfaith marriage rate among Neo-Pagans is a reflection of this group's emphasis on tolerance and diversity. For Neo-Pagans, there is no contradiction or problem with cohabiting with or marrying someone of another religious tradition or a humanist. There is no imperative for Neo-Pagans to marry or live with another Neo-Pagan. The rate of intermarriage may decrease as more children are raised in the religion and seek out others like themselves. The emphasis on personal freedom and on honoring diverse spiritual paths among Neo-Pagans makes the notion of Neo-Pagan parents pressuring their children to marry within the religion seem absurd, although there may eventually be more subtle forms of pressure.

There is some variation among sects of the degree to which their partners share Neo-Pagans' spiritual practices. Shamans have the highest proportion of partners who share their spiritual path. Of the Shaman respondents, 40.8 percent state that they share their spiritual path with their partners, and an additional 23.1 percent have partners who are tolerant or sympathetic to the Shaman's spiritual path. If we consider only those Shamans who answer this question, 59.4 percent share their spiritual path with their partners, and 33.8 percent have partners who are sympathetic or tolerant. As previously discussed, Shamans claim that they involve their children in the parental spiritual path. Shamanism as practiced in the United States does not appear to be a solitary path but instead commonly involves romantic partners and children. Druids are only slightly less likely than Shamans to involve their partners in their spiritual path. Less than half (40.6 percent) of all Druids report having partners who share their spiritual path. Considering only those Druids who answer this question, 58 percent share their spiritual path with their romantic partners, and 35.5 percent report having romantic partners who are either sympathetic or tolerant of the Druids' spiritual path. Wiccans and Pagans have approximately the same proportion of romantic partners who share their spiritual path. Approximately one-third (37.3 percent) of all Wiccans and 51.2 percent of those who answer this question share their spiritual path with their partners. These percentage can be compared with Pagans, of which 35.6 percent of all Pagans and 51.2 percent of those who answer this question share their spiritual path with their partners. Of those who answer this question, 42.2 percent of Wiccans and 41.3 percent of Pagans state that their romantic partners are either sympathetic to or tolerant of their spiritual path.

Goddess Worshipers and UU Neo-Pagans are the least likely to share their spiritual path with their romantic partners. Of those who answer this question, 49.2 percent of Goddess Worshipers and 46.8

percent of UU Neo-Pagans share their spiritual path with their romantic partners. Although some women-only groups are radical separatists in which all their members are either lesbians or bisexual, other groups welcome heterosexual women. These women, particularly in groups whose rituals are exclusive of men, participate in their religious worship without their husbands or male partners. In some cases their spouses or romantic partners are supportive of the women's spiritual quests; in other cases the romantic partners are not. Of all the sects examined, UU Neo-Pagans have the lowest rate of sharing their spiritual path with their romantic partner. One of the appeals of Unitarian Universalism for these Neo-Pagans may be the inclusion of many religious traditions and teachings. The UUA has always been a haven for couples of mixed marriages. Today such mixed marriages may also include one partner who is a Neo-Pagan.

Other People's Children

> I'm 18 years old and have recently begun working in a coven-like group w/ three girls . . . one 17 and two 15. My three "companions" attend Catholic school and have been openly harassed by students, teachers, and clergy. . . . I belong to an informally organized Pagan support group at my college. Why can't we work to organize truly dedicated high school students in this way? (Survey 1461)

An increasing number of teens have become interested in Witchcraft. This interest has both fueled and is fueled by the growing number of television shows, movies, books, websites, Internet chat rooms, and magazines geared toward the teenage Witch. Although many youths who become interested remain content to dabble in occult magical practices, such as casting love spells or burning incense to bring money to them, some of these teenagers become drawn to Witchcraft, Wicca, or Neo-Paganism as a religion, resulting in some underage individuals seeking out coven training. Underage seekers raise a number of problems and issues for Neo-Pagans. As Judy Harrow describes the dilemma, "If you are a coven leader or other Pagan teacher, and the child of bigoted parents comes to you for training, you will find yourself caught between principle and self-preservation. While in principle you should be upholding freedom of spiritual choice, you may have to walk carefully to avoid trouble for yourself—and for the young person involved" (1994:94).

Harrow, furthermore, notes that groups with underage seekers in a coven that works skyclad (that is, nude) may face charges of corrupting a minor. Even in groups that are robed, the parents may become worried and seek legal action against the coven because they confuse Wicca, Witchcraft, or Paganism with Satanism. These parents may fear for their child's well-being or be opposed to their child's participation in any nontraditional religion or any religion other than the one practiced by the family. In turn, underage seekers may find themselves in difficulty if they are financially dependent on their disapproving parents. Harrow counsels that group leaders should not risk training underage seekers without parental approval. She suggests that the young person should be told to see this period of waiting as a challenge and as a time of personal development in which she or he can read books, learn to meditate, work with and in nature, and prepare for a career that is consistent with Neo-Pagan principles. Amber K similarly warns those covens contacted by minors for instruction: "Your first step should be to contact the parents or guardians, and if possible have a face-to-face discussion about Wicca and their child's interest. Never assume that it is all right to share information with a minor or invite them to events. . . . If you have talked with the parents or guardians and they are genuinely supportive then you may ask them to sign a permission slip and waiver of liability for their young person to participate in whatever programs you think are appropriate" (K 1998:283–84).

In her book *Teen Witch: Wicca for a New Generation* Silver RavenWolf writes two prefaces, one for parents and the other for the adolescents for whom her book is written. In the first preface she aims to calm the potential fears of parents whose children are interested in her book. She states: "If you feel that the Craft is against your belief system after you've read the book don't panic. I've written this book so that your teen (or you) can take any of the techniques herein and use them in your own religious background" (1999:xiv).

Our survey asks respondents the degree to which they agree or disagree with the statement "People who are under the age of 18 whose parents are not Pagan/Witches should not be trained in the Craft." As table 40 demonstrates, the majority of Neo-Pagans and members of the six sects that we have examined is opposed to this statement, albeit the largest proportion of all the groups hold this belief with qualifications. Similarly, the majority of those who agree with this statement does so with qualifications. In other words, most Neo-Pagans, regardless of the sect to which they belong, believe that seekers under the age of eighteen should be given instruction in Neo-Paganism. Of all the sects, Shamans are the most likely and UU Neo-Pagans the least likely to believe that underage seekers should be given spiritual instruction. As on other issues, UU Neo-Pagans appear somewhat more conservative than the rest of the Neo-Pagan community, although again the difference is small, as the majority of UU Neo-Pagans, like the majority of the Neo-Pagans, supports instructing underage seekers.

The wisdom, presented by well-known Neo-Pagan authors, of involving minors in Neo-Paganism seems at odds with the more general attitude among the majority of Neo-Pagans that underage seekers should be trained. For Neo-Pagans, the issue of religious freedom is important. Because theirs is a minority religion, and one whose very name often elicits heckles, Neo-Pagans are concerned with issues of discrimination. This concern, it appears, has resulted in books that suggest caution when dealing with minor seekers. However, most Neo-Pagans defend their right, although the majority of these does so with qualifications, to teach their religion to anyone who seeks them out in the same manner that mainline churches are free to instruct those seeking their spiritual guidance. A substantial minority of the Neo-Pagans does not believe underage seekers should be trained. The majority of both those who agree and disagree with the notion of underage seekers being trained does so with qualifications. This reservation suggests that most Neo-Pagans are concerned both with protecting themselves and their families against litigation by angry parents or community members and with supporting the rights of minors to choose their own spiritual path.

The extent to which Neo-Pagans believe that underage seekers should be trained varies by region. As shown in table 41, Neo-Pagans who reside in the Bible Belt are least likely to support teaching underage seekers. In only one region, the West South Central, do less than 50 percent of Neo-Pagans support, even with reservations, teaching minors who seek instruction. In the other southern regions, and in

TABLE 40: Sects' Attitudes toward Training Underage Seekers

Response	GNPP %	Druid %	Goddess %	Pagan %	Shaman %	Unitarian %	Wiccan %
Strongly disagree	15.3	20.8	15.8	15.7	18.7	8.8	16.1
Disagree	16.7	10.7	15.0	16.8	17.1	12.4	17.5
Qualified disagree	26.3	28.4	27.9	28.8	27.5	28.5	27.5
No opinion	8.6	6.1	3.0	8.1	6.9	11.9	5.9
Qualified agree	19.4	23.4	19.2	18.5	18.2	25.4	19.5
Agree	6.1	6.1	5.5	5.4	5.2	7.8	6.2
Strongly agree	5.5	4.1	5.9	4.7	3.3	3.6	6.1
No response	2.1	0.5	1.7	2.0	3.0	1.6	1.3

the culturally conservative East North Central and West North Central regions, the majority of respondents supports training minors, although the rate of support is lower than the national average. Those individuals residing in New England, Mid-Atlantic, Mountain, and Pacific regions give the greatest support for teaching underage seekers.

Members of covens or groups, those most likely to be confronted with the issue of having an underage seeker request training, are the least likely to support the proposition that underage seekers should be trained. Table 42 shows that although the majority of those individuals who work in covens (like those who work with one partner and solitaries) supports educating underage seekers, only 52.9 percent of coven members—adding together all degrees of support—advocate training these individuals. This figure can be compared with those working with a partner and solitaries, in which respectively, 57.5 percent and 62.4 percent to some degree support training underage seekers. Furthermore, solitaries are the most likely, and coven members the least likely, to strongly support training underage seekers. Our data suggest that those who are most likely to suffer the consequences of lawsuits or public hostility if parents of an underage seeker were to protest are also the least likely to view the practice as acceptable.

Conflicts and Contradictions

Neo-Paganism, although still a relatively new religion, is aging. As part of the aging process, some conflicts within and contradictions of the religion, which may have not been apparent previously, have come to the fore. Neo-Paganism, particularly as it has evolved in the United States, prides itself on extolling diversity, being nonauthoritarian, accepting alternative life-styles and ways of dealing with issues and problems, and celebrating all forms of sexuality. Members of the religion are sexually and socially experimental. We find, however, that group marriage, which is frequently spoken about within Neo-Paganism as offering an alternative to the exclusivity of monogamy, is only infrequently practiced.

Neo-Pagans, nonetheless, are as a whole sexually experimental. The sexual openness of Neo-Pagans, which some view as a hallmark of their emphasis on nature and on being life affirming, has also

Table 41: Regional Attitudes toward Training Underage Seekers

Response	GNPP %	ENC %	ESC %	MA %	MO %	NE %	PA %	SA %	WNC %	WSC %
Strongly disagree	15.3	13.1	21.7	14.6	21.2	17.7	13.9	13.9	11.5	12.9
Disagree	16.7	14.4	15.2	20.1	16.0	19.2	16.9	16.9	11.5	14.7
Qualified disagree	26.3	24.4	15.2	26.8	26.3	26.4	28.3	28.3	28.2	18.1
No opinion	8.6	10.7	8.7	7.5	5.8	9.4	6.3	6.4	6.4	8.6
Qualified agree	19.4	23.7	19.6	18.5	16.7	16.2	21.1	21.0	25.6	26.7
Agree	6.1	7.6	10.9	3.9	7.7	6.0	6.6	6.6	3.8	9.5
Strongly agree	5.5	5.2	8.7	6.3	4.5	2.3	5.7	5.7	9.0	8.6
No response	2.1	1.0	0.0	2.4	1.9	2.6	1.2	1.2	3.8	0.9

TABLE 42: Attitudes toward Underage Seekers for the Three Forms of Spiritual Practice

Response	GNPP %	Group %	SP %	SO %	NR %
Strongly disagree	15.3	10.4	16.6	18.7	11.9
Disagree	16.7	15.9	18.1	17.0	15.7
Qualified disagree	26.3	26.6	22.8	26.7	27.0
No opinion	8.6	7.7	7.8	9.2	8.8
Qualified agree	19.4	24.8	21.8	16.4	14.5
Agree	6.1	5.9	4.7	6.2	7.5
Strongly agree	5.5	6.5	6.7	4.1	8.8
No response	2.1	2.1	1.6	1.7	5.7

resulted in some tensions developing. Embracing a feminist form of spirituality, Neo-Pagans envision creating an alternative community that strives to be free of domination. However, the openness of sexuality has resulted in some individuals feeling sexually exploited. The issue of spiritual teachers and students having sexual relations has raised the question of whether it is possible to have free and open sexuality between two individuals of different statuses, even if they are both adults and do not work in the same office. The Pagan Census finds a clear gender division on this issue, with more women concerned that sex between spiritual teachers and students can be exploitative and more men concerned with maintaining sexual freedom. UU Neo-Pagans and Goddess Worshipers are also more likely than other Neo-Pagans to question the ethics of teacher-student sexual relations.

Although there are differences among sects, regions, and between mothers and fathers, we find that the majority of Neo-Pagans who are parents of minors involves their children in the parental spiritual path. The inclusion of children in Neo-Paganism has raised questions of how the religion should be taught to the next generation and whether or not it is appropriate to include children in covens or groups. For some Neo-Pagans, there is a need for a new form of training and group practice that is open and friendly to parents and children. For others, there is a concern that the inclusion of children will distort the religion, as the needs of the adults and the rigor of coven training become ignored or watered down to allow children participation.

As a large percentage of Neo-Pagans' spouses and romantic partners are not Neo-Pagans, there is no clear sense of a family religion until the birth of children to participants. Although there is a mythology of Neo-Paganism as the old religion, the religion of the community, until recently it has been a religion of adults who choose to join as individuals. However, with the birth of children and the desire of parents to introduce those children to Neo-Paganism, a tension that always existed within the religion has come to the fore—that is, how should Neo-Paganism be envisioned? Should it be a religion of adult seekers, or as the family-oriented religion of a community? For some Neo-Pagans, the inclusion of children within Neo-Paganism violates the child's freedom of choice. For others, it is important that their children be introduced to what they view as a life-affirming, ecologically attuned, magical and spiritual path. The tension between Neo-Paganism as a spiritual path freely chosen and as a community religion has existed since its foundation. However, the contradiction has not become apparent until there were enough children born to adherents to bring the issue into focus. The notable proportion of Neo-Pagans who are parents and the large proportion of those who want to raise their children as Neo-Pagans will undoubtedly force the religion, or at least some forms of it, to change.

While the inclusion of Neo-Pagans' children into circles has raised one set of issues, the potential training of minors from non–Neo-Pagan families raises other issues. On the one hand, Neo-Pagans strongly support religious freedom and freedom of choice in most matters, particularly freedom of religious choice. On the other hand, many Neo-Pagans, most notably leaders within the community, are concerned that training underage seekers will make Neo-Pagans vulnerable to lawsuits and might increase "witch-hunts" in communities that are hostile to Neo-Paganism. Most Neo-Pagans support the right of underage seekers to be trained, although the majority of these does so with qualifications. Those who work in groups and therefore are most likely to be confronted with the issue of training underage seekers are the least likely to support the notion that minors from non–Neo-Pagan families should be trained in Neo-Paganism.

As long as there remains hostility toward Neo-Pagans in the larger community, it will be a risk to train those who are minors. However, books, magazines, and the Internet continue to provide a venue through which teenagers find out about Neo-Paganism, and many choose to self-initiate.

The identified conflicts and contradictions are unlikely to dissipate completely. However, it is probable that the religion will continue to change as it responds to these conflicts and contradictions. It will be interesting to see what occurs in the religion as participants age, more become parents, and there is increasing interaction with the larger society.

5

POPULARIZATION AND INSTITUTIONAL CHANGES

I am firmly convinced that if Pagans want to be more than just an irritating voice on the fringes of religious thought, they need to develop a mainstream approach to the dissemination and development of their religious convictions. . . . For example, the Methodist congregation down the street has a piece of property with a building on it. It has a mailbox, a sign and a symbol of Christianity clearly displayed. People go there on Sunday morning in droves. Therefore, it must be a legitimate church and religion. Pagans need that sort of "instant recognition." We need temples, ministerial schools, public bank accounts, and (gasp!) a real theology that goes beyond "the Earth is our Mother—Hail Goddess." A little dogma won't hurt either . . . but very little. . . . Unfortunately it seems that Pagans in general are reluctant to open their wallets and give money to support a church-like organization. (Survey 1080)

This respondent is advocating that the Neo-Pagan movement become better organized, more standardized, and ultimately more mainstream. James Richardson (1985) argues that all new religions go through a process of change as they age and are affected by both internal and external factors. The internal factors mentioned by Richardson include such developments as the aging of the participants, the birth of a second generation to those who joined in their youth, and new seekers entering the religion. External factors, which include such developments as the popularization of Witchcraft and Neo-Paganism in the media and on the Internet, and conflicts with larger society that result in the truncation of Neo-Pagans' civil rights or in court cases, are also pushing Neo-Paganism in new directions.

Neo-Paganism is different from the new religious movements used as case studies by Richardson. Since it arrived on American soil, Neo-Paganism has been decentralized with no single leader or organized group of leaders, or even with one set of shared beliefs or practices. As noted in chapter 1, the borders and boundaries of this new religion are permeable. Nonetheless, the movement is being confronted with many of the same issues and problems that all social movements face as they age. Some of the answers that Neo-Pagans suggest are traditional ones, such as that offered by the respondent quoted at the beginning of this chapter who advocates the development of congregationalism among Neo-Pagans. Data from our survey suggest that on the whole Neo-Pagans give guarded support for the creation of at least some aspects of congregationalism, such as the development of a paid clergy. However, three notable trends—the traditional way in which the religion has been transmitted to new seekers, the amorphous structure of the religion, and the unwillingness of Neo-Pagans to make large donations to support their religion—appear to mitigate against the creation of traditional congregations.

Among Wiccans, the religion traditionally has been taught in small groups that usually meet in members' homes. Druids similarly meet in small groups, often called groves or circles, that are organized from the leaders' homes. Other spiritual paths have normally relied on free training or on individuals gaining their knowledge from books, correspondence courses, or classes at local occult bookstores or adult education centers for which individuals pay a fee.

Groups that meet in homes are by necessity small and tend to not last for many years with the same participants. Those that define themselves as training groups encourage their members to leave after they are deemed competent to begin their own group. Others fall apart because of internal conflicts, while still others disintegrate as people move or have children. These groups typically form, survive for a while, and then disintegrate, possibly to be re-created with some new and some original members. Thus, Neo-Pagan groups tend to be too small and too unstable to transform themselves into a congregation.

A number of national umbrella organizations that provide services for groups or individual Neo-Pagans have developed. These organizations arrange festivals, produce newsletters and magazines, provide a legal network for Neo-Pagans involved in court cases because of their religious adherence, and/or furnish credentials for Neo-Pagans to become legal clergy. Some of the groups, such as Circle Sanctuary and Elf Lore Family (ELF) have bought land, which is used for Neo-Pagan gatherings and centers. These centers and their work are supported mainly through Neo-Pagans paying a fee for specific services or products. Donations, when they are made, tend to be small. Most newsletters and journals have advertisements for occult supplies, services, or books and are sold to subscribers. Producing and distributing newspapers and magazines is usually costly for a group and rarely, if ever, generate profits. Festivals, open rituals, and membership fees do generate money for groups to survive and at times to support full-time or part-time staff. Although monetary donations made by Neo-Pagans tend to be small, individuals do give their time to ensure that the group survives and that their work is done. Of the Neo-Pagans in our survey, 61.6 percent claim that they donate time to their religion. The most common activities through which Neo-Pagans donate time are by sending mailings and working on newsletters and magazines, and at festivals.

Most of these organizations are well respected within the Neo-Pagan community, and their leaders are often spokespersons for the religion. Through their writings and editing of journals, these individuals often play an important role both in North American Neo-Paganism and in Neo-Paganism throughout the English-speaking world. These organizations have not, however, formed into traditional denominations or congregations, as they remain at this time primarily service organizations for the larger Neo-Pagan community. For those groups that have access to land, legal ownership is usually in the hands of the group members. These groups are not like churches with a congregation or denomination that can decide to call a new spiritual leader or ask an existing one to leave.

For some Neo-Pagans, the lack of churches with land is symbolic of the marginality of their religion. For those who see this lack as a problem, their concerns have several roots. As members of a minority religion, particularly one whose very name raises the heckles of some religious or cultural conservatives, many feel vulnerable. For example, Neo-Pagans report having legal action taken against them for holding rituals on their own property and having their religious affiliation used against them in custody cases (Pike 2001). One respondent reports: "I would like to see more positive public relations with the rest of society. We really need to try and lift the pressure of prejudice and religious persecution that we, as Pagans must live with daily. As a college student I am afraid to wear my pentagram openly in class for fear the professor will use his position against me and give me less than standard grades. (By the way I live in the Bible belt)." (Survey 1452). As this quote suggests, even for those individuals not caught up in court cases, there is a concern among Neo-Pagans that their religion will not be viewed as legitimate, and they fear that remaining on the fringe can have negative consequences for them. This concern is magnified for parents who fear that their children may suffer discrimination.

Other Neo-Pagans fear that their religion will become diluted as more individuals join and are trained through books or correspondence courses. These individuals are less concerned with building churches than creating a clergy that is well trained and knowledgeable. However, the call for clergy who are better trained and educated also has resulted in some Neo-Pagans talking of creating a group of paid clergy. The notion of churches, paid clergy, and with it the concept of hierarchy is an anathema to many Neo-Pagans. As another respondent notes, "I left Christianity in my late teens because I didn't like having a clergyperson mediating my experience of the sacred. I still don't. While I respect people who spend more time than I do studying and practicing a spiritual tradition, I don't give them power to tell me what to believe or how to practice" (Survey 1804).

Although some Neo-Pagans are embracing greater routinization of their religion, others strongly oppose such changes. They view Neo-Paganism's lack of structure as its strength, as there is no authority to mediate their spiritual practice or their relationship with the Divine. Being marginal for these individuals is viewed as preferable to becoming solidified, unchanging, and out of tune with the spiritual needs of practitioners. John Lofland and James Richardson (1984) argue that the tendency of new religions within a democratic society is to move toward congregationalism, and, as a result, to become less radical and innovative. Those Neo-Pagans who oppose the creation of churches, paid clergy, and hierarchy fear that the radical edge of Neo-Paganism will become blunted as the religion becomes more accepted.

To determine the degree to which Neo-Pagans support or oppose routinization of their religion, we ask respondents to give their opinion on a series of questions about the creation of hierarchy, the development of paid clergy, the popularization of the religion, and training neophytes. On the whole our survey finds that Neo-Pagans are advocates for the religion becoming more mainstream.

Money and Neo-Paganism

Among Wiccans, all those who are initiated are clergy. Although as noted in the last chapter, some Wiccans consider themselves to be clergy to the larger Neo-Pagan community, many within that community define themselves as following an alternative path. The notion of some or all Neo-Pagans being clergy is noncontroversial; what is controversial is the idea of some Neo-Pagans becoming paid clergy. Traditionally within Wicca, a Witch was not allowed to accept money for teaching someone else the religion. Teaching traditionally took place within coven settings, in which there were small groups of people trained by a high priestess and high priest, or in women-only groups by a high priestess or priestesses. Each individual who had been taught the Craft was obliged to pass that knowledge on as he or she had received it—as a gift (Ezzy 2001). Most other Neo-Pagan traditions similarly have accepted the notion that individuals should not be paid for teaching spiritual or magical teachings. As the religion has grown, this stance has changed somewhat. Some Neo-Pagans offer workshops at adult education centers or occult book-shops, for which they are paid, albeit modestly. As the respondent quoted at the beginning of this chapter illustrates, some Neo-Pagans are questioning whether the religion should continue to rely on unpaid labor of its clergy. To determine attitudes toward payment of clergy, we ask respondents to state the degree to which they agree or disagree with two statements: "Full-time paid clergy should be financially supported by their community" and "A Witch should not accept money for teaching the Craft."

Table 43 illustrates that the majority of Neo-Pagans, regardless of sect, believes that full-time clergy should be supported. There is basically no gender difference in response to this question, with 50.9 percent of women and 50.1 percent of men supporting the creation of paid Neo-Pagan clergy to some degree. UU Neo-Pagans give the strongest endorsement, with 61.1 percent supporting the notion to some degree. Druids and Shamans, among whom respectively 57.3 percent and 55.4 percent support this proposition to some degree, express slightly weaker support than UU Neo-Pagans but greater support than other sects in their approval of full-time clergy being economically supported. Neo-Pagans who belong to the UUA choose to participate in a church and to help support and pay for a clergy person's salary and benefits. It is, therefore, not surprising that this group is the most likely to support the notion of full-time Neo-Pagan clergy becoming salaried. The strong support among Druids for Neo-Pagan clergy being paid a salary is consistent with Druids' development of a rigorous training program for their religious leaders. As individuals gain credentials and invest time in training, it may be expected that they will be freed from mundane work to do spiritual or religious work. Shamans' stronger-than-average support for paid clergy is somewhat more surprising. However, this finding may be explained by our earlier finding that Shamans in the United States, despite their reputation as isolated practitioners, are a religious group.

The strongest support for the creation of paid Neo-Pagan clergy comes from the West North Central, the New England, and South Atlantic regions, in which respectively 57.6 percent, 55.5 percent, and 53.8 percent of Neo-Pagans support to some degree the creation of paid clergy. The weakest support is from the West South Central, Mid-Atlantic, and East South Central regions, in which respectively 44.6 percent, 46.9 percent, and 47.8 percent support to some degree the creation of a paid Neo-Pagan clergy. Although less than half of

TABLE 43: Sects' Attitudes toward Paid Clergy

Response	GNPP %	Druid %	Goddess %	Pagan %	Shaman %	Unitarian %	Wiccan %
Strongly disagree	5.2	5.1	5.4	5.1	5.0	3.6	4.7
Disagree	9.2	8.1	8.9	9.0	6.9	5.7	9.7
Qualified disagree	11.0	8.1	11.0	11.3	8.0	7.8	12.8
No opinion	21.8	20.8	21.4	22.1	21.5	20.2	19.5
Qualified agree	24.4	28.4	25.6	24.6	30.3	26.9	25.0
Agree	18.5	21.8	17.9	18.4	16.8	26.9	18.0
Strongly agree	7.9	7.1	8.0	7.6	8.3	7.3	8.9
No response	2.1	0.5	1.8	2.1	3.3	1.6	1.4

the Neo-Pagans in these three regions supports the creation of paid clergy, many more support this proposition than oppose it. In the West South Central region 25.9 percent oppose the creation of paid Neo-Pagan clergy to some degree; in all other regions less than 25 percent of Neo-Pagans oppose the creation of paid clergy.

Among the three forms of worship the strongest support for paid clergy comes from those who work in groups, among whom 55 percent support to some degree and 23.6 percent oppose to some degree the creation of a paid clergy. The weakest support is from those who work with a partner, among whom 47.2 percent support to some degree and 33.1 percent oppose to some degree the creation of paid clergy. Of solitary practitioners, 49.1 percent support to some degree, and 27 percent oppose to some degree the creation of paid clergy. Although there is some variation among the three forms of spiritual practice, in all instances more Neo-Pagans support than oppose the creation of paid clergy. Those in groups, who are the most likely to find themselves in the position of either becoming or supporting paid clergy, are the ones most likely to endorse this proposition.

Although there is strong support for the idea of the creation of paid clergy, only 0.6 percent of our sample claim that they are full-time paid clergy, and 1.3 percent state they are part-time paid clergy. A slightly higher percentage of men (1.8 percent) than women (1.1 percent) claims to be part-time clergy. The disparity between the theoretical support for the creation of paid clergy and the actual small percentage of individuals who are supported in their role as Neo-Pagan clergy suggests that there are structural barriers to the development of paid clergy. Although some groups are attempting to create church or denominational structures, these are still quite nascent. As the quote at the beginning of this chapter suggests, Neo-Pagans have been hesitant to give money to support organizations or individuals.

Table 44 shows that most Neo-Pagans (66.9 percent) claim that they give between $0 and $250 a year to their religion. There are 27.9 percent who state that they give nothing and an additional 15.3 percent who claim to donate $75 or less per year to their religion. The GSS asks a similar question: "About how much do you contribute

TABLE 44: Comparison of the General Neo-Pagan Population's and the General American Public's Religious Donations

Donation	GNPP %	GSS %
$0	27.9	—
$0–$250	66.9	63.4
$251–$500	11.9	8.3
$501–$1,000	5.0	8.6
$1,001–$9,999	4.5	8.6
$10,000–$99,994	0.1	0.2
No response	11.4	8.1

to your religion every year (not including school tuition)?" As seen in table 44, most GSS respondents (63.4 percent) state they gave between $0 and $250 a year.[1] Unfortunately, GSS does not report the percentage of their respondents who claim to give nothing. Although slightly more Neo-Pagans fall into the low end of giving than the general American public, the real difference can be seen by comparing our results to the greater amounts of donations reported in the GSS. In that survey, a larger proportion of the general American public makes donations between $501 to $1,000 and $1,001 to $9,999 a year than Neo-Pagans do. The largest contribution that any individual reports donating to Neo-Paganism is $6,000. The GSS reports that 0.2 percent of their sample contribute over $10,000 a year, and 8.6 percent contribute between $1,001 and $9,999 a year. These statistics can be compared with Neo-Pagans, among whom only 4.5 percent donate between $1,001 and $9,999 annually. Those surveyed in the GSS are a cross section of Americans, some of whom have no religious affiliation. Our survey, to the contrary, was distributed only to those who self-identify as Neo-Pagans.

There are several reasons seemingly fewer Neo-Pagans make large contributions to their religion than members of the general American public. Very few, if any, Neo-Pagans are wealthy. One survey respondent notes, "I'd like to see the Pagan Community at large be more accepting of those among them who earn a larger-than-average income. For some reason Pagans tend to equate wealth with conspicuous consumption and Earth-harming practices, but that is not necessarily so. . . . If these people were accepted, they might contribute some of that wealth to our causes" (Survey 2576). Although, as our survey illustrates, Neo-Pagans on the whole have a high education level and there is variation in earnings, the movement has a countercultural image. For some Neo-Pagans, this image results in their choosing lower paid jobs that will permit them to do work they see as consistent with their spiritual ideals or that will allow them extra time for their spiritual quests.

Neo-Pagans have qualms about giving money directly to individuals or organizations to support paid clergy. In part this is because, at least among the largest sect, Wicca, all participants are considered priestesses or priests; hence all can equally claim the right of support for their spiritual quests. Within the religion, clergy have traditionally ministered to their small covens, rarely to larger groups. Those who have created umbrella organizations rely on volunteer labor and/or are paid for services such as running a festival and either do not attempt or are unable to become full-time clergy supported by a congregation. Neo-Pagans are leery of giving money to an individual or group, particularly if there is no clear sense of the organization as belonging to the members who can, if they so choose, vote the founders out of office. Helen Berger (1999a) describes the struggle of one such Neo-Pagan umbrella organization, the Earth-Spirit Community, to have paid clergy. Among the reasons individuals give for not supporting EarthSpirit Community's quest for funding from the larger Neo-Pagan community is concern that the organization is run by an inner circle of individuals who are ultimately unaccountable to the membership.

Although different from the first statement about the establishment of paid clergy, the second statement, about whether it is acceptable for a Witch to accept payment for teaching the Craft, raises the related question of whether it is legitimate for some Neo-Pagans to be paid for work associated with their spiritual path. However, concerning the second statement—"A Witch should not accept money for teaching the Craft"—our respondents are nearly evenly split on the issue, with 41.7 percent disagreeing to some degree and 42.5 percent agreeing to some degree.

TABLE 45: Women's and Men's Attitudes toward Witches Accepting Payment

Response	Total %	Female %	Male %	No Gender Listed %
Strongly disagree	5.1	5.5	4.2	7.1
Disagree	14.6	16.9	10.5	14.3
Qualified disagree	22.0	23.1	20.2	14.3
No opinion	13.8	12.2	16.2	28.6
Qualified agree	17.2	17.1	17.2	21.4
Agree	12.9	12.2	14.5	3.6
Strongly agree	12.4	11.0	15.1	7.1
No response	2.1	2.1	2.0	3.6

As table 45 indicates, there is a gender divide on this issue, with more women (45.5 percent) than men (34.9 percent) disagreeing to some degree with the proposition. More men than women have no opinion, and 40.3 percent of women and 46.8 percent of men agree with the proposition. As shown in table 46, among the sects examined, Goddess Worshipers are the most likely to disagree to some degree with the notion that Witches should not accept money for teaching the Craft. Although both female and male Witches can and do teach the Craft within covens, the high priestess is a more important figure than the high priest (H. Berger 2000). It might then appear that Neo-Pagan women in general, and Goddess Worshipers specifically, view the free labor provided primarily by women as problematic. However, as table 46 also indicates, Wiccans are the most likely to agree that Witches should not be paid for teaching their spiritual path. Among members of this sect, 47.7 percent agree to some degree, and 39.7 percent disagree to some degree with the proposition. Although not the only ones to do so, Wiccans are the most likely to accept the label *Witch*. They are, therefore, the ones who would most likely either profit by selling their knowledge or to potentially feel exploited by giving it away for free. As previously noted, there is a strong feeling among Wiccans that it is unethical for teachers to accept money for their teachings. This ethic may mitigate against desires to be paid for their work. Nonetheless, it must

TABLE 46: Sects' Attitudes toward Witches Accepting Payment

Response	GNPP %	Druid %	Goddess %	Pagan %	Shaman %	Unitarian %	Wiccan %
Strongly disagree	5.1	2.5	6.6	5.0	6.9	3.1	4.9
Disagree	14.6	10.2	16.6	15.4	11.3	12.4	14.1
Qualified disagree	22.0	27.9	21.6	20.6	24.5	24.4	20.7
No opinion	13.8	17.8	13.0	14.5	12.9	20.2	11.3
Qualified agree	17.2	20.3	17.3	17.5	18.2	15.5	18.8
Agree	12.9	9.1	11.0	12.1	11.3	13.5	14.6
Strongly agree	12.4	11.7	12.1	12.9	12.1	8.8	14.3
No response	2.1	0.5	1.8	2.0	2.8	2.1	1.3

TABLE 47: Regional Attitudes toward Witches Accepting Payment

Response	GNPP %	ENC %	ESC %	MA %	MO %	NE %	PA %	SA %	WNC %	WSC %
Strongly disagree	5.1	3.1	6.5	5.5	5.1	6.8	5.7	4.8	2.6	3.4
Disagree	14.6	18.6	8.7	12.2	13.5	15.1	18.8	9.6	12.8	8.6
Qualified disagree	21.9	19.6	21.7	20.5	19.9	27.5	24.1	22.0	21.8	18.9
No opinion	13.8	15.8	19.6	14.2	9.6	14.0	11.7	13.9	19.2	12.9
Qualified agree	17.2	15.5	15.2	15.7	16.0	17.4	15.7	20.5	17.9	21.6
Agree	12.9	12.4	19.6	14.2	16.0	10.2	10.6	15.4	11.5	17.2
Strongly agree	12.4	13.4	8.7	15.0	17.9	6.8	10.8	13.0	11.5	15.5
No response	2.1	1.7	0.0	2.8	1.9	2.3	2.6	0.9	2.6	1.7

TABLE 48: Attitudes toward Witches Accepting Payment by the Three Forms of Spiritual Practice

Response	Total %	Group %	SP %	SO %	NR %
Strongly disagree	5.1	3.7	6.7	5.5	6.3
Disagree	14.6	15.3	12.4	14.4	16.4
Qualified disagree	22.0	22.6	23.8	21.1	23.3
No opinion	13.8	11.7	8.3	16.5	10.7
Qualified agree	17.2	16.5	19.7	16.8	19.5
Agree	12.9	15.3	13.0	12.2	6.9
Strongly agree	12.4	13.1	15.0	11.5	11.9
No response	2.1	1.8	1.0	2.0	5.0

be noted that less than half of all Wiccans agree with the proposition that Witches should not accept money. This view suggests that as more and more people enter the religion, the older ethic is becoming transformed.

Pagans, Druids, and Shamans are almost equally divided between those who support and those who oppose the notion of Witches being paid for teaching their spiritual path. UU Neo-Pagans are the least likely to have an opinion on this issue. Those who do have an opinion are almost evenly divided between those who agree (31.5 percent) and those who disagree (39.9 percent) with the proposition.

Regionally, as demonstrated in table 47, Neo-Pagans in the New England and the Pacific regions are the most likely to view Witches accepting money to teach the Craft as acceptable. Respectively, 49.4 percent and 48.6 percent of Neo-Pagans in these regions disagree to some degree with the proposition that "a Witch should not accept money for teaching the Craft." Slightly more than a third of Neo-Pagans in both these regions agree with the proposition to some degree. Neo-Pagans in the Mountain region express the strongest support for the idea that it is inappropriate for Witches to accept money for teaching the Craft. In this region 49.9 percent of the respondents agree to some degree, and 38.5 percent disagree to some degree with the proposition. Both the Pacific and New England regions have major urban centers in which there is both the potential market for Witches to teach the Craft for a fee and in which initiated Witches, who teach for free, may feel overwhelmed by seekers. Although the existence of urban centers helps to explain the difference between the New England and Pacific regions and the Mountain region, other regions, such as the Mid-Atlantic region, which includes New York City and Philadelphia, also have high population density but do not indicate as strong a level of support of Witches accepting money. Regional differences cannot be explained simply by differences in density but also must reflect local variations among Neo-Pagans.

Individuals who practice with one partner are the most likely to support the proposition that Witches should not receive pay for teaching the Craft. As is indicated in table 48, 47.7 percent of these individuals agree to some degree with the proposition and 42.9 percent disagree with it. The weakest support comes from solitaries, among whom 40.5 percent agree to some degree and 41 percent disagree to some degree. Those working in groups, the most likely to be trained for free, are in the middle, with 44.9 percent agreeing to some degree and 41.6 percent disagreeing to some degree with the proposition. Both solitaries and those working with only one partner are the most likely to seek out teachers outside the coven setting. However, Neo-Pagans in these two forms of spiritual practice differ on whether or not they believe it is acceptable for Witches to receive payment for their teachings.

Training

When asked if it is important for a Witch to have high standards of training, over 80 percent of Neo-Pagans say yes. Although there are some minor variations among sects, regions, and forms of spiritual practice, they are very small. We unfortunately do not ask the same question about training for other spiritual paths, although we suspect that there would be a general consensus that all Neo-Pagans, particularly those in leadership, teaching, or ministerial roles, should be well trained. However, there is disagreement concerning what constitutes good training. As those who are trained through books and correspondence courses are often viewed as not having equivalent training to those in covens, we ask respondents to react to the statement "Correspondence courses are an acceptable way to learn the Craft." As with the other statements in this chapter, respondents are asked to state the degree to which they agree or disagree. Our data indicate that more Neo-Pagans find correspondence courses an acceptable way to learn the Craft than those who feel that such courses are not acceptable. Among the general Neo-Pagan communities, 48.4 percent agree to some degree with this proposition, 30.6 percent disagree to some degree, and 21 percent have no opinion.

As it is more likely that solitaries and those working with a partner are trained through correspondence courses, we anticipated greater interest in and support for this proposition among these two cohorts. In part our expectation was met, as solitaries are the least likely to disagree with the statement, with only 26.7 percent disagreeing to some degree. Those working with a partner have a somewhat higher rate of disagreement, with 31.7 percent disagreeing to some degree, and those working in groups have the highest disagreement, with 36.6 percent disagreeing to some degree. However, solitaries are also the most likely to have no opinion on this issue. Among this cohort, 20.7 percent have no opinion, which can be compared with those working with a partner, among whom 14 percent have no opinion and those working in groups, among whom 17.5 percent have no opinion. Those working with a spiritual partner are the most likely to support the notion that correspondence courses are an acceptable way to learn the Craft. Of those working with a spiritual partner, 53.9 percent support this proposition to some degree. This statistic can be compared with solitaries, among whom 50.8 percent support this proposition and those working in groups, among whom 44.1 percent support the proposition.

Table 49 illustrates some variance among the sects. The majority of Druids, Shamans, Wiccans, and Pagans supports correspondence courses as an acceptable way to learn the Craft. Respectively, 56.9 percent, 52.8 percent, 50.8 percent, and 50.2 percent of each sect support to some degree the proposition that correspondence courses are an acceptable way to learn the Craft. UU Neo-Pagans and Goddess Worshipers are the least likely to support this proposition, with 47.1 percent and 47.9 percent respectively agreeing to some degree

TABLE 49: Sects' Attitudes toward Correspondence Courses

Response	GNPP %	Druid %	Goddess %	Pagan %	Shaman %	Unitarian %	Wiccan %
Strongly disagree	6.3	6.1	6.0	5.9	6.3	5.7	5.7
Disagree	10.9	8.1	11.5	10.6	8.0	9.3	11.2
Qualified disagree	13.4	17.8	13.9	12.7	14.1	9.3	14.3
No opinion	19.2	10.1	19.1	18.8	15.4	27.0	17.0
Qualified agree	26.3	32.0	27.4	27.1	30.0	28.5	28.3
Agree	16.5	18.3	15.7	16.9	17.3	15.5	16.8
Strongly agree	5.5	6.6	4.8	6.2	5.5	3.1	5.7
No response	1.8	1.0	1.5	1.7	3.3	1.6	0.9

that correspondence courses are an acceptable way to learn the Craft.

The biggest differences are regional, as illustrated in table 50. Although in all regions more Neo-Pagans support the proposition that correspondence courses are a legitimate way to learn the Craft, the weakest support comes from New England and the Pacific region, which include 42 percent and 43 percent respectively of their respondents agreeing with this proposition, and from the Mid-Atlantic states, which include 47.7 percent agreeing with the proposition. In all other regions a majority of our respondents agrees with the proposition, although the strongest support came from the East South Central region, in which 74 percent agree to some degree. The three regions in which support is weakest for correspondence courses are also the areas that have a high density of Neo-Pagans and, therefore, an increased opportunity for individuals to learn the Craft through participation in a coven, a group, or a class. In other areas, where it might be harder to find a teacher, and hence the reliance on correspondence courses may be higher, there is greater acceptance of the practice.

Hierarchy

> I know of no historical example that supports the idea that hierarchy can be a non-oppressive structure—even feminist institutions that strive to be non-oppressive suppress individual freedoms because they are hierarchical. (Survey 1777)

A dread of the development of hierarchy and with it the curtailing of individual freedom and spiritual expression is one of the reasons that some Neo-Pagans oppose the creation of paid clergy and the development of institutions. Among Neo-Pagans there is simultaneously a strong ethic of individual freedom and, at least among many, a desire to see their religion grow and change. One survey respondent notes, "From my experience with Judaism, I appreciate the fact that there's no 'enforcer' in the Craft. If we disagree, we can disavow and disassociate, but we're not Papist, setting down what is 'right' and what's heresy. I would like to see more organized community, a clergy, and a place of worship" (Survey 1831). Many Neo-Pagans are caught between the desire to remain a religion whose focus is on individual

TABLE 50: Regional Attitudes toward Correspondence Courses

Response	NPP %	ENC %	ESC %	MA %	MO %	NE %	PA %	SA %	WNC %	WSC %
Strongly disagree	6.3	3.8	2.2	5.9	4.5	8.3	7.3	6.6	9.0	7.8
Disagree	10.9	8.9	4.3	13.4	9.0	12.8	12.1	11.1	3.8	10.3
Qualified disagree	13.5	12.0	8.7	12.2	17.9	12.8	15.9	12.0	15.4	11.2
No opinion	19.2	23.0	10.9	18.5	11.5	21.9	19.2	18.7	15.4	19.8
Qualified agree	26.3	27.8	34.8	21.3	34.0	20.4	26.7	29.2	26.9	26.7
Agree	16.5	17.9	19.6	18.9	15.4	17.4	14.1	16.3	16.7	11.2
Strongly agree	5.6	5.2	19.6	7.5	6.4	4.2	2.2	5.1	10.3	12.1
No response	1.8	1.4	0.0	2.4	1.3	2.3	2.4	0.9	2.6	0.9

expression and experience and the desire to have their religion bene-
fit by greater organization and better-trained clergy. Neo-Pagans
pride themselves on not having a guru or leader. Although isomorphism is occurring through the sharing of magical and spiritual rituals at festivals and other gatherings, and through individuals reading
the same books and interacting on the Internet, there has never
been a central organization or leader who speaks for the entire community in condemning or extolling practices. Some individuals'
voices are heard more often, and listened to more than others, but
they do not have the institutional power to include or exclude others from the Neo-Pagan community.

As the institutionalization and development of paid clergy imply
the creation of hierarchy, we ask respondents to state their degree of
agreement or disagreement with the statement "Hierarchy can be an
organic, non-oppressive organizational structure." The majority of
Neo-Pagans (50.3 percent) agrees to some degree with this statement, 19.2 percent have no opinion, and 30.4 percent disagree and
the rest did not answer this question. Although there is some variation among the sects, the two most notable responses are from
Druids and Goddess Worshipers. Druids give the strongest support
for this proposition (60. 4 percent agree to some degree, and 21.3
percent disagree to some degree). Goddess Worshipers, on the other
hand, are the only sect in which less than half (47.9 percent) of the
respondents supports this statement, although even in this group
more respondents agree with the statement than disagree with
it (34.6 percent disagree). Among the other four sects examined,
between 50.8 percent and 52.3 percent agree to some degree that
hierarchies can be organic and nonoppressive, and between 24.3
percent and 29.6 percent disagree to some degree with this proposition.

Druids' stronger-than-average support for the notion that hierarchies can be organic and nonoppressive is consistent with the
structure of their circles or groves, which tend to be more openly
hierarchical than other Neo-Pagan sects, and Druids' attempts to
develop standardized training for their clergy. The response of Goddess Worshipers echoes that of Neo-Pagan women in general,
among whom 47.1 percent agree to some degree, and 33.3 percent

disagree to some degree with the statement, and 20.4 have no opinion. However, women Goddess Worshipers have a stronger response to this statement than do Neo-Pagan women in general. Of female Goddess Worshipers, 43.6 percent agree to some degree, and 37.9 percent disagree to some degree with the idea that hierarchy can be organic and nonoppressive. This response can be compared with male Goddess Worshipers, who more strongly support the proposition than do Neo-Pagan men in general. Among male Goddess Worshipers, 62.4 percent agree to some degree that hierarchies can be organic and nonoppressive as compared with Neo-Pagan men in general, among whom 57 percent agree with this statement.

Goddess Worshipers tend not to form into groups that are structurally hierarchical. Unlike Wiccans whose covens are typically headed by a high priestess and high priest, most Goddess Worshipers' groups do not have official leaders. At times one or two women do take the unofficial position of leadership within these groups. Women who enter Neo-Paganism from feminism bring with them a concern about anyone having power over others, thus being able to dominate their subordinates. Within Wiccan groups, in which the high priestess is regularly seen as the group leader, concern is frequently expressed that this unofficial leadership might result in one person gaining power over others. It is often simultaneously stated that the groups are nonhierarchical and egalitarian, and that the high priestess is the group leader (H. Berger 2000). Starhawk (1987) makes a distinction between three types of power: power-over, or domination; power-from-within, or self empowerment; and power-with, or influence. She finds the distinction useful in differentiating between oppressive forms of power and those that are helpful to the individual or group. Starhawk uses this distinction to reconcile a desire for egalitarianism among Neo-Pagans and the reality of leaders forming within groups. Because Goddess Worshipers on the whole are the least likely to have either official leaders, or, like Wiccans, three levels or degrees of attainment, it is not surprising that they give the weakest support for the notion that hierarchies can be nonoppressive. More surprising is that the small group of men who define themselves as Goddess Worshipers are more likely than other Neo-Pagan men to support the notion that hierarchies may be a positive structural form. In all the other questions we find that male Goddess Worshipers' responses are closer to those of Neo-Pagan women than other Neo-Pagan men's responses.

In four regions—East North Central, Mid-Atlantic, New England, and Pacific—less than half of our respondents support the proposition that hierarchy can be an organic, nonoppressive organizational structure. In these regions more respondents agree to some degree with the proposition than disagree with it; the rest have either no opinion or do not answer the question. The weakest support for the proposition comes from the East North Central region, in which only 38.2 percent of the respondents agree to some degree, and 37.8 percent disagree to some degree with the proposition. Among the other three regions, slightly less than 50 percent support this proposition (the Pacific region has 49.7 percent, Mid-Atlantic 48.8 percent, and New England 48.7 percent agreeing with the proposition). The strongest support comes from the West South Central region, in which 57 percent agree to some degree, and 17.2 percent disagree to some degree with the proposition. The slightly weaker support on the two coasts is not surprising, as both tend to be more liberal and hence might be more concerned with the corrosive elements of hierarchy.

Among the three forms of spiritual practice, the weakest support comes from solitaries, 45.7 percent of whom disagree with the proposition that hierarchies can be nonoppressive. This figure can be compared with those who work in a group, of whom 57.4 percent disagree to some degree, and those who work with a partner, among whom 55.9 percent disagree to some degree with this proposition. Solitaries are the least likely to have an opinion on this issue. Of solitaries, 20.9 percent report having no opinion, compared with those that work in a group, among whom only 10.7 percent have no opinion, and those who work with a partner, among whom only 13 percent have no opinion. Solitaries are the least likely to have contact with hierarchical groups and hence are the least concerned with the issue. Solitaries who do express an opinion are the most likely of the three forms of spiritual practice to find hierarchy of any sort unacceptable. Their distrust or dislike of hierarchies may be one of the reasons that these individuals choose to work alone.

Going Mainstream

> Well it seems to me that Pagan (or very Pagan-sounding) ideas are
> entering the mainstream at a tremendous rate—particularly Goddess
> awareness. Watered-down, non-specific rituals are being formed not
> just at New Age gatherings, but before business meetings [and] city
> council sessions. . . . I don't know if it's just another pop trend or if
> we're seeing the beginnings of real change, and I'm ambivalent about
> the diluted rituals, but I do feel in my bones that Neo-Paganism is
> about to make major inroads in public consciousness even with our
> non-proselytizing tendencies. (Survey 1469)

The number of books, television programs, newspaper articles, and
images that abound in popular culture bears witness to the spread
of Neo-Paganism and its ingress into mainstream culture. There is
ambivalence within the Neo-Pagan community about the religion's
popularization. On the one hand, many Neo-Pagans are pleased that
their religious and magical beliefs protect the earth and that their
concern for individual rights, including women's and gay rights, are
permeating mainstream culture. On the other hand, they worry
that popularization may result in their religion becoming diluted—
particularly for serious seekers who may be put off by its popularization.

Ezzy (2001) argues that the growing reliance on Wicca how-to
books, videos, and training courses with a fee, although making the
religion open to more people, is also creating an alternative version
of Wicca that differs from the older initiatory religion. According to
Ezzy, unlike the older version, which focuses on spiritual practices
that enhance individuals' personal development and connections to
nature, the new version emphasizes magical practices and the casting of spells outside of a larger spiritual framework. Ezzy acknowledges that not all books or correspondence courses result in the
reduction of the spiritual teaching of Wicca to magical techniques
but notes that the commercialization of Wicca is an outgrowth of
this change.

To determine whether our respondents view popularization as
a problem, we ask them to state the degree to which they agree or
disagree with the statement "The popularization of Witchcraft has

diluted its standards and identity." Responses indicate that 43.4 percent of Neo-Pagans disagree with this statement, 34.3 percent agree, and 19.9 percent have no opinion; the rest do not respond to this statement. Neo-Pagan men are as likely to disagree with this statement as agree with it. Neo-Pagan women, however, are more likely to disagree than disagree with it (46.percent disagree, and 31.8 percent agree).

Table 51 indicates that the larger sects—Wiccans, Pagans, and Goddess Worshipers—are more likely to believe that popularization has not diluted the identity and standards of Witchcraft than are the other three sects examined—Druids, Shamans, and UU Neo-Pagans. Wiccans most strongly disagree with this statement, with 50.2 percent disagreeing to some degree, 33 percent agreeing to some degree, and 15.5 percent having no opinion. Slightly fewer Goddess Worshipers (47.8 percent) and Pagans (46.9 percent) disagree to some degree with this statement than do Wiccans. Druids are the only sect in which more respondents agree with the statement to some degree than disagree to some degree (47.7 percent agree to some degree, and 34 percent disagree with it). UU Neo-Pagans are the least likely to have an opinion on this issue. Among those who do state an opinion, 38.9 percent disagree, and 31.6 percent agree to some degree with the statement.

Our survey results suggest that on the whole most Neo-Pagans do not see popularization as a problem. Particularly among Wiccans, the majority does not see the standards of Witchcraft being weakened by the religion's popularization. The one notable exception is Druids, who are more likely to see popularization as a problem. This finding is consistent with the movement among Druids for long-term training of their leaders. Although other groups also have increased their training and standards, Druids have been the most outspoken and consistent in doing this.

In all regions except New England, more respondents disagree with the proposition that "popularization of Witchcraft has diluted its standards and identity" than agree with it. In New England 34.4 percent disagree, and 40 percent agree with this proposition, 23 percent have no opinion, and 2.6 percent do not respond to the statement. In two regions, West South Central and Mountain, the majority

TABLE 51: Sects' Attitudes toward Popularization

Response	GNPP %	Druid %	Goddess %	Pagan %	Shaman %	Unitarian %	Wiccan %
Strongly disagree	8.4	8.6	10.3	10.0	8.3	8.3	9.8
Disagree	21.2	14.7	21.4	22.1	21.2	16.6	24.1
Qualified disagree	13.8	10.7	16.1	14.8	11.3	14.0	16.3
No opinion	19.9	17.8	18.4	17.9	18.5	28.0	15.5
Qualified agree	17.8	24.4	17.8	17.4	19.6	15.0	18.7
Agree	10.7	15.2	9.2	10.1	10.5	10.4	9.6
Strongly agree	5.7	8.1	4.5	5.3	7.2	6.2	4.7
No response	2.3	0.5	2.2	2.4	3.6	1.6	1.4

TABLE 52: Regional Attitudes toward Popularization

Response	GNPP %	ENC %	ESC %	MA %	MO %	NE %	PA %	SA %	WNC %	WSC %
Strongly disagree	8.4	8.2	17.4	7.9	9.0	7.9	8.4	9.0	6.4	9.5
Disagree	21.2	23.0	10.9	18.5	23.7	14.3	22.5	24.1	17.9	29.3
Qualified disagree	13.8	11.3	13.0	13.8	17.9	12.1	13.7	15.0	15.4	15.5
No opinion	19.9	18.2	19.6	19.7	12.2	23.0	22.5	19.3	19.2	12.1
Qualified agree	17.9	20.3	21.7	18.9	25.0	17.7	14.8	15.7	17.9	19.8
Agree	10.7	11.3	6.5	9.1	6.4	17.0	11.3	9.3	11.5	7.8
Strongly agree	5.7	5.8	10.9	9.1	4.5	5.3	4.0	6.0	7.7	4.3
No response	2.3	1.7	0.0	3.2	1.3	2.6	2.9	1.5	3.8	1.7

of our respondents disagrees with this statement (54.3 percent and 50.6 percent respectively). In the South Atlantic and Pacific regions notably more individuals disagree with this proposition (48.2 percent and 44.6 percent respectively) than agree with it (31 percent and 30.1 percent respectively). In all the other regions the difference between those who disagree and those who agree with this statement is small. Those who work in groups as opposed to working with one partner or solitaries are more likely to disagree to some degree with the statement. The reason popularization of the religion seems more acceptable to those working in groups than in other forms of worship is not clear.

Popularization of the religion has resulted in its becoming more recognized and, at least within some segments of the society, acceptable. Two areas in which Neo-Pagans through their interaction with the larger society may create dissonance is in calling themselves Witches and the way they dress, particularly when giving media interviews. Both children's fairy tales and historic accounts of witch trials paint a picture of witches as ugly, harmful people who have made a pact with the Devil to do his work. While some individuals do not refer to themselves as Witches simply because they follow a different spiritual path, others eschew the term because of its negative connotations. For others, accepting the term *Witch* is an important element of self-definition either because they view it as linking them to what they see as an old religion or because they want to reclaim the word. Among some feminists in particular, taking a word, such as *Witch,* that has traditionally been used negatively against women and giving it a positive image is a political act in itself. One respondent states, "I believe that Wiccans and Witches should reclaim the name *witch* from its imposed negative connotations. Ditto for *Pagans* and for *Heathens.* Ditto for Odinists, who do *not* want to be equated with any racism or other imposed negative connotation" (Survey 2610).

When we asked respondents to state the degree of agreement or disagreement with the statement "The term *Witch* is inappropriate today and should not be used," most Neo-Pagans (78 percent) state they disagree to some degree with this proposition. Neo-Pagan women are somewhat more likely to reject the proposition than are

Neo-Pagan men—80.1 percent of women and 74.4 percent of men disagree to some degree with the statement. Wiccans, the group most likely to use the label *Witch,* are also the most likely to reject this proposition. Among Wiccans, 85.4 percent disagree with the statement to some degree. Druids are the sect most likely to agree with this proposition, although even in this group only 10.9 percent of respondents agree to some degree with the statement. There is some minimal variation geographically with the strongest support in the East South Central region, in which 15.2 percent of the respondents agree with the statement, and the majority, 67.4 percent, disagrees with it; 17.4 percent have no opinion.

Although support is greatest among Neo-Pagan women and Wiccans, there is in general strong support for maintaining use of the term *Witch.* At the same time that there is a desire to become more accepted and recognized by many within the Neo-Pagan movement, most continue to support use of the name *Witch.* Whatever other compromises Neo-Pagans are willing to make to gain public acceptance, they are not willing to drop the term *Witch.* Instead, many Neo-Pagans want to educate the public that Witches are not Devil Worshipers or evil. We do not ask how many individuals within the Neo-Pagan movement use the term *Witch* as a self-description, nor would we have comparative data to determine if there has been a decrease or increase in the proportion of Neo-Pagans who accept that label.

With growing popularization there has been increased media coverage of Neo-Pagan rituals, particularly around Halloween. Most news stories report on the meaning of the holiday, its focus on the natural cycles, and the fact that the participants are not Satanists. Some Neo-Pagans who have been interviewed do so in ritual robes and jewelry. Others believe that it is important to dress as mundanely as possible when making public appearances to decrease the sense of Witches or Neo-Pagans being odd or very different. As one respondent to our survey contends, "flamboyant costumes tend to lessen credibility" (Survey 2629). The issue of dress is important because, through their presentation of self, Witches can either choose to emphasize that they are part of the mainstream despite participating in a minority religion or they can choose to emphasize that they are part of the counter-culture. Dressing in ritual robes and jewelry can be seen as political act in the same manner that taking the label *Witch* is a political act.

When asked to state the degree to which they agree or disagree with the statement "'Public Witches' should dress conservatively when giving media interviews," Neo-Pagans are split almost evenly on the issue: 39.1 percent disagree to some degree, 37.9 percent agree to some degree, 20.9 percent have no opinion, and the rest do not respond to this statement. Neo-Pagan women are more likely to answer this question negatively than are Neo-Pagan men. Among women, 41.6 percent disagree with the statement, 36 percent agree, and 20.4 percent have no opinion. These statistics can be compared with men, among whom 33.9 percent disagree, 41.7 percent agree, and 22.5 percent have no opinion.

Goddess Worshipers and UU Neo-Pagans stand out in their response to this question from the other sects, as more Goddess Worshipers disagree with the statement and more UU Neo-Pagans agree with the statement. Among Goddess Worshipers, 42.9 percent disagree, 35.9 percent agree, and 19.4 percent have no opinion. A larger percentage of female than male Goddess Worshipers disagree that public Witches should dress conservatively when giving interviews. In comparing the two, 44.4 percent of women Goddess Worshipers and 38.2 percent of men Goddess Worshipers disagree with this proposition. More than one-third (34.3%) of women and 40.7 percent of men agree with the statement, and 19.5 percent of women and 19.7 percent of men have no opinion. Although as with Neo-Pagans in general, women in this sect are more likely to disagree with the statement than men, both are more likely to disagree than their counterparts in the larger Neo-Pagan community.

UU Neo-Pagans are the only group in which a larger percent of respondents agree with the statement than disagree with it. Among UU Neo-Pagans, 31.1 percent disagree, 44.5 percent agree, and 22.8 percent have no opinion about this statement. As with other questions in the survey, UU Neo-Pagans tend to be more culturally conservative than other Neo-Pagans. By participating in a church, UU Neo-Pagans are, to some degree, more mainstream than others within the Neo-Pagan community. It is, therefore, not surprising that they are the most likely to support the proposition that Witches should dress conservatively when making public appearances.

As demonstrated in table 53, two regions, New England and Pacific, are the most likely to disagree with the statement that public Witches should dress conservatively when giving media interviews. In New England 48.3 percent of respondents disagree with this statement, 32.4 percent agree, and 16.2 percent have no opinion. Among respondents in the Pacific region, 42.2 percent disagree, 34.2 percent agree, and 21 percent have no opinion. These are the two regions where the largest percent of Neo-Pagans reside. Both areas are also culturally liberal regions in which dressing differently or having an alternative religious affiliation is most likely to be socially acceptable. In these regions Neo-Pagans appear concerned than in other areas of the United States that public Witches giving interviews not distinguish themselves through their dress. Consistent with this finding, Neo-Pagans in the East South Central region are the most likely to agree with the statement. In this region 47.8 percent agree with the statement, 24 percent disagree with the statement, and 28.3 percent have no opinion. Similarly, in the West South Central region 48.3 percent of the respondents agree with the statement, and 31.9 percent disagree; 18.1 percent have no opinion. In the South Atlantic region 42.5 percent agree with the proposition, 36.4 percent disagree, and 20.5 percent have no opinion. On the whole, those in the southern United States are more likely to believe that Witches giving media interviews should dress conservatively. Neo-Pagans in these areas are the most likely to be concerned that they and their families might be ostracized because of their religious practices. One respondent, for example, notes, "Paganism in the *Bible Belt* is still very much in the closet due to fears of persecution. (I am quite guilty of this too!) I hope that we can find a way to be *out* without fear of major retribution" (Survey 2645). A more conservative presentation by public Witches is more likely to help allay their neighbor's fears than seeing a Witch in ritual garb on the local television news station.

Popularization of Witchcraft and Neo-Paganism is affecting the religion. Although fewer Neo-Pagans view this effect as a problem than do not, the difference is small. There is concern that popularization

TABLE 53: Regional Attitudes toward Attire of Public Witches

Response	GNPP %	ENC %	ESC %	MA %	MO %	NE %	PA %	SA %	WNC %	WSC %
Strongly disagree	8.4	7.9	2.2	6.7	9.0	12.1	9.3	6.3	9.0	6.9
Disagree	15.6	15.8	10.9	12.2	17.3	21.1	15.7	15.0	10.3	14.7
Qualified disagree	15.1	14.1	10.9	18.1	12.8	15.1	17.2	14.8	14.1	10.3
No opinion	20.9	22.7	28.3	22.8	21.8	16.2	21.0	20.5	25.6	18.1
Qualified agree	18.8	18.9	23.9	16.1	19.9	18.5	18.5	18.4	23.1	20.7
Agree	11.0	10.7	15.2	12.2	12.2	9.4	9.3	13.0	7.7	12.9
Strongly agree	8.1	8.6	8.7	9.4	5.8	4.5	6.4	11.1	7.7	14.7
No response	2.1	1.4	0.0	2.4	1.3	3.0	2.6	0.9	2.6	1.7

might result in the religion losing its focus or becoming so inundated with seekers (only a small percentage of whom are seriously interested in the spirituality) that the more committed will become disillusioned. The growing media attention on Neo-Paganism has raised other concerns. Some have experienced and fear discrimination, and others fear a backlash in the more culturally conservative areas of the United States. However, the vast majority of Neo-Pagans continues to support the use of the word *Witch* to describe at least some of their members. Eliminating the name *Witch,* for many Neo-Pagans, suggests too great an accommodation with the larger society. However, in terms of presentation of self in public, particularly for those Witches speaking to the media, Neo-Pagans are almost evenly split on whether these individuals should dress conservatively. Popularization is one of the forces encouraging accommodation, but for many Neo-Pagans there appears to be a concern that in the process of creating an acceptable persona for the larger community, they not distort their own religion and possibly dull its critical edge.

The Aging of a Late Modern Religion

John Lofland and James Richardson (Lofland and Richardson 1984; Richardson 1985) note that the organizational form of new religions is volatile, shifting rapidly from one form to the next as the religions respond to pressures from both within and outside. Neo-Paganism is in the process of responding to many of the same pressures that other new religions experience—the birth of children, the aging of the early participants, the influx of neophytes, and tensions with the larger society. The responses of Neo-Pagans, however, do not follow the model suggested by Lofland and Richardson's research. Their study creates a typology of five ideal organizational forms of new religions. Three of these types require adherents of the religion to withdraw from some or all of "the four main areas of everyday functioning: work, residence, eating, and family/personal support circles" (36). Although there are some Neo-Pagans who live communality, by and large this arrangement is rare. Most Neo-Pagans remain within the larger society—albeit some choose to do so on the fringes.

The other two organizational forms described by Lofland and Richardson, client clinics and congregations, although sharing some aspects with Neo-Paganism, do not describe this new religion. Client clinics, which Rodney Stark and William Bambridge (1985) refer to as client cults, are based on fees for service. These clinics resemble the relationship between a therapist and patient, or a consultant and a client, and according to Lofland and Richardson, do not result in the development of a community of celebrants. Although market exchanges exist for classes on magic, Witchcraft, Shamanism, and creation of rituals, such exchanges are not the essence of the religion. Neo-Pagans regularly join together for the celebration of sabbats, for other magical workings, and at festivals. Neo-Paganism, furthermore, preexists the creation of classes with fees or correspondence courses and goes beyond them.

Our data indicate that on the whole Neo-Pagans endorse changes in their religion. The majority of our respondents states that they support, at least in theory, the creation of a paid clergy and believe that there are, and can be, nonoppressive forms of hierarchy. A greater proportion of our respondents agrees than disagrees that correspondence courses are an acceptable way to learn the Craft and that the popularization of Witchcraft is not weakening the religion. Although there are indicators that Neo-Pagans do not want to give up their radical edge—for instance, the majority support for the retention of the name *Witch*—even though it often creates misunderstandings with the larger public, there is also a desire to become more respected and accepted by the larger society. Respondents are almost evenly split on the issue of Witches dressing conservatively when giving interviews. Our survey questions focus on opinions and do not ask if respondents have or are willing to work for or financially support changes in their religion. Nonetheless, our results do indicate Neo-Pagans' willingness to see their religion change.

The low level of donations by Neo-Pagans to their religion suggests that it is unlikely that traditional congregations will be formed by this new religion. Contemporary organizational theory contends that there have been changes in organizational forms in late modernity, or as some authors refer to, the contemporary period postmodernity (Clegg 1990; Dimaggio and Powell 1983). These changes include decentralization, the creation of marketing niches, the development of networks, and the need for workers to have multiple skills. Nancy Ammerman (1993) suggests that contemporary denominations, like other organizations, are responding to the changes wrought by the transition to late modernity and, at least in some instances, are redefining and reorganizing themselves.

Neo-Paganism as a religion of late modernity has never developed traditional institutional structures. Instead it has developed umbrella organizations that provide specific services (such as festivals, open rituals, the granting of clerical status) and products (such as magazines, journals, books, and manuals) to Neo-Pagan groups and individuals, usually for a fee. These umbrella organizations form a network, as individuals are free, and are even encouraged, to use the services and buy the products from more than one umbrella organization. Those running each of these organizations know one another, usually support each other's work, and use each other's services and products, but the organizations remain distinct. Although these organizations have a good deal of influence and can help shape the future of the religion, they cannot exclude specific individuals, practices, or ideas from the religion. Unlike congregational religions, the focus for Neo-Pagans is not on a specific place such as a church but instead abides by what Neo-Pagans regularly refer to as their community. This community is the network of Neo-Pagans who interact at festivals, on the Internet, and at open rituals, and most of those who have read the same seminal books and share, at least broadly, similar rituals and myths. The growth and increased influence of umbrella organizations is resulting in increased isomorphism (H. Berger 1999a). However, we argue that they will never have the institutional power of traditional denominations. These umbrella organizations provide an alternative, late modern approach to institutionalization—one that is decentralized and allows for flexibility and diversity.

6

FESTIVALS

> There is much dissension, it seems, as to whether or not festivals and open gatherings are really healthy for the spirit of the Craft. One side claims that festivals serve as a valuable meeting place for different covens and traditions, to discuss their ways, to learn and grow. The opposing side, consisting mainly of elder or more reserved Wiccans, says that making the Craft more accessible to the public will only dampen the spirit of it. Too many people attempting to perform a ritual together, with too many varied traditions, cannot get a powerful focused result. (Survey 2188)

Festivals are large gatherings of Neo-Pagans that normally occur in a rural setting at the same time each year and that usually last for a week or a weekend. Varying in size, the most popular festivals draw hundreds of people from all over the United States and Canada, and a handful of Neo-Pagans from around the world. These events are normally open to all those who pay the registration fee. Most attendees are Neo-Pagans or people with Neo-Pagan friends who invite them to the festival. However, some individuals attend festivals out of curiosity, some participate as merchants, and some appear in the role of academic researchers. Organizers maintain the right to ask participants to leave if they are disruptive, although this rarely occurs. The laissez-faire attitude of Neo-Pagans usually results in organizers and participants erring on the side of individual freedom. At times disruptive individuals are asked to change their behavior by the organizers or by other participants, and the threat or possibility of being expelled may serve as a lever to encourage the individual to alter his or her behavior.

Some groups, such as ELF and Circle Sanctuary, own land and hold their festivals in the same place each year. Sacred spaces and altars can be formed and later enlarged, maintained, and revisited from year to year (Pike 2001). Other groups, such as EarthSpirit Community, rent space from summer camps and must dismantle anything that was built for the festival, store it, take it home, or dispose of it. Festivals that are held annually tend to draw some individuals back each year, although there is normally some turn over, with new individuals coming and previous attendees taking a year off or choosing not to return. This turnover, however, as illustrated in table 54, does not result in festivals drawing a disproportional number of individuals in their twenties. The modal age range for those attending festivals is between thirty and thirty-nine. However, the turnover of those attending festivals does give a sense of an ever-changing and growing community as new faces intermingle with old ones and some people fade from the scene.

Those who attend festivals describe entering a different world. Individuals wear ritual robes, capes, and elaborate jewelry in the image of goddesses, gods, the moon, trees, or pentagrams. Others walk around nude. Sarah Pike places festivals within the American tradition of religious retreats, which regularly take place in the countryside and in which individuals join together in a spiritual quest. As most of the events occur in the spring or summer, and the participants live in tents or cabins, there is a summer camp atmosphere to festivals. Adults leave behind their normal lives, jobs, and responsibilities to participate in workshops, learn new magical techniques, discuss issues (such as Neo-Pagan child rearing and workplace discrimination), learn new or different ways to perform a ritual, participate in some large and other small rituals, rest, interact, or dance around campfires until late in the night. Festivals are places in which Neo-Pagans come together for a short time but also make new friends and acquaintances. Some of these relationships continue past the festival, and others are renewed each year at one festival or another (Pike 2001).

The respondent quoted at the beginning of this chapter offers the opinion that some members of the Neo-Pagan community, particularly

TABLE 54: Age of Festival Attendees and Nonattendees

Age	GNPP %	Do Not Attend %	Attend %
8–9	0.1	0.1	0.1
10–19	3.6	4.7	1.4
20–29	29.1	30.4	24.1
30–39	34.3	32.1	33.9
40–49	24.5	21.1	26.7
50–59	7.9	7.0	6.7
60–69	2.1	1.7	2.2
70–79	0.2	0.3	0.2
80 and older	0.0	0.0	0.0
No response	2.7	3.0	2.3

some of the elders, view festivals as potentially harmful because they help to popularize the religion. However, our survey finds very little difference in the responses of those who attended a festival or festivals in the previous year and those who did not to the statement "The popularization of Witchcraft has diluted its standards and identity." A larger percentage (23.1 percent) of those who did not attend have no opinion on this issue. This figure can be compared with those who attended a festival in the previous year, among whom 15.5 percent have no opinion. Among those who attended a festival, 45.8 percent disagree with the statement to some degree, and 35.9 percent agree with the statement to some degree. Slightly fewer (41.7 percent) of those who did not attend agree with the statement, and 33.3 percent disagree with the statement. The concern that popularization will dilute the religion clearly is not a reason that individuals either attend festivals or stay home. This absence of concern about festivals diluting Neo-Paganism's standards and identity does not mean that there is no concern or discussion among Neo-Pagans, particularly those defined as elders, about the appropriateness or usefulness of festivals for the religion. However, there has been no concerted or unified attempt to curtail festivals. To the contrary, the number of festivals that occur every year has grown, and attendance remains high.

Neo-Pagans attend festivals for many reasons. For neophytes, it is an opportunity to meet elders and teachers. For all participants, it is a time to share information about ritual and magical practices and to feel part of a larger group, thus validating their spiritual and magical worldview. In their everyday lives, Neo-Pagans are part of a minority religion whose practices and beliefs may appear alien or even threatening to those around them. At festivals Neo-Pagans find themselves surrounded by those with the same basic spiritual and magical beliefs and practices.

Festivals are often described by Neo-Pagans as providing an image of a future Neo-Pagan society or community (Pike 2001; Adler 1992). One respondent notes, "I love the 'clan' feeling one gets at a gathering, and the sense of openness that cannot be felt in a closed room" (Survey 2188). Neo-Pagans often relish the sense of freedom at festivals and the intensity of magical experiences. Individuals speak of feeling free to be fully who they are. They can openly display symbols of their religion and walk around in ritual clothing or skyclad. Magical experiences are particularly encouraged and taken seriously at festivals. Indeed, the intensity of interactions, rituals, and magical rites at festivals results in Neo-Pagans speaking of becoming psychically or magically "burned out." There is a sense of being overwhelmed and needing time to "ground"—that is, to come back to a more mundane less magical mind-set. Healing huts and listeners are provided at many festivals to help those who are overwhelmed by the intensity.

Efforts to maintain the collective help participants to create an image of festivals as microcosms of future Neo-Pagan communities. Although organizers of the festivals normally are responsible for the gathering, everyone is expected to do some work, such as helping with parking, picking up trash, watching children, running workshops, and (at festivals that provide food) working in the kitchen. Many festivals have a merchants row at which one can buy services, such as body painting, massages, or tarot readings, and buy goods oriented toward Neo-Pagans, such as jewelry, books, tarot decks, handmade cloaks, leather boots, or images of goddesses, and to a lesser degree, gods. The merchants are independent tradespeople who have rented space from the festival organizers. These merchants, however, always sell goods that are reflective of the interests and concerns of Neo-Pagans and are frequently Neo-Pagans themselves. For some merchants, sales merely help to offset the cost of festival attendance and do not result in a profit.

Since most of the food, clothing, and other necessities are brought to the festival from the mundane world, the work done at these gatherings by participants are tokens and not a reflection of how a face-to-face community of Neo-Pagans might maintain themselves economically. Festivals do help to create a community among Neo-Pagans by providing one of the avenues through which Neo-Pagans throughout the country can meet one another and share information. Although they help to create a sense of community among Neo-Pagans, festivals are only one element in this process. The Internet, Neo-Pagan newsletters and magazines, and large open rituals are other ways community is created (Berger 1999a). Nonetheless, festivals provide an image of a potential face-to-face Neo-Pagan community.

For social science researchers, festivals appear to be a gold mine. They provide a place to make contact with groups and individuals and to distribute surveys to a large number of Neo-Pagans. As noted earlier, most surveys whose results have been published were distributed at festivals. One respondent to our survey states the opinion "Festivals are *not* important to most Pagans—they are attended by less than 5 percent of the Seattle 'Community'" (Survey 1904). We do not know how this respondent determined the percentage of Neo-Pagans from Seattle that attend festivals, nor can we say that most Neo-Pagans share his view about how important festivals are for the religion. The influence of the festivals may well go beyond those who attend, since attendees return to their home communities and share magical techniques, rituals, and information about Neo-Paganism that they learned at the festivals (Adler 1986). However, the majority (58.4 percent) of respondents states that they did attend a festival in the previous year. Only 38.1 percent state that they did attend at least one festival in the previous year. The rest of our respondents do not answer this question. Among those Neo-Pagans who attended a festival in the previous year, 43.9 percent went to only one, and 24.7 percent attended two. Only 7.4 percent of those who attend festivals participated in five or more festivals in the previous year. The percentage of Neo-Pagans attending festivals is significantly higher than the Seattle respondent suggests but still represents a minority of Neo-Pagans.

There are multiple reasons individuals choose not to attend festivals. Some may be new to Neo-Paganism and may not know about festivals. Others may not go because the festivals are far from their homes and the travel is either inconvenient or prohibitively expensive. One respondent to our survey notes, "Most of the people in our group are rather low-income. I find it unfortunate that so many Pagan gatherings are beyond our price range" (Survey 1986). Some festivals offer scholarships for low-income individuals, sometimes in exchange for scholarship holders doing extra work at the festival site. These scholarships are limited, often requiring that the individual pay something toward the admission fee. Although limited resources may influence individuals' decisions to attend festivals, we find no difference in the median income between those who attended a festival in the last year and those who did not. One respondent offers another reason for not attending festivals: "I do not feel comfortable with the large number of what I refer to as 'marginal people' (i.e., people with obvious emotional/social problems) found at most Pagan gatherings. I feel too 'normal' or 'conventionally' well adjusted to fit in, although my spiritual beliefs are often in synch with theirs. Also, there seems to be too many couples" (Survey 2194). Other people may feel shy about attending alone, feeling that others will be either with their romantic partners or with their coven mates.

Surveys that are distributed and collected at festivals reach only those who attend and may overrepresent those who attend multiple festivals. In our survey, we find that Neo-Pagans who work in groups are the most likely to attend festivals and those who work alone are the least likely to attend. Of those attending festivals, 43.1 percent work in groups, 9.2 percent work with a spiritual partner, and 35.8 percent are solitaries. Solo practice is the most popular form of spiritual practice among Neo-Pagans, but it is underrepresented at festivals. More than half (55.8 percent) of those practicing in a group attended a festival in the previous year. The majority of those working with a partner, 94.9 percent, attended a festival in the previous year. In comparison, a minority, 29.1 percent, of those working alone attended a festival in the previous year.

Our data do not permit us to say why those who practice alone are the least likely to attend festivals. It may be that their preference to work alone extends to participating in group rituals at festivals, or that they do not have a group or friend with whom to attend the festivals and they fear that they will be lonely or isolated. Solitaries may be less gregarious by nature and not enjoy being in large groups. Neo-Pagans who work in groups may be encouraged to attend by other group members and be able to organize a car pool to get to the festival site. The high percentage of those who work with only a spiritual partner and attend a festival is harder to explain. Individuals in this cohort may be more interested in finding other Neo-Pagans in their area and in working at least for a short time in larger groups.

Our survey suggests that the results of surveys distributed at festivals may be misleading. Compared with our findings, surveys distributed at festivals may overrepresent those who work in groups and with one spiritual partner and underrepresent those who work alone. We find that there are marked differences between those who attended a festival in the previous year and those who did not. These differences, however, echo the variations we find among the different forms of practice. On the whole we find that those who attended a festival in the previous year, like those who work in groups, tend to encourage their children to follow their spiritual path, to have a high rate of voting, and to be politically active. Just as there is no difference between the three forms of spiritual practice in terms of the types or numbers of paranormal experiences reported, there is also no difference between those who attend and those who do not attend festivals in terms of the type or form of paranormal experiences they report.

Our survey question asks respondents about their attendance at festivals in the previous year only, thus providing the most accurate information, as individuals may have forgotten how often they attended festivals over a longer period of time. However, this limited question does mean that at least some portion of those who state they did not attend a festival in the previous year may have attended one or more festivals at some earlier period.

Demographics and Politics

Very few demographic differences exist between those who attended a festival in the previous year and those who did not. As table 54 illustrates, most Neo-Pagans who either attended or did not attend a festival in the previous year are between the ages of twenty and forty-nine. The most notable difference between those who attend and those who do not attend festivals is that the former tends to be somewhat older, which is somewhat surprising, because attending a festival gives the impression that most participants are young. It may be that salient activities, such as late-night drumming and ecstatic dancing around campfires, which are typical of festivals, attract more young participants. Our data indicate that just under a quarter of those who attended a festival in the previous year are in their twenties. Festivals are, therefore, populated by enough young adults who, when joined by those in their thirties, forties, or older who are interested, keep the late-night drumming and dancing lively.

Although men are the minority at festivals, a higher proportion of men attends festivals, and particularly attends multiple festivals a year, than the proportion of men in the Neo-Pagan community. Our survey finds that men comprise 35.8 percent of festival participants, women comprise 62.6 percent of festival participants, and we received no response from 1.5 percent of our sample for this question. Danny Jorgensen and Scott Russell (1999) suggest that the actual proportion of women to men within the religion may be exaggerated by survey results distributed at festivals. As Jorgensen and Russell note, the subjective sense of some observers and participants of Neo-Paganism is that women do outnumber men in the movement, but that difference is less than what surveys indicate. Our results suggest, to the contrary, that previous surveys do not exaggerate the difference. The disparity between the statistical data and the subjective sense of observers may be explained by two factors: the existence of women-only groups and a larger number of women than men working as solitaries. Inclusive groups may, therefore, have a lower imbalance between the genders than the statistics suggest. However, as noted in chapter 3, members of all the

Neo-Pagan sects examined, except for Druids, have a higher proportion of women than men.

Our data indicate that those who attended a festival in the previous year are more politically active than those who did not attend. As shown in table 55, with the exception of holding public office, those who attended festivals in the previous year are more politically active than those who did not attend a festival for each of the criteria for political participation. So few Neo-Pagans have held public office that it is impossible to see any difference in this area. Although more of those who attended a festival in the previous year were active in political lobbying and campaigning, very few individuals were involved in these activities. The differences in political activity is more clearly evident in attending special events, such as demonstrations and marches, grassroots organizing, and serving as spokespeople for a cause. The differences in political activity between those who did and those who did not attend a festival in the previous year reflect the differences in political activity between group participants and solitaries. Among those who work in groups, 51.9 percent report that they attended a special event, such as a march or demonstration, in the previous year. This figure can be compared with 44 percent of those who work with a partner and 41.2 percent of solitaries who participated in special events. Of those who work in groups, 15.5 percent state they are or have been public spokespeople for a cause, compared with 15 percent of those working with a partner and 12.8 percent of solitaries who are or have been public spokespeople.

Of those who attended a festival in the previous year, 90.5 percent state they are registered to vote, and 74.6 percent note that they did vote in the last national election. This statistic can be compared with those who did not attend a festival, among whom 85.9 percent are registered to vote, and 74.6 percent state they did vote in the last national election. This difference is consistent with the differences found among the three forms of practice. Among those who practice in groups, 90.2 percent are registered to vote, and 76.5 percent did vote in the last national election. Eighty-seven percent of those who work with a partner and 84.8 percent of solitaries are registered to vote. Respectively, each of these forms of practice report that 77.2

TABLE 55: Comparison of Political Activity between Those Who Attended and Those Who Did Not Attend a Festival in the Previous Year

Registered to Vote

Response	Total %	Did Not Attend %	Attend %
No	11.4	13.3	8.7
Yes	87.8	85.9	90.5
No response	0.8	0.7	0.8

Voted in Last National Election

Response	GNPP %	Did Not Attend %	Attend %
No	16.2	18.6	12.8
Yes	70.9	68.3	74.6
No response	12.9	13.1	12.6

Voted in Last State Election

Response	GNPP %	Did Not Attend %	Attend %
No	27.4	30.8	22.6
Yes	58.8	55.2	64.0
No response	13.7	14.0	13.4

Voted in Last Local Election

Response	GNPP %	Did Not Attend %	Attend %
No	36.2	38.8	32.6
Yes	49.5	46.8	53.3
No response	14.3	14.4	14.1

Writes Letter to Federal Legislators

Response	GNPP %	Did Not Attend %	Attend %
No	45.0	48.2	40.5
Yes	49.1	45.5	54.0
No response	5.9	6.2	5.4

Writes Letter to State Legislators

Response	GNPP %	Did Not Attend %	Attend %
No	49.7	50.8	48.3
Yes	44.1	42.8	45.8
No response	6.2	6.4	5.9

Writes Letter to Local Government

Response	GNPP %	Did Not Attend %	Attend %
No	61.2	62.5	59.4
Yes	31.6	30.3	33.5
No response	7.2	7.2	7.2

Participates in Grassroots Local Organizing

Response	GNPP %	Did Not Attend %	Attend %
No	67.5	70.5	63.3
Yes	24.8	21.7	29.1
No response	7.7	7.8	7.6

Participates in Town Meetings, Hearings, Forums, and Open Meetings

Response	GNPP %	Did Not Attend %	Attend %
No	67.4	69.8	63.9
Yes	25.0	22.6	28.4
No response	7.7	7.6	7.7

TABLE 55 *(continued)*

Participates in Special Events

Response	GNPP %	Did Not Attend %	Attend %
No	48.3	52.2	42.7
Yes	45.7	41.7	51.4
No response	6.0	6.1	5.9

Public Spokesperson for Causes of Personal Concern

Response	GNPP %	Did Not Attend %	Attend %
No	76.9	79.2	73.7
Yes	14.6	11.9	18.2
No response	8.5	8.8	8.1

Active Lobbier

Response	GNPP %	Did Not Attend %	Attend %
No	86.9	86.8	87.2
Yes	4.0	3.8	4.3
No response	9.1	9.5	8.5

Active in Campaigning

Response	GNPP %	Did Not Attend %	Attend %
No	83.1	83.9	82.0
Yes	8.2	7.1	9.8
No response	8.7	9.0	8.2

Hold/Have Held Public Office

Response	GNPP %	Did Not Attend %	Attend %
No	88.9	88.6	89.4
Yes	1.9	1.9	1.8
No response	9.2	9.5	8.8

percent and 66.8 percent of their members did vote in the last national election.

A larger proportion of those who work in groups (and hence of those who attend festivals) is registered as Democrats. Among those who attended a festival in the previous year, 45.4 percent are registered Democrats, 5.9 percent are Republicans, and 27.9 percent are not registered. Democrats comprise 50.7 percent of those who work in groups, 42 percent of those who work with a partner, and 36.4 percent of solitaries. Republicans comprise only 7.8 percent of solitaries and comprise an even lower percentage of the other two forms of worship. There are more Neo-Pagans registered as Independents than as Republicans. Among solitaries, 32.2 percent are registered as Independents. Twenty-two percent of those who work in groups and 28 percent of those who work with one partner are registered as Independents.

As noted in chapter 2, Neo-Pagans on the whole are politically active; those who attend festivals tend to be drawn from the more politically active subsection of the Neo-Pagan population—i.e., those who work in groups. Political concerns are sometimes voiced at festivals, with individuals mentioning forthcoming gay-pride parades, women's issues, and environmental problems, but on the whole, politics is not central to the festivals. As previously noted, Adler (1986), who conducted a survey at festivals, contends that Neo-Pagans on the whole are not involved in traditional political activities. However, our data suggest that Neo-Pagans, particularly those who attend festivals, are politically active when compared with the general American public. Festivals are primarily spiritual and magical gatherings in which political concerns are reflected in rituals—e. g., in discussion of how gender is portrayed in those rituals, or in celebration of the earth. Politics is not the central element of gatherings or of Neo-Pagans' focus. Nonetheless, the concerns raised at these gatherings may be part of the process by which Neo-Pagans, particularly those who work in groups, become politically energized.

Creating a Temporary Community: Paradoxes and Disparities

As temporary communities, festivals offer Neo-Pagans a positive image of what a community based on Neo-Pagan norms and values might be. Festivals, however, also help bring to light paradoxes, disparities, and potential conflict both within the Neo-Pagan community and between Neo-Pagans and their neighbors. Festival organizers must help to maintain a sense of harmony with festival neighbors, with the local police, and within the festival community. Practices including drug use, nudity, and sexuality can result in conflicts with the larger society and disagreements within the Neo-Pagan community.

Sarah Pike (2001) notes that festival organizers regularly include warnings in their literature, which state that illegal substances are not permitted on the festival grounds. The organizers take care both to maintain good relations with neighbors, who are often leery of having a Neo-Pagan gathering in their neighborhood, and to avoid potential conflicts with the police. College campuses similarly have restrictions against, and concerns about, the use of illegal drugs in dormitories. However, for Neo-Pagans the issue is more complex, as for some Neo-Pagans the use of drugs, as well as drumming, chanting, dancing, and meditating, is a legitimate method of entering into an alternative consciousness that puts one in touch with the spirit world. The use of illegal drugs by Neo-Pagans is controversial, particularly within the context of festivals, as it not only places the individuals involved in legal jeopardy, but might also result in the festival being closed and prohibited in subsequent years.

We ask respondents to state the degree to which they agree or disagree with the statement "The use of mind-altering chemicals is a valid magical practice." On the whole, more Neo-Pagans (52.2 percent) agree to some degree with this statement than disagree. Those who attend festivals are more likely than other Neo-Pagans to view the use of mind-altering drugs as legitimate. Among those who attended a festival in the previous year, 56.9 percent agree to some degree, 31.8 percent disagree to some degree, and 9.1 percent have no opinion about this statement. These statistics can be compared with the responses of those who did not attend festival in the previous year, among whom 48.6 percent agree to some degree, 36.5 percent disagree to some degree, and 13.3 percent have no opinion about this statement. Consistent with all the data in this chapter, the responses of those who attended a festival in the previous year reflect the responses of those who work in groups, among whom 57.6 percent agree to some degree, 31.5 percent disagree to some degree, and 11.6 percent have no opinion about the statement. Among those who work with a partner, 53.9 percent agree to some degree, 36.3 percent disagree to some degree, and 9.3 percent have no opinion about this proposition. Among solo practitioners, 49.1 percent agree to some degree, 35.4 percent disagree to some degree, and 13.9 percent have no opinion about this proposition.

Our statement questions the validity of the use of mind-altering substances. We do not ask if the respondents use these substances or if they support their use at public gatherings. Nonetheless, the high rate of support for the use of mind-altering substances—particularly among those who attend festivals—suggests that a tension exists between the desires of festival organizers to avoid conflicts with the law and with the larger society, and the view held by the majority of participants that the use of mind-altering substances is a legitimate form of spiritual quest. This tension is reflective of a larger tension that exists within the Neo-Pagan community between the desire to accommodate societal norms in order to become a recognized and accepted religion and the wish for the religion to maintain its critical edge. Support for the use of mind-altering chemicals is one area in which this tension can be seen. The use of these drugs in some indigenous cultures, particularly by shamans in those cultures, is viewed by some Neo-Pagans as justification for their use of mind-altering substances. Nonetheless, it puts Neo-Pagans in conflict with the larger society and potentially jeopardizes gatherings.

Ritual fires provide another avenue of potential conflict between festival participants and the surrounding community. Pike describes the atmosphere around ritual fires:

> Boundaries at ritual fires are permeable; they allow for both freedom
> of expression and a sense of safety. Not everyone attends the fires to
> do transformative ritual work. Some come to "trance dance" or engage
> in what they call shamanic journeying; others approach the fire to
> express themselves with a physical freedom impossible in other social
> contexts; while other late-night fire participants may be looking for a
> party atmosphere, provided by the spectacle of dancing bodies and
> fire-jumping. People with diverse intentions come and go all night
> and are disruptive in ways they would never be in a more formal rit-
> ual. (1996:128)

The diversity of interests around the ritual fire results in friction at
times. The development of a "party atmosphere" is resented by some
of those doing spiritual work. They feel distracted from their spiritual quests by what they define as the wrong type of energy. Others
believe cigarette butts being placed in or near the ritual fire dese-
crates this sacred site.

Pike notes that rare but nonetheless annoying instances of
women being sexually harassed have occurred at festivals, specifically around ritual fires. Sexual freedom and celebration of the body,
which are enjoyed by Neo-Pagans, also may result in sexual exploitation (Jencson 1998). This potential exploitation is particularly true at
festivals where large groups of individuals gather, many of whom are
unknown to one another. Neo-Pagans pride themselves on being tolerant and supportive of each other's freedom of expression. They
envision a society of caring individuals, but one with few rules. However, issues of sexual harassment, particularly at festivals, force Neo-
Pagans to confront the limitations of having few rules with little or
no enforcement.

As noted previously, our survey results suggest that Neo-Pagans,
particularly women Neo-Pagans, are concerned that sex not be
exploitative of one party. At festivals, women in particular are concerned that they be safe when dancing semidressed or undressed
around the ritual fire. For many women, dancing around the fire is
liberating, helping them get in touch with their body and their sensuality without necessarily being sexual. If others intrude on that
space by touching them or pursuing them after they stop dancing,
then not only the women who are harassed but all women at the

festival may feel vulnerable and therefore not fully enjoy the trans-
formative effects of dancing around the ritual fire. Festival organizers have attempted to deal directly with the issue of sexual harassment
by distributing written statements about what constitutes inappropriate sexual behavior at festivals. In one such document the organizers urge, "How do you know when your flirting is 'Bad touch?' One
easy way to tell is if the person says, 'Stop,' 'No thank you, I'm not
interested' or 'Get your hands off me.' It is less easy to tell if the person tries to be 'polite' and just avoids you. . . . When in doubt ask"
(as quoted in Pike 1993:135).

The open sexuality and nudity at festivals also may place the participants at odds with neighbors who complain that they can see
Neo-Pagans sunbathing or swimming in the nude from across lakes
or from roadsides. Nudity and open sexuality, particularly at festivals, challenge the norms of surrounding communities and may create tensions between Neo-Pagans and neighbors. Even if the festival
organizers restrict going skyclad to areas that cannot be seen from
outside the festival compound, some surrounding communities feel
that their own ethical and moral principles are challenged by the
knowledge that Neo-Pagans are practicing sexual and bodily freedom, whether they can be seen or not.

Drugs and sexuality can create tensions both within the Neo-
Pagan community and between Neo-Pagans and the larger society.
The intensity of people living together for a week, often in relatively
close proximity, can also result in tensions, specifically within the
festival community. The needs of parents and children to sleep and
the desire of others to spend the night around the ritual fire may create some conflicts. Problems with some individuals not showing up
for their work assignments or not cleaning up after themselves also
create tensions and problems. Although Neo-Pagans often speak of
festivals as possible blueprints for a future society, the fact that these
gatherings exist only for a short time, albeit repeatedly each year,
permits potential problems to be ignored or only partially dealt with.
For Neo-Pagans, festivals remain an image of an alternative, and better, society, but they also provide a view of some of the issues and
tensions that are embedded within Neo-Paganism. Any long-term,
face-to-face Neo-Pagan community ultimately needs to confront

and deal with these issues. Some of these issues, particularly those involving drugs, sexuality, and conflict between individuals' freedom and group needs, surface within the more disperse Neo-Pagan community, although in a less intense manner. The ability and tendency of Neo-Pagans to break away from groups, form new ones, or work alone without ceasing to be a member of the community, have permitted Neo-Pagans to postpone dealing with many of these problems in a comprehensive manner. As the religion ages, grows, and comes more clearly into the public eye, there may be an increased concern and a need for a more systematic approach to dealing with these and other problems.

Festival Participation and Religious Commitment

Jorgensen and Russell (1999) hypothesize that those who attend festivals are among the most committed members of the religion. Determining an individual's level of commitment to his or her religion is difficult, more so for Neo-Pagans, among whom much of their spiritual work can be and is performed alone. Several of our indicators, such as donations of time and money, and involving children in their parents' spiritual path, suggest a greater religious commitment from those who attend festivals. However, our data, when more fully examined, suggest that Neo-Pagans who work in groups or with a partner are more likely than solitaries to attend festivals, to encourage their children in their spiritual path, and to make larger donations of money and time to their religion. Contrary to Jorgensen and Russell, we believe that those who work in groups or with one partner are more committed to viewing Neo-Paganism as a family and community religion. Solitaries, who are the least likely to attend festivals and involve their children in their spiritual path, have the lowest rates for donating time and money to their religion, because they are more likely to envision their religion as an individual spiritual path. This observation, however, does not mean that solitaries are less committed to their religion or spiritual path than those who work in groups.

Our data indicate that Neo-Pagans who have children are slightly more likely to attend festivals than their numbers in our sample suggest. The difference is very small. Among those who attended a festival in the previous year, 42.1 percent are parents, as compared with

40.5 percent of those who did not attend a festival in the previous year. The data are consistent with the disproportional representation of those who work in groups. Nonetheless, the figures do indicate that having children does not discourage Neo-Pagans from attending festivals.

We do not ask parents if they brought their children to the festivals. It is possible that only one parent attended the festival or that the child or children were left at home with other family members or friends. As many festivals welcome children and provide some provisions for childcare, festivals also may provide countryside spiritual vacations for families. Attending festivals is also a way that parents can help introduce their children to Neo-Paganism and other Neo-Pagan children, thus helping to normalize their religious experience, particularly for families living in areas with few or no other Neo-Pagans.

A larger proportion of parents who attended a festival in the previous year claim to encourage their children to follow their spiritual path than those who did not attend a festival. Among parents who attended a festival in the previous year, 73.5 percent encourage their children to participate, as compared with parents who did not attend a festival, among whom 67.3 percent encourage their children to participate. These numbers are consistent with the proportion of Neo-Pagan parents who work in groups or with one partner who encourage their children to follow their spiritual path.

Festival attendees also are more likely to claim that they donate time and money to their religion. Among those who attended a festival in the previous year, only 20.3 percent have not donated money to their religion that year. This number can be compared with those who did not attend a festival in the previous year, among whom one-third state they donated no money to their religion in the previous year. Similarly, those who attend festivals are more likely to have donated time to their religion in the previous year than those who did not attend festivals. Among those attending festivals in the previous year, 66.2 percent state they donated time to their religion, as compared with those who did not attend a festival, among whom 58.3 percent donated time. These statistics are reflective of the donation patterns among the three forms of practice discussed. Only

17.8 percent of those who work in groups and 26.9 percent of those who work with a partner did not donated money to their religion. Among solitaries, 34.6 percent state that they donated no money. Solitaries also claim to donate the least amount of time to their religion. Although a majority of solitaries (52.2 percent) states they have donated time to their religion, this is a smaller proportion than in the other two forms of practice. Of group participants, 73.4 percent donated time to their religion in the previous year; 69.4 percent of those working with a spiritual partner donated time.

The larger proportion of donations of time and money by those festival attendees in the previous year, compared with those who did not attend a festival, can be viewed as a greater commitment to Neo-Paganism. However, solitaries are the least likely to attend festivals, and, as shown in chapter 5, to support the institutionalization of the religion. Their lack of interest in institutionalization explains their low rate of donating time and/or money to organizations or groups that provide services to or represent Neo-Pagans to the larger society. The smaller proportion of solitaries who involve their children in their spirituality also can be viewed as a commitment to seeing Neo-Paganism as an individual and personal spiritual path.

This interpretation is supported by our findings that there are no notable differences in response to questions about paranormal experiences between those who attended and those who did not attend a festival in the previous year. We anticipated that attending a festival in the previous year would result in our respondents having more paranormal experiences, as these respondents have recently been immersed in workshops and rituals aimed at creating these types of experience. It is possible that if we had asked other questions about paranormal experiences phrased in language that Neo-Pagans use to speak about their magical experiences, we would find some differences. Nonetheless, our data suggest that although festivals are viewed by Neo-Pagans as providing intense magical experiences, attendance at festivals does not affect the types or frequency of paranormal occurrences reported. Similarly, we find no notable differences in paranormal experiences among the three forms of spiritual practice. The lack of difference between those who attended a festival in the previous year and those who did not and among the three forms of spiritual practice suggests that magical or spiritual experiences, which are the heart of religious practice within in Neo-Paganism, are equally shared throughout the Neo-Pagan community. Solitaries, who disproportionately do not attend festivals, may not be less committed to Neo-Paganism as a religion or spiritual path, but less committed to its social and institutional development. Those working in a group or with a spiritual partner appear, to the contrary, to envision Neo-Paganism as community religion.

Festivals and Social Science Research

Festivals provide an intense introduction to Neo-Paganism for social science researchers. Numerous workshops, rituals, and discussions around dining tables and ritual fires all afford researchers insights into Neo-Pagans' worldview, magical practices, life-styles, and images of an alternative or better world. Festivals also provide researchers with contacts, interviewees, and respondents for surveys. The large number of Neo-Pagans gathered in one place for a length of time appears ideal for the distribution of surveys. The composition of festivals, however, as our survey indicates, is not representative of the Neo-Pagan community. Those who work in groups and with a partner are overrepresented, while solitaries are under represented. Differences exist in terms of political attitudes and behavior, demographics, and notions about Neo-Paganism among those who work in a group, with a partner, or alone that skew results of surveys distributed solely or primarily at festivals.

Festivals remain an important research site, as many Neo-Pagans view festivals as a central part of their self-image as Neo-Pagans and as an important element of community building. Festivals bring together Neo-Pagans from all over the country and some from others countries to meet fellow Neo-Pagans, interact, play, and participate in rituals. These festivals will continue to provide researchers with a quick immersion course in Neo-Paganism and contacts within the Neo-Pagan community. However, festivals are not an accurate microcosm of the Neo-Pagan community, the majority of whose participants work as solitaries and do not attend festivals.

7

VOICES OF CONSENSUS AND
DISSENSION; VOICES OF
CONCERN AND JOY

Thank you for giving me the chance to voice my opinion and
thoughts. (Survey 3009)

Through an analysis of over two thousand voices, as recorded in
responses to our survey questions and in additional written remarks
from approximately half of the respondents, we gained a unique
view into Neo-Paganism. Unlike previous surveys distributed primarily at festivals, our survey was published in Neo-Pagan journals,
reproduced on the Internet, mailed to participants by Neo-Pagan
organizations, distributed hand to hand by respondents, as well as
made available at festivals. Although like all previous surveys, ours
was not a random sample, it had the largest and most varied distribution of any study of Neo-Pagans in the United States. This broad
distribution permits a wider view of the community and allows us to
hear voices often missed in research, such as those of solitaries who
are the hidden majority of Neo-Pagans because of their low rate of
festival attendance.

Our study is unique in another manner. All other published surveys include no questions that permit a direct comparison between
Neo-Pagans and other Americans. To enable us to compare Neo-
Pagans to their neighbors, we ask questions from the GSS concerning political beliefs, activities, paranormal experiences, and
images of the afterlife. We find that on the whole Neo-Pagans are

more liberal than the general American public but have lower confidence in government and social institutions. Neo-Pagans are also, on the whole, more politically active than the average American. This finding is contrary to Margot Adler's 1986 analysis of the Neo-Pagan movement and to traditional sociological views of the relationship between mysticism and politics. Our data support Robert Wuthnow's 1978 study, which demonstrates that contemporary mystics are not dissociated from politics. Our findings also bring into question the belief, most recently presented by Cynthia Eller (2000), that women's spirituality removes women's focus from traditional political activity by transfixing their gaze on the goddess. To the contrary, our data indicate that Goddess Worshipers, particularly women Goddess Worshipers, are among the most politically active Neo-Pagans.

By comparing Neo-Pagans' and the general American public's paranormal experiences and images of the afterlife, we find that Neo-Pagans share aspects of their mystical worldview with other Americans. A larger proportion of Neo-Pagans reports having paranormal experiences and tends to have more of them than does the average American. Nonetheless, these experiences are relatively common throughout the United States. The frequency of paranormal experiences varies by regions for both the general Neo-Pagan population and the American public. However, there is no apparent relationship between region of residence and the paranormal experiences of the two populations.

When asked to describe the likelihood of different images of the afterlife, not surprisingly, fewer Neo-Pagans hold these images to be accurate than does the general American public—probably because the wording of the questions reflect the influence of Christianity on American popular culture. However, the relative likelihood of each of these images of the afterlife is quite similar for the two populations. This similarity suggests that Neo-Pagans have a distinct religious worldview, but one that is influenced by images of the afterlife that are prevalent in the society and to which many Neo-Pagans were exposed in their youth as members of Christian churches.

In their written responses Neo-Pagans speak of the importance of and distinctions among different traditions or spiritual paths. However, based on our study, the three primary forms of Neo-Paganism—Wiccans, Pagans, and Goddess Worshipers—appear to be remarkably similar. All three sects are composed of primarily white, middle-class, well-educated adherents. Although the proportion is higher for Goddess Worshipers, all the sects are disproportionately composed of women. Goddess Worshipers show the strongest commitment to issues of gender and sexual orientation equity, although the commitment to these issues is high for all the sects. All three sects also report similar levels of paranormal experience.

The other three sects examined—Druids, Shamans, and UU Neo-Pagans—share many qualities with the general Neo-Pagan population. Druids distinguish themselves by having a larger proportion of men than the other sects of Neo-Paganism and by reporting having more paranormal experiences. Shamans are among the most likely to involve their romantic partners in their spiritual path. Unlike the image of Shamans as reclusive individualists marked for their calling, our data suggest that Shamanism in the United States is a religion. UU Neo-Pagans are the most politically active and the most socially conservative of all forms of Neo-Paganism examined. It is unclear if the UUA draws the more politically interested and socially conservative Neo-Pagans to their churches or if the interaction of Neo-Pagans with other Unitarian Universalists influences Neo-Pagans' worldview and political activity. Although our results do indicate that there are differences among Neo-Pagan sects, we find that there are more similarities than differences. It is possible that another set of questions that focuses exclusively on theology and the specifics of ritual practices may tease out greater variances and help to support Neo-Pagans' view of significant differences among spiritual paths.

After completing the survey, one respondent offers the opinion: "Your survey sounds like you're trying to arrive at some conclusion on who a typical Pagan is. . . . That's BULLSHIT!" (Survey 2425). Our intention in presenting these survey results is both to show the range of opinions and views among Neo-Pagans and, more importantly, to present the more common views that form the center of the beliefs and practices of the Neo-Pagan community. As in any survey, there is variation among our respondents on all issues. For example, in commenting on the issue of gender equity, one respondent offers the opinion: "Men should be required to clean house for the next 5,000 or 6,000 years. You've had your turn—now sit down and hush up" (Survey 1307). Another states: "The E.R.A. as it stands doesn't give equal rights, it puts women above men. I just want a level playing field" (Survey 2207). Such diversity of opinion is found on nearly every item of the survey.

In some instances our data help to illuminate tensions that exist within the Neo-Pagan community, particularly around the issues of sexuality, popularization of the religion, and institutionalization. All ethnographic accounts of Neo-Paganism describe the celebration of sexuality as a central element of Neo-Pagan practices, beliefs, and life-styles (see, for example, Scarboro et al. 1994; Orion 1995; Berger 1999a; Pike 2001). Our data, in part, support this image. For example, even though we find that a very small percent of Neo Pagans live in a group marriage, a larger proportion of Neo-Pagans believes that polygamy should be legalized than opposes to its legalization. However, Neo-Pagans, as participants in a feminist form of spirituality, are also aware that sexuality can be exploitative. Women and UU Neo-Pagans appear to be the most concerned about controlling the exploitative aspects of sexuality within their community. For instance, they more strongly believe that it is unethical for spiritual teachers to have sexual relations with their students. Neo-Pagan men, on the other hand, are more likely to emphasize another ethic within Neo-Paganism—that of individual freedom. One respondent offers the opinion, "I believe in getting rid of all the shoulds" (Survey 2593). The tensions around open sexuality, responsibility, and free dom are likely to increase as more children are born and grow up in the community and as more teenagers join the movement. Although these tensions predate the second generation of Neo-Pagans becoming teenagers, parental concerns for the safety of their children exacerbate these tensions. The increased eye of the media on Neo-Pagans and the desire, at least among some members of the religion, to be accepted by the mainstream society will, we suspect, also help to fuel these debates.

The birth of children to Neo-Pagans also has helped to illuminate the tension that exists in the religion between a personal spiritual path and the religion of a community (Berger 1999a, 1999b). Although some individuals note in their written responses that they would encourage only those Neo-Pagans' children who express interest, our data indicate that the majority of Neo-Pagan parents does encourage their children to follow in the parental spiritual path. Women and UU Neo-Pagans are even more likely to encourage their children to follow in the parental spiritual paths than other Neo-Pagan parents. Personal experience with child rearing is resulting in one view of Neo-Paganism—that is, as a religion of the community —becoming more prominent, at least among a growing number of Neo-Pagans.

Neo-Pagans are working to have their religion accepted and acknowledged within the larger society. Some Neo-Pagans want their religion to become more mainstream. As one respondent states: "The Pagan community does not work hard enough at showing that Neo-paganism is compatible with a 'mainstream' lifestyle, rather than the sole province of 'alternative' life-styles" (Survey 3228). Another respondent presents the opposite view: "I think it is important for the Pagan movement to keep its 'cutting-edge,' politically and socially" (Survey 3002). Our data suggest that although Neo-Pagans are willing to make some concessions to become accepted within the larger society, they are not willing to eliminate their critical edge.

Two of our questions ask Neo-Pagans the degree to which they believe that their movement should present a more mainstream or a more alternative image to the public. We also ask if they think that those representing their religion to the public should dress conservatively and if the word *Witch* should still be used, as it often creates misunderstandings with the larger society. In response to the first question, our respondents are almost evenly split between those who believe that representatives of the religion should dress conservatively when addressing the media and those who feel that it is unnecessary. Women are the most likely to uphold the notion that the clothing worn by representatives of the religion should not be an issue, and UU Neo-Pagans are the most likely to state that those coming into the public eye should dress conservatively.

Approximately three-quarters of all Neo-Pagans, and even a larger proportion of women, contend that the term *Witch* should be retained. For most Neo-Pagans, the term needs to be reclaimed and not eliminated. As one respondent states, "There has been a lot of controversy in the Wiccan/Witch community on what we should call ourselves because of the bad 'press' given to the word 'Witch.' It is my belief that if we were to drop the word, to ignore the 9,000,000 who have died, we would just be giving up" (Survey 2087). For many Neo-Pagans, the use of the term *Witch* is a political act either in acknowledging and remembering those killed during the witch trials of the early modern period or because the term has traditionally been used as a negative image of women.

Debates have raged within Neo-Pagan journals and websites and at festivals about the acceptability of some individuals being paid for their work as clergy. Our research indicates that the majority of Neo-Pagans supports the notion of paid clergy, but only a minority of Neo-Pagans donates money to their religion. Fewer Neo-Pagans support the idea of a Witch accepting money to teach the Craft. The notion that Witchcraft or Wicca should be taught to initiates as a gift is embedded in the early writings and teachings of the religion. Nonetheless, our data indicate that Neo-Pagans are flirting with more traditional forms of organization. This finding is suggested by the fact that the majority of those surveyed accepts the notion of paid clergy and by the predominance of those who believe that it is possible to have hierarchies that are organic and nonoppressive.

Our study also attests to countervailing trends toward greater support for institutionalization. Two such areas are evident in answers to questions about whether or not the popularization of their religion and the development of correspondence courses are detrimental to Neo-Paganism. In both instances the majority of respondents does not view either of these trends as a problem. Those who fear popularization are concerned that it will result in inferior training of neophytes and ultimately dilute the spiritual, magical, and mystical elements of the religion. One respondent describes the dilemma with which Neo-Pagans are confronted: "Unfortunately a problem modern Paganism faces, possibly because it is more and more public, is people who are in the Craft for 6 months and decide they are ready to be teachers and want to start their own 'church.' These people set themselves up as ['counselors'] and 'guides' and can not only hurt individuals but the Pagan and Wiccan communities as a whole. I don't know what can be done without threatening our individuality but it is an issue that I am concerned about" (Survey 2365). Popularization is one of the forces that work against consistent and systematic training, resulting in some individuals being poorly trained and also in a free and open market in spiritual innovation. Similarly, correspondence courses remove training from the group and make them available on the Internet or through the mail. Although some of these courses are quite rigorous and available from reputable organizations, others are not.

Possibly the largest challenge to institutionalization within this new religion is the growth of solitary practitioners. Slightly more than half of respondents practice alone. These individuals are less likely to attend festivals where most surveys are distributed and some ethnographic research is conducted. They are, therefore, less likely to have their views, spiritual practices, and beliefs known. Our research indicates that those who practice alone are the least supportive of institutionalization. They are the least likely to share their spiritual path with their romantic partner and, for those who are parents, with their children. Solitaries are as likely as other Neo-Pagans to have paranormal experiences, but are on the whole younger, less politically active, and less liberal than other Neo-Pagans. Our research suggests that solitaries visualize this new religion as an individual spiritual path and not as a community religion. This vision, which has always been an element of Neo-Paganism, serves to counteract routinization.

Neo-Pagans are composed of many different spiritual paths, with no central organization or leader. Umbrella organizations provide leadership within the community, liaisons with the larger society, and at times information and training for other Neo-Pagans. Association with these organizations remains voluntary, but their influence has permeated the religion. Solitaries are influenced by such organizations, even though they have a low rate of attendance at festivals, which are run by these organizations. Solitaries read the journals and newsletters produced by these organizations and interact on the Internet with others who are members. The growth of umbrella organizations among Neo-Pagans is consistent with the development of new forms of organizational structures in late modernity. However, the growing number of solitary practitioners, particularly among the young, and their alternative vision of the religion may ultimately challenge both the way Neo-Pagan organizations develop and function and ultimately the future of this religion.

Voices of Concern, Voices of Joy

In their written statements Neo-Pagans share concerns about discrimination and their desire to educate the public about the religion. They write about problems they observe in their own community, particularly the problem that Neo-Pagans do not consistently live up to their own ideals. But many respondents, including those who feel there is a need for improvement within the Neo-Pagan community, share their joy in being members of this community.

Discrimination

> I think most people are afraid to come out of the "broom closet" in everyday life. It is wonderful to see a movement to help legitimize our religions. (Survey 1857)

Several other respondents similarly note that they fear discrimination. Others mention their own need to keep the religion hidden from some or all non–Neo-Pagans. One woman writes: "I still cannot tell my future mother-in-law for fear of breaking her purely Christian heart for her only son whom she assumes is a good Christian boy. My own father accepted it and I even did a [tarot] card reading for him. At this point, I have to wear my pentagram in my shirt and keep my altar in my closet. I want to be open, but it would cause too many problems in my life because of other people's misconceptions about my religion" (Survey 1102). Other respondents note the particular problems they experience or their fear of living in what they describe as either conservative areas or the Bible Belt. Another states that the "greatest obstacle/frustration in my participation in the Pagan movement is fear of public harassment and retribution. . . . It is hard to enjoy outdoor rituals when you're afraid of being stopped by someone unfriendly such as a cop or worse" (Survey 2390).

One respondent argues, "I think it's time we quit hiding and 'come out.' The current rising tide of right-wing fundamentalism is dangerous to us, the human race, and the planet—we should provide alternatives and knowledge to 'combat' it [fundamentalism]"

(Survey 2599). After the September 11, 2001, terrorist attacks on the World Trade Center and the Pentagon, Rev. Jerry Falwell asserted that these attacks are a display of God's wrath. As he states: "The pagans and the abortionists and the feminists, and gays and lesbians—I point a finger in their face and say, 'You helped this happen'" (as quoted in Infield 2001). Although those Neo-Pagans living in culturally conservative areas are the most likely to come into conflict with fundamentalist Christian groups, all Neo-Pagans are aware of and many are concerned about being portrayed by these groups as Satanists or, at the very least, in the employ of Lucifer. They fear that this prejudice may affect them in child-custody cases, may hurt their prospects for career advancement, and may result in violent attacks.

Neo-Pagans are sensitive to the media's depiction of their religion and of them. One respondent notes, "I think that the Pagan community should unite and fight the prejudice and misconceptions of Craft use that the media and TV impose. Witches are always depicted as sex crazed, drug taking, mentally ill, baby killers or devil worshippers" (Survey 2606). Neo-Pagan networks have been active in organizing letter-writing campaigns to television stations or to movie studios when they believe that they or their religion is being slandered. However, not all media coverage has been negative. Many newspapers, including the *New York Times,* have published articles about Witches and Neo-Pagans—particularly around Halloween—that are positive (see, for example, Cavafajal 1998; Niebuhr 1999; Reisberg 2000). *Sabrina the Teenage Witch* and *Charmed,* although not accurate portrayals of Witchcraft, do provide positive images. Nonetheless, Neo-Pagans remain watchful of portrayals of their religion in the media.

Many of our respondents describe the need to address the issue of discrimination. One respondent states: "I highly object to 'Bunker Mentality' Paganism, i.e., We are such an oppressed minority. *All* minorities are oppressed, *all* differences can and will be used against you. No one is singling us out [as] special" (Survey 1366). This respondent, it should be noted, does not deny that Neo-Pagans have been the object of discrimination, only that such discrimination is a common problem for all minorities. Her response is unique. The vast majority of other respondents, although not seeing themselves as the only targets of discrimination, expresses interest in exploring ways in which to eliminate or fight the discrimination they experience.

Several of our respondents suggest that the Neo-Pagan community needs to unite to protect itself. One respondent offers this opinion: "I think we need to stand together to come out of the broom closet and bring about Public Education, which will facilitate that acceptance. We should focus on our similarities, not our differences—there is enough working against us already without us weakening ourselves from inside by quarreling among ourselves" (Survey 2305). Repeatedly, Neo-Pagans speak about the need for public education and for unity within the Neo-Pagan community. Some suggest that the Neo-Pagan community also needs to reach out to other religious groups and work with them. Some respondents relate their groups' outreach and charity works within their communities as part of both the spiritual commitment and the attempt to be integrated into their larger community. One respondent states: "There needs to be a Pagan/Witch anti-defamation league that is active and aggressive" (Survey 1868). Many antidefamation leagues exist, but at least this respondent believes that they are not well enough known and organized.

Gay Rights, Feminism, and Environmentalism

> I feel that religions that support the "Earth as mother" concept are important in this time. Through being in touch with the feminine principle we can address issues of dominance and violence and living in a throwaway society, and help to achieve more balance. Religions that are Goddess centered have more respect (I believe) in general, for earth, environment, family, balance, animals, and more tolerance for alternative life styles. (Survey 2617)

Issues concerning gay rights, feminism, and environmentalism are common themes in the written responses. One respondent contends that there is too much emphasis among Neo-Pagans on social issues. He writes, "Too much time and energy (read bickering) is wasted on political agendas wearing cloaks of paganism. *It's time to get back to the spiritual.* . . . P.S. Yes Virginia there are 'conservative' Pagans. (Well at least one)" (Survey 1205). Although, as noted in their responses, Neo-Pagans are disproportionately liberal, Neo-Paganism is a religion, not a political movement, and there are many variations of political views among Neo-Pagans. And even though Neo-Pagans on the whole support gay rights, women's rights, and environmentalism, not all do, and even among those who do, not all agree on what is the correct manner or degree of support.

We ask survey respondents the extent to which they agree or disagree with the statement "Homophobia is as prevalent in the Pagan movement as anywhere else in society." Although half (50.9 percent) disagree to some degree with this statement, and only 23.2 percent agree to any degree with the statement, we are surprised that the expressed disagreement is not stronger. Ethnographic accounts and Neo-Pagan writings both describe the celebration of all forms of sexuality within this religion (see, for example, Orion 1995; Berger 1999a; Pike 2001; Starhawk 1982; Adler 1986). One respondent offers this explanation: "Yes—Homophobia is more prevalent outside the [Neo-Pagan] community, but [is] particularly offensive to me in a religion, whose worldview must by nature encompass everything in the cosmos as sacred" (Survey 1425).

Many Neo-Pagans hold themselves, and others in their community, to a higher standard. They believe that the hallmark of their spirituality is its celebration of diversity in all its forms. Another respondent, referring to our question on homophobia, more concisely notes, "Pagans have their share of crackpots just like any other group" (Survey 1035). For many Neo-Pagans, the "crackpots"—that is, those who are homophobic within their community—are particularly offensive because they go against Neo-Pagans' image of their community and its ideals.

One respondent claims: "Pagan/Wiccan men are more likely to respect all women and treat them with dignity" (Survey 3209). Another notes: "There is an important connection between Paganism and Feminism, which men need to understand, accept and act upon" (Survey 2597). One woman provides an alternative opinion: "Our toleration of alternate religions, sexual orientations, and lifestyles are admirable and something mainstream society could learn from. But our utter lack of tolerance for sexism has led certain members of our community to do things that shame us all. If people

are gong to engage in male-bashing they should qualify their statement to make it clear they are only bashing one particular male,
without making said male a scapegoat for the entire gender" (Survey
1162). This woman believes that there is too strong a feminist element within Neo-Paganism. Some women, in turn, contend that
men are still "taking up too much space." That is, men are having
everyone focus on them and their discussion of their emotions. Similarly, as with homophobia, those within the Neo-Pagan movement
are critical of what they see as their own—and other members of the
community's—failings in this area. Sexism, however, is more complex than homophobia for this group. The ideal of treating all alternative life-styles with respect is accepted by most if not all
Neo-Pagans. Those who show homophobic behavior are judged
against this clear ideal. There is a general contention that women
should be treated with dignity. But what that means specifically, particularly in romantic or sexual relationships, varies among groups
and individuals. Although Neo-Pagans are in the process of experi-
menting with alternative gender roles, the Neo-Pagan community
has no single concept of what these should be (Berger 1999a).

The Limits and Joys of Community

> Paganism seems to be a wide enough religion to encompass even
> cranky skeptics like me, who see more of the Divine in astronomy
> than astrology. The majority of the people I've encountered are very
> sincere and energetic, and that is a joy to be around. Taking a larger
> view what are "flaws" to me can also be seen are proof of diversity—
> and certainly proof of our own humanness. I certainly would not
> trade the folks I've met for any homogenized, single-belief, unified . . .
> group. (Survey 1854)

This respondent begins her comments with a list of complaints
about Neo-Pagans: that some members are too superstitious, that
some are too dogmatic in their beliefs or practices, and that some
charge large sums for training. Nonetheless, she sees her community as one of joy.

Respondents note their disdain for infighting between Neo-
Pagans or among traditions. One woman calls for "the need for tolerance in the Pagan community. I was shocked at the in-fighting

between traditions and the intolerance for those whose beliefs or rituals were different" (Survey 3146). Other respondents express similar sentiments in different words. For example, one respondent reports: "The more I read of the increasing proliferation of malicious and malignant gossip between members of and groups of Pagan persuasion, the more I am reminded of Christian organizations" (Survey 1776). For Neo-Pagans, the tensions that are common within groups become intolerable, because the ideal, which is impossible to sustain, is "perfect love and perfect trust."

Future Research

Our analysis of The Pagan Census provides insights into the Neo-Pagan community, contributes to growing literature in the field, corrects some misconceptions from survey research conducted solely at festivals, and compares Neo-Pagans with what they refer to as their "cowan" (non-Pagan) neighbors. Our research also helps to raise additional questions that future research should address. The decision to include the GSS questions means that we had to limit the number of Neo-Pagan–related questions. Several respondents comment on the length of the survey, noting that they did not include a more detailed written statement because the survey had already consumed too much of their time or, in one case, remarking that she had not completed the entire survey because of its length. In their free responses, individuals list questions they believe should be asked in future surveys. Although these suggestions do not provide us with formal survey data, we include a discussion of some of these suggestions because they provide an interesting picture of issues that Neo-Pagans believe are important for future research.

Several individuals suggest that future surveys should ask respondents if they are "in the broom closet"—that is, to what degree individuals are open about their religious participation. Have they, for instance, told their parents, siblings, extended families, neighbors, or coworkers about their spiritual involvement? Our research indicates that Neo-Pagans in culturally conservative parts of the United States are less likely to be politically active, more likely to maintain a traditional life-style, and less approving of public Witches dressing in ritual garb when speaking to the media than other Neo-Pagans. We suspect from our findings that there are significant differences in the degree to which Neo-Pagans are open about their religious practices in different regions of the United States.

Several respondents suggest the inclusion of more questions on Neo-Pagan theology and practices. One such respondent notes, "This census needs more detailed and customized sections on Pagan theology, politics, and practices. You don't seem to cover many subjects at all, or only glancingly, such as: vegetarianism, violence, sacrifice, scholarship, relations with other religions, relations with the state, ecology, and what people's *ideals* and *goals* are for the Pagan Movement (as opposed to what we have to put up with now)" (Survey 2032).

Similarly, another respondent states, "The survey seems to focus more on socio-economic descriptions rather than on those aspects of Pagan belief and practice that distinguishes us from other religious paths. I am far less concerned with an afterlife and what it might be like than I am with religious/spiritual practices that root and center me in *this* life, *this* planet, and *this* time" (Survey 2216). Questions that may help illuminate distinctions among spiritual paths are of particular import for all Neo-Pagan traditions, but are essential for Odinists. The growth of a neo-Nazi branch of Odinists may be a threat to Neo-Pagans' open acceptance of all spiritual expressions and result in a hardening of boundaries and borders within this amorphous religion. More research is needed to determine the extent to which Nazi Neo-Pagan groups exist in the United States and to help differentiate those Odinist groups and individuals who are neo-Nazis or racists and those who fit more comfortably within the mainstream of Neo-Paganism.

Other areas for future inquiry that respondents propose include:

1. How many Neo-Pagans are healers, even if this is not the way in which they earn a living?
2. To what extent are respondents earning their living through their spiritual skills?[1]
3. For those Neo-Pagans who have adult children, are they Neo-Pagans or do they participate in another religion? Or no religion at all?
4. What are the religious practices of other members of Neo-Pagans' families—their partners, parents, and siblings?

5. Have respondents experienced discrimination because of their affiliation with Neo-Paganism? If so what form has it taken?
6. Do respondents use Internet chat rooms or other computer networks? If so how often?
7. Do Neo-Pagans practice safe sex?
8. Do respondents engage in rituals skyclad, in robes, or in street clothing?
9. For students, what is their major or area of study?

One respondent suggests that a subsection of questions be included in future surveys specifically for children to answer. Although some of the questions, which our respondents recommend, would be difficult if not impossible to pose in a survey, and might best be answered by ethnographic research, others could successfully be incorporated into future surveys. Answers to all of these questions would give us a better understanding of Neo-Pagans and Neo-Paganism.

Our own study suggests that qualitative as well as quantitative research on solitaries is essential. Finding and contacting these individuals will be a challenge to future researchers. One method of contact may be through Neo-Pagan newsletters, magazines, and, most importantly, websites. One of our respondents offers the advice: "*Many* pagans are rather un-affiliated with 'the Pagan movement': Bulletin boards (computer networking) is a way that many unconnected Pagans communicate" (Survey 1033). Solitaries, although a hidden majority, are an important subsection of Neo-Pagans. More research is required on these practitioners to gain a better understanding of them, their practices, and beliefs and to determine their influence on the larger movement.

Although demographically Neo-Pagans are quite similar to one another, this is not a monolithic group. There are variations in behavior, beliefs, and spiritual practices. This book provides one set of voices from the Neo-Pagan community. More surveys that study the diversity and similarities within the Neo-Pagan movement and compare Neo-Pagans with mainstream Americans are needed. Neo-Paganism is an aging and growing religion. These changes need to be chronicled in future research.

APPENDIX

The Questionnaire Used
in the Reported Research

Introduction
Please read the following paragraphs carefully before filling out the form.

What is the Pagan Census Project?
The Pagan Census Project is an attempt to document the size and diversity of the contemporary Pagan movement as accurately as possible. Over the past thirty years, Paganism has experienced a considerable growth in membership, but, given such factors as the lack of centralized organization within the Pagan movement and the relative anonymity sought by many of its adherents, it is very difficult to estimate how many of us there are. Several attempts have been made over the past fifteen years to survey contemporary Pagans. These attempts, however, have either been very limited in the size of the sampling or have targeted a very specific and therefore limited population within the Pagan movement. The Pagan Census Project seeks to survey a larger and more diverse sampling of Pagans.

Why is it needed?
There are several reasons why such a project is important. If we can document our numbers in some tangible way, we will be in a stronger position to attain more credibility as a religion and as a community.

Greater credibility would enable us to better address issues of religious discrimination and social prejudice (the Helms Bill, or movies such as *The Craft,* for instance); would give us more weight in addressing anti-Pagan stereotypes (for example, we might finally be able to convince the publishers of encyclopedias and dictionaries to include more contemporary definitions of the terms Witch and Pagan); and it would give us greater access to influential forums (such as academia, interfaith councils, etc.) from which Pagans have mostly been excluded.

Who is organizing the Census?

The Census form has been compiled by Andras Corban Arthen and Helen Berger, Ph.D. Andras Arthen is a founder and director of the EarthSpirit Community, one of the largest Pagan networks in the country. He has been a practicing Witch since the late 1960's and has given lectures and workshops on Witchcraft and Paganism for many years. Helen is a professor of sociology at West Chester State University in Pennsylvania. She has been a member of the Earth-Spirit Community for many years and is very interested in this project because of the statistical significance of the survey for her work in documenting the modern Pagan movement.

In addition, the following Pagan leaders have reviewed the census form, offered valuable suggestions, and endorsed this project (organizations of affiliation are named for purposes of identification only; endorsement by these individuals does not imply endorsement by the organization itself): Margot Adler, author; Susun Weed of the Wise Woman Institute; M. Macha NightMare and Starhawk of Reclaiming Collective; Otter G'Zell, Diane Darling, Morning Glory Zell and Anodea Judith of Church of All Worlds; Selena Fox and Dennis Carpenter of Circle Sanctuary; Phyllis Curott, Judy Harrow, Russell Williams, Rowan Fairgrove and Michael Thorn of Covenant of the Goddess; Lynn Stone of Circle in the Greenwood; Isaac Bonewits and Colleen Dómí O'Brien of Ár nDraíocht Féin; Ellen Evert Hopman of Keltria; Doborah Ann Light, hedgewitch; Rhiannon Bennett of Heartland Spiritual Alliance; John Brightshadow Yohalem of *Enchanté;* Jade and Lynnie Levy of *Of a Like Mind;* Kyril Oakwind of *Converging Paths;* Gavin and Yvonne Frost of Church and School of Wicca.

How is the Census structured?

The Census form is divided into five sections: the first four sections ask for basic demographic data, sociopolitical views, spiritual beliefs, and specifically Pagan-related information. Some of the questions included throughout this form are taken verbatim from a University of Chicago public opinion poll that has been ongoing since the 1950's as a way to compare Pagan views to those of the mainstream society. Although the language and assumptions found in those particular questions leave a lot to be desired from a Pagan perspective, we cannot make any changes in them if we wish to preserve statistical comparability; we ask for your indulgence in this matter. Section 5 is an open-ended request for any other information or opinions that you would like to share with us, including your impressions of the Census itself—please feel free to use additional sheets as necessary.

Although the Census is set up to insure complete anonymity for all respondents, you have the option of returning to us the Census Update form found at the bottom of the last page if you would like to be informed of census results as they become available. If you fill out the Census Update form, *please be sure to mail it to us separate from the Census form itself* in order to maintain anonymity.

How will the information be used?

Census results will be shared with other Pagan networking organizations and publications at their request. They will also be made available to statistical bureaus, academic researchers, interfaith organizations, and other institutions and individuals interested in documenting the growth of contemporary Paganism. Under no circumstances will the names or addresses of individuals returning Census Update forms be shared with anyone.

How is the census funded?

Initial funding for the Pagan Census Project has been provided by monies allocated by The EarthSpirit Community and West Chester State University for this purpose, as well as by a donation from Covenant of the Goddess. We anticipate that this project will cost several thousand dollars more in printing, postage, and computer time. We are currently investigating possible grant sources, and greatly welcome any suggestions or leads in this regard. Other financial contributions of any size are also much needed and appreciated; if you would like to make such a contribution, please make out your check to "The EarthSpirit Community—PCP" and send it to the address above.

Many thanks for your participation in the Pagan Census Project!

I. General Demographic Information

A. 1. Sex_____ 2. Date of birth_____

B. Marital status (please check all that apply):
___ 1. Never married
___ 2. Married legally
___ 3. Married ritually (not legally)
___ 4. Live with lover(s)
___ 5. Divorced
___ 6. Widow/er
___ 7. Separated
___ 8. Group marriage
___ 9. Other (please specify)

C. Sexual orientation:
___ 1. Heterosexual
___ 2. Lesbian
___ 3. Gay
___ 4. Bisexual
___ 5. Other (please specify)

D. Highest level of education completed so far:
___ 1. Less than high school diploma
___ 2. High school diploma
___ 3. Some college
___ 4. College degree
___ 5. Professional or technical school
___ 6. Postgraduate work

___ 7. Postgraduate degree/s (please specify)
___ 8. Other (please specify)

E. 1. What is your race?_____
   2. What is your ethnic background?_____

F. What religion(s)/religious denomination(s) were you raised in?_____

G. Which most closely describes your current home neighborhood?
___ 1. Secluded rural
___ 2. Large town
___ 3. Rural community
___ 4. Suburb
___ 5. Small town
___ 6. Metropolitan area
___ 7. Other (please explain)

H. 1. If you live in the U.S., in which state do you presently reside?_____
   2. If you live outside of the U.S., where do you reside?_____

I. 1. What is your main or principal occupational title?_____
  2. In what type of industry or business do you work?_____

J. What was the combined income before taxes of all members of your family/household for the past year?
___ 1. Less than $10,000
___ 2. $10,000–$20,000
___ 3. $20,001–$30,000
___ 4. $30,001–$40,000
___ 5. $40,001–$50,000
___ 6. $50,001–$60,000
___ 7. $60,001–$70,000
___ 8. $70,001–$100,000
___ 9. Above $100,000

K.   1. Do you have children (biological or adopted)? Yes___ No___
         2. Grandchildren? Yes___ No___
         3. Please list the age and sex of each of your children:

         _____

L.   If you are a single parent, do you have primary custody of your child/ren? Yes___ No___
         2. Joint custody? Yes___ No___

M.   What type of school does/did your child/ren predominantly attend? If you have more than one child, please note what type of school each of them goes/went to by indicating the number of children who attend/ed that type of school:
         ___   1. Public school
         ___   2. Parochial school
         ___   3. Home educated
         ___   4. Private, nonparochial school
         ___   5. Other (please specify)

N.   Do/did you encourage your child/ren to be involved in your spiritual path? Yes ___ No ___

II.   Political Information

A.   Are you a registered voter? Yes___ No___

B.   1. If yes, are you registered as: 2. Did you vote in the last
         ___   a. Democrat   ___   a. national elections?
         ___   b. Republican   ___   b. state elections?
         ___   c. Independent/unenrolled   ___   c. local elections?
         ___   d. Other (please specify) _____

C.   Do you participate, for any reason, in any of the following political activities?
         ___   1. Do not participate in any activities special events
         ___   2. Write or telephone legislators in Washington
         ___   3. Write or telephone state legislators

____ 4. Write or telephone local government

____ 5. Participate in grassroots local organizing

____ 6. Participate in town meetings, hearings, forums, and open meetings

____ 7. Participate in special events (e.g., marches, rallies)

____ 8. Public spokesperson for causes of personal concern

____ 9. Active lobbier

____ 10. Active in campaigning

____ 11. Hold/have held public office

D. We are faced with many problems in this country, none of which can be solved easily or inexpensively. Listed below are some of these problems. For each one, please indicate whether you think we are spending too much money on it, too little money, or about the right amount.

1 – Too much
2 – The right amount
3 – Too little
4 – Don't know

____ 1. Space exploration program

____ 2. Improving and protecting the environment

____ 3. Improving and protecting the nation's health

____ 4. Solving the problems of the big cities

____ 5. Halting the rising crime rate

____ 6. Dealing with drug addictio

____ 7. Improving the conditions of Blacks

____ 8. The military, armaments, and defense

____ 9. Foreign aid

____ 10. Welfare

____ 11. Highways and bridges

____ 12. Social Security

____ 13. Mass transportation

____ 14. Parks and recreation

____ 15. The arts

____ 16. AIDS research

____ 17. The homeless

____ 18. Education

E. Listed below are some institutions in this country. Some
people have complete confidence in the people running these
institutions. Suppose these people are at the end of the scale
at point number 1. Other people have no confidence at all in
the people running these institutions. Suppose these people
are at the other end, at point 7. And, of course, other people
have opinions somewhere in between at point 2, 3, 4, 5, or 6.
Where would you place yourself on this scale?

Complete confidence [1 2 3 4 5 6 7] No confidence at all

____ 1. Banks and financial institutions
____ 2. Major companies
____ 3. Organized religion
____ 4. Education
____ 5. Executive branch of the federal government
____ 6. Organized labor
____ 7. The press
____ 8. Medicine
____ 9. Television
____ 10. U.S. Supreme Court
____ 11. Scientific community
____ 12. U.S. Congress
____ 13. Your state government
____ 14. Your local (city, town) government

F. Do you favor or oppose the death penalty for a person
convicted of murder?
___Favor ___Oppose

G. 1. Do you believe there should be legal access to abortion?
Yes___ No___
2. If so, should there be any restrictions regarding age of the
woman, length of the pregnancy, or other circumstances?
Please specify: _____

H. Please indicate your opinion on the following social issues using the scale below:
0 – Very strong disagreement with statement
1 – Disagreement with statement
2 – Qualified disagreement with statement
3 – No opinion about statement
4 – Qualified agreement with statement
5 – Agreement with statement
6 – Very strong agreement with statement

___ 1. There should be an Equal Rights Amendment to the U.S. Constitution.
___ 2. Women should not be included in a military draft.
___ 3. Same-sex marriages should be legal.
___ 4. To redress previous discrimination, there should be preferential hiring of women at all levels of employment.
___ 5. Women in the military forces should be included in combat positions.
___ 6. Nondiscrimination on the basis of sexual preference should be part of any civil rights legislation.
___ 7. The right to religious freedom should not include human sacrifice.
___ 8. Marijuana should be legally available on the same basis as alcohol or tobacco.
___ 9. Homosexuals should be excluded from the military.
___ 10. Polygamy should be legal in the U.S.

III. Religious/Spiritual Beliefs

A. 1. Do you believe there is a life after death?
Yes___ No___ Not sure___
2. Do you believe in reincarnation?
Yes___ No___ Not sure___

B. Of course no one knows exactly what life after death would be like, but here are some ideas people have had. How likely do you feel each possibility is? For the next ten questions, please use the following scale:

1 – Very likely
2 – Somewhat likely
3 – Not too likely
4 – Not at all likely

____ 1. A life of peace and tranquility
____ 2. A life of intense action
____ 3. A paradise of pleasures and delights
____ 4. Reunion with loved ones
____ 5. A pale shadowy life, hardly a life at all
____ 6. A spiritual life, involving our mind but not our body
____ 7. A life like the one here on Earth, only better
____ 8. A place of loving intellectual communion
____ 9. Union with God (or Gods and Goddesses)
____ 10. A life without many things that make our present life enjoyable

C. How often have you had any of the following experiences? Please use the following scale:

1 – Never in my life
2 – Once or twice
3 – Several times
4 – Often

____ 1. Thought you were somewhere you had been before, but knew that it was impossible.
____ 2. Felt as though you were in touch with someone when they were far away from you.
____ 3. Saw events that happened at great distance as they were happening.
____ 4. Felt as though you were really in touch with someone who had died.
____ 5. Felt as though you were very close to a powerful, spiritual force that seemed to lift you out of yourself.

D. 1. Approximately how much money did you contribute to you
    religion during the past twelve months_____

    2. How much time or other resources do you contribute
    annually to your religion_____

    3. Are you paid clergy?_____   If so, are you:

                                       Full time?_____

                                       Part time?_____

IV. Pagan-Related Information

A. Do you primarily consider yourself to be: (if you list more than
    one, indicate which is most important, 2nd, 3rd, etc.)

    ____   1. Agnostic
    ____   2. Atheist
    ____   3. Buddhist
    ____   4. Ceremonial magician
    ____   5. Christian
    ____   6. Druid
    ____   7. Goddess worshiper
    ____   8. Jewish
    ____   9. Magic worker
    ____   10. Neo-Pagan
    ____   11. New Age
    ____   12. Odinist
    ____   13. Pagan
    ____   14. Satanist
    ____   15. Shaman
    ____   16. Spiritual, but dislike labels
    ____   17. Thelemite
    ____   18. Unitarian-Universalist
    ____   19. Witch (non-Wiccan)
    ____   20. Witch (Wiccan)
    ____   21. Other (please specify)_____

B. What is the primary manner in which you work/worship?

    ____   1. In a group
    ____   2. With a magical/spiritual partner (including
               apprenticeships)
    ____   3. As a solitary

C. What is/are your tradition/s or orientation/s (e.g., Eclectic, Gardnerian, Dianic, Keltrian, etc.)? If more than one, please prioritize if possible: _____

D. If you have a mate or spouse, how does he/she relate to your spiritual orientation?
    ____ 1. Shares your orientation
    ____ 2. Does not share but is tolerant/indifferent
    ____ 3. Does not share but is sympathetic
    ____ 4. Does not share and is antagonistic to your orientation
    ____ 5. Does not know about your orientation

If more than one mate or spouse, please indicate this information for each individually.

E. During the last year, how many Pagan festivals or gatherings lasting more than one day, if any, have you attended?_____. Please list, giving festival name, date, and place:

    _____
    _____
    _____

F. If you did not attend any festival during the last year, why didn't you?_____

G. Since what year have you been an active member of the Pagan/Witch community (i.e., participated in a coven, took part in a Pagan ritual, attended a festival, joined a pagan organization, etc.)?_____

H. Please indicate with a check mark (✓)which Pagan publication you read regularly:
    ____ 1. *Circle Network News*
    ____ 2. *C.O.G. Newsletter*
    ____ 3. *Druid's Progress*
    ____ 4. *EarthSpirit Newsletter*
    ____ 5. *Enchanté*

____ 6. *FireHeart*
____ 7. *Green Egg*
____ 8. *Keltria*
____ 9. *Of a Like Mind*
____ 10. *PSA Newsletter*
____ 11. *Panegyria*
____ 12. *Reclaiming Newsletter*
____ 13. *Sage Woman*
____ 14. *Survival*
____ 15. *Thesmophoria*
____ 16. *Tides*
____ 17. Other (please specify)_____

I. Of the publications you indicated, which are your favorites, and why?_____

J. If you have ever let a subscription to a Pagan publication lapse, what qualities of the publication caused you to drop it?

_____

K. Briefly, how did you become involved in Paganism/Witchcraft?

_____

L. What Pagan-oriented books or teachers have been specially influential for you?_____

M. The following are community issues that have arisen in Pagan publications and at gatherings over the past few years. Please indicate your own personal reaction to the statements below based on the following scale:

0 – Very strong disagreement with statement
1 – Disagreement with statement
2 – Qualified disagreement with statement
3 – No opinion on statement
4 – Qualified agreement with statement
5 – Agreement with statement
6 – Very strong agreement with statement

____ 1. People who are under the age of 18 whose parents are not Pagan/Witches should not be trained in the Craft.

____ 2. The use of mind-altering chemicals is a valid magical practice.

____ 3. The words "Witch" and "Pagan" have and should retain significantly different meanings.

____ 4. The term "Witch" is inappropriate today and should not be used.

____ 5. Satanism can be a valid form of Paganism.

____ 6. "Public Witches" should dress conservatively when giving interviews to the media.

____ 7. Correspondence courses are an acceptable way to learn the Craft.

____ 8. Hierarchy can be an organic, non-oppressive organizational structure.

____ 9. Full-time Pagan clergy should be financially supported by their community.

____ 10. A Witch should not accept money for teaching the Craft.

____ 11. Sex between a spiritual teacher and a student is unethical.

____ 12. It is important that Witches have high standards of training.

____ 13. The popularization of Witchcraft has diluted its standards and identity.

____ 14. Witches and Pagans should actively seek connections with the "New Age" community.

____ 15. Homophobia is as prevalent in the Pagan movement as anywhere else in society.

____ 16. Compulsory military service is incompatible with Pagan religious beliefs.

V. Other Information

A. Is there any additional information, perspective, or opinion relevant to your participation in the Pagan movement that you would like to share with us? Please use the space below or attach additional sheets as necessary. Thanks again for your participation in this survey.

To receive information on census results and other Pagan-related projects, please detach the form below and mail separately.

The Pagan Census Project — Census Update Form
(*please print*)

Name_____

Address_____

Street_____

City_____ State_____ Zip_____

Mail to
The EarthSpirit Community
P.O. Box 365
Medford, MA 02155

Telephone (617) 395–1023
Facsimile (617) 396–5066

The Pagan Census Project

(Copyright 1993, Andras Corban Arthen and Helen Berger, Ph.D.)

NOTES

Preface

1. One of the initial people to help us with the survey began numbering them from 1,000; hence, although we received only 2,089 surveys, some are numbered 3,000 or above. The numbers given to surveys are not an indication of when they were received but are arbitrary identification codes.

Chapter 1

1. Throughout this text we will capitalize *Neo-Pagan, Pagan,* and *Witch* when referring to practitioners of this contemporary religion. We do not capitalize these words when referring to the historic pagans or witches, as they were not practitioners of a specific religion. Historically, pagans were rural people who practiced a number of different local religions.

2. Ronald Hutton (1999:28) attributes the creation of the term *Neo-Pagan* in nineteenth-century Britain to W. F. Barry, who used it to disparage those who were drawn to classical pagan mythology.

3. The results of this participant observation study have been published in Berger 1999a. As noted in the preface, the views presented in this book are those of the authors and not those of Andras Corban Arthen or EarthSpirit Community.

4. Some of these authors refer to this period as postmodern while others refer to it as late modern.

5. See, for example, Rose 1962.

6. Dion Fortune is the pen name for Violet Firth.

7. Although the acronym remains the same, the name sometimes changes. For example, it has also stood for Women Infuriated at Taking Care of Hoodlums. For more examples, see Eller (1993:53).

8. For a discussion of the historic witch trials see, Russell 1972 and 1980, Trevor-Roper 1969, Kern 1993.

Chapter 2

1. From the fifteenth through the seventeenth centuries, witch trials occurred throughout most of Europe and to a lesser degree in the American colonies and Quebec.

2. The GSS has a large repertoire of questions, only some of which are included in their survey in any given year. The closest date to the administration of our survey that the GSS includes the questions we ask on the paranormal is 1993.

3. These data are from the 1988–91 GSS.

4. Circle Sanctuary is a well-known and influential Pagan umbrella organization located in Wisconsin.

5. These data are from the 1991–93 GSS.

6. The last years the GSS includes these questions are 1983–87.

7. In order to make the question relevant to Neo-Pagans, our survey adds in parentheses "or Gods and Goddess" to the question that asks if the afterlife is a union with God.

8. This question was last asked by the GSS in 1983–87.

9. These data are from the 1996 GSS results.

10. These data are from the 1983–87 GSS results.

11. A question on the arts is not included in the 1993 GSS but is included in 1988–91.

12. These results are from 1972–82 GSS.

13. Theses results are from the 1996 GSS.

14. This question is included in the 1983–87 GSS.

15. Fort Hood received media coverage in 1999 when the military leadership came under attack by the religious right for permitting Neo-Pagan soldiers to have an altar and participate in rituals on military property.

16. These data are from the1988–91 GSS.

17. These data for 1991, the last year the GSS recorded the political affiliation of their sample.

Chapter 3

1. A 66.3 percentage of UU Neo-Pagans and a 29.7 percentage of the general Neo-Pagan community believes we are spending too little on mass transit.

2. A percentage of 46.6 of UU Neo-Pagans and 54 percent of the general Neo-Pagan community believe that we are spending too little on big cities; 42.4 percent of UU Neo-Pagans and 49.8 percent of the general Neo-Pagan community state that we are spending too little on crime; and 44.6 percent of Neo-Pagans and 49.7 percent of the general Neo-Pagan community believe we are spending too little on drug addiction.

Chapter 5

1. These data are from the 1988–91 GSS.

Chapter 7

1. Although we do not ask this specific question, by requesting that respondents list their occupation, we find that some respondents earn their living in a manner related to Neo-Paganism, such as owning or running an occult bookstore. Please see table 7.

BIBLIOGRAPHY

Adler, Margot. 1986. *Drawing Down the Moon*. Rev. and enl. Boston: Beacon Press.

———. 1992. "Interview." *FireHeart* 5: 25–33.

Alfred, R. H. 1976. "The Church of Satan." In *The New Religious Consciousness,* edited by Charles Glock and Robert Bellah. Berkeley and Los Angeles: University of California Press.

Ammerman, Nancy. 1993. "SBC Moderates and the Making of a Post-Modern Denomination." *Christian Century* (September 22–23).

Babbie, Earl. 2000. *The Practice of Social Research.* 9th ed. Belmont, Calif.: Wadsworth Publishing.

Bambridge, William. 1978. *Satan's Power: A Deviant Psychotherapy Cult.* Berkeley and Los Angeles: University of California Press.

Beckford, James. 1992. "Religion and Modernity, Post-Modernity." In *Religion: Contemporary Issues,* edited by Bryan Wilson. London: Bellew.

Berger, Helen A. 1994. "Witches and Scientists." *Sociological Viewpoints* 10 (fall): 56–65.

———. 1999a. *A Community of Witches: Contemporary Neo-Paganism and Witchcraft in the United States.* Columbia: University of South Carolina Press.

———. 1999b. "Witchcraft: The Next Generation." In *Children in New Religious Movements,* edited by Susan J. Palmer and Charlotte E. Hartman. New Brunswick, N.J.: Rutgers University Press.

———. 2000. "High Priestess: Mother, Leader, Teacher." In *Daughters of the Goddess: Studies of Healing, Identity and Empowerment,* edited by Wendy Griffin. Lanham, Md.: AltaMira Press.

Berger, Peter L. 1967. *The Sacred Canopy: Elements of a Sociological Theory of Religion.* Garden City, N.Y.: Doubleday.

Beslaw, Elaine G. 1992. *The Salem Witch from Barbados: In Search of Tituba's Roots. Essex Institute Historical Collections* 128 (October): 217–39.

Bonewits, Isaac. 1989. *Real Magic.* York Beach, Maine: Samuel Weisner.

Budapest, Zsuzsanna. 1986. *The Holy Book of Women's Mysteries.* Rev. ed. Oakland, Calif.: Susan B. Anthony Coven 1.

Butler, Jon. 1979. "Magic, Astrology, and the Early American Religious Heritage, 1600–1760." *American Historical Review* 48: 317–46.

———. 1986. "The Dark Ages of American Occultism, 1760–1848." In *The Occult in America: New Historical Perspectives,* edited by Howard Kerr and Charles L. Crow. Urbana: University of Illinois Press.

Carpenter, Dennis D. 1996. "Emergent Nature Spirituality: An Examination of the Major Spiritual Contours of the Contemporary Pagan World View." In *Magical Religion and Modern Witchcraft,* edited by James R. Lewis. Albany: State University of New York Press.

Cavafajal, Doreen. 1998. "Better Living through Sorcery." *New York Times,* October 26: E1, 4.

Cave, Alfred A. 1992. "Indian Shamans and English Witches in Seventeenth-Century New England." *Essex Institute Historical Collections* 128 (October): 239–54.

Chaves, Mark. 1997. *Ordaining Women: Culture and Conflict in Religious Organizations.* Cambridge: Harvard University Press.

Clegg, Stewart R. 1990. *Modern Organizations.* London: Sage.

Clifton, Chas S. 2000. "Fort Hood's Wiccans and the Problem of Pacifism." Paper presented at the American Academy of Religion annual meeting.

Covenant of the Goddess. 2000. Wiccan/Pagan poll. October 7. http://www.cog.org

Crowley, Vivianne. 2000. "Healing in Wicca." In *Daughters of the Goddess: Studies of Healing, Identity, and Empowerment,* edited by Wendy Griffin. Walnut Creek, Calif.: AltaMira Press.

Cunningham, Scott. 1988. *Wicca: A Guide for the Solitary Practitioner.* St. Paul, Minn.: Llewellyn Publications.

———. 1993. *Living Wicca: A Further Guide for the Solitary Practitioner.* St. Paul, Minn.: Llewellyn Publications.

Davis, James A., and Tom W. Smith. 1992. *The NORC General Social Survey: A User's Guide.* Newbury Park, Calif.: Sage.

de Blécourt, Willem. 1999. "The Witch, Her Victim, the Unwitcher and the Researcher: The Continued Existence of Traditional Witchcraft." In *Witchcraft and Magic in Europe: The Twentieth Century,* edited by Willem de Blécourt, Ronald Hutton, and Jean La Fontaine. London: Athlone Press.

DiMaggio, Paul, and Walter Powell. 1983. "The Iron Cage Revisited: Institutional Isomorphism and Collective Rationality in Organizational Fields." *American Sociological Review* 48 (April):147–60.

Durkheim, Emile. 1965. *The Elementary Forms of Religious Life*. New York: Free Press.

Easlea, Brian. 1980. *Witch-Hunting, Magic and the New Philosophy: An Introduction to Debates of the Scientific Revolution, 1450–1750*. Atlantic Highlands, N.J.: Humanities Press.

Eilberg-Schwartz, Howard. 1989. "Witches of the West: Neo-Paganism and Goddess Worship as Enlightenment Religions." *Journal of Feminist Studies of Religion* 5: 77–95.

Eland-Goossensen, M. A., et al., 1997. "Snowball Sampling Applied to Opiate Addicts outside the Treatment System." *Addiction Research* 5: 317–30.

Eller, Cynthia. 1993. *Living in the Lap of the Goddess: The Feminist Spirituality Movement in America*. New York: Crossroads.

———. 2000. *The Myth of Matriarchal Prehistory: Why an Invented Past Won't Give Women a Future*. Boston: Beacon Press.

Ellwood, Robert S. Jr. 1979. *Alternative Altars: Unconventional and Eastern Spirituality in America*. Chicago: University of Chicago Press.

———. 1986. "The American Theosophical Synthesis." In *The Occult in America: New Historical Perspectives*, edited by Howard Kerr and Charles L. Crow. Urbana: University of Illinois Press.

———. 1994. *The 60s Spiritual Awakening*. New Brunswick, N.J.: Rutgers University Press.

Ezzy, Douglas. 2001. "The Commodification of Witchcraft." *Australian Religious Studies Review* 14: 31–44.

Feher, Shoshanah. 1992. "Who Holds the Card? Women and New Age Astrology." In *Perspectives on the New Age*, edited by James R. Lewis and J. Gordon Melton. Albany: State University of New York Press.

Fenwick, Ben. 2000. "Oklahoma School Suspends Girl for Casting Spell." *Reuters*, October 27.

Finley, Nancy J. 1991. "Political Activism and Feminist Spirituality." *Sociological Analysis* 52: 349–62.

Foltz, Tanice G. 1996. "Divine Divorce: Healing Wounded Relationships through Goddess Ritual." Paper presented at the annual meeting of the Society for the Scientific Study of Religion.

Frost, Garvin and Yvette Frost. 1975. *The Witch's Bible*. New York: Berkley Books.

Gardner, Gerald. 1954. *Witchcraft Today*. London: Rider.

Giddens, Anthony. 1987. *Social Theory and Modern Society*. Stanford, Calif.: Stanford University Press.

———. 1990. *The Consequences of Modernity*. Stanford, Calif.: Stanford University Press.

———. 1991. *Modernity and Self-Identity: Self and Society in the Late Modern Age*. Stanford, Calif.: Stanford University Press.

Greeley, Andrew. 1987. "Mysticism Goes Mainstream." *American Health* (January/ February), 47–49.

Griffin, Wendy, ed. 2000. *Daughters of the Goddess: Studies of Healing, Identity, and Empowerment*. Lanham, Md.: AltaMira Press.

———. 2003. "Returning to the Mother of Us All: Goddess Spirituality in the West." In *Her Voice, Her Faith: Women Speak on World Religions*, edited by Arvind Sharma and Katherine Young. Boulder, Colo.: Westview Press.

Harner, Michael. 1982. *The Way of the Shaman*. New York: Bantam.

Harrow, Judy. 1994. "Other People's Kids: Working with the Underaged Seeker." In *Modern Rites of Passage: Witchcraft Today*, bk. 2, edited by Chas S. Clifton. St. Paul, Minn.: Llewellyn Publications.

———. 1996. "The Contemporary Neo-Pagan Revival." In *Magical Religion and Modern Witchcraft*, edited by James R. Lewis. Albany: State University of New York Press.

———. 1999. *Wicca Covens: How to Start and Organize Your Own*. Secaucus, N.J.: Citadel Press.

Harvey, Graham. 1997. *Contemporary Paganism: Listening People, Speaking Earth*. New York: New York University Press.

Heelas, Paul. 1996. *The New Age Movement*. Oxford: Blackwell.

Hochschild, Arlie. 1990. *The Second Shift*. New York: Avon Books.

Huber, Joan, and Glenna Spitze. 1983. *Sex Stratification: Children, Housework, and Jobs*. Philadelphia: Temple University Press.

Huizinga, Johan. 1950. *Homo Ludens: A Study of the Play Element in Culture*. Boston: Beacon Press.

Hutton, Ronald. 1999. *The Triumph of the Moon: A History of Modern Pagan Witchcraft*. Oxford: Oxford University Press.

Infield, Tom. 2001. "Falwell's Finger-Pointing Draws Caution, Outrage." *Philadelphia Inquirer*, September 17: C4.

Jencson, Linda. 1998. "In Whose Image? Misogynist Trends in the Construction of Goddess and Woman." In *Spellbound: Women and Witchcraft in America*, edited by Elizabeth Ries. Wilmington, Del.: Scholarly Resources.

Jorgensen, Danny L., and Scott E. Russell. 1999. "American Neo-Paganism: The Participants' Social Identities." *Journal for the Scientific Study of Religion* 38 (September): 325–38.

K, Amber. 1998. *Covencraft: Witchcraft for Three or More*. St. Paul, Minn.: Llewellyn Publications.

Kaplan, Jeffrey. 1996. "The Reconstruction of the Asatru and Odinist Traditions." In *Magical Religion and Modern Witchcraft,* edited by James R. Lewis. Albany: State University of New York Press.

Kelly, Aidan A. 1991. *Crafting the Art of Magic.* Bk. 1. St. Paul, Minn.: Llewellyn Publications.

Kern, Louis J. 1993. "Eros, the Devil, and the Cunning Woman: Sexuality and the Supernatural in European Antecedents and in the Seventeenth-Century Salem Witchcraft Cases." In *Perspectives on Witchcraft: Rethinking the Seventeenth-Century New England Experience,* edited by William T. LaMoy. Salem: Essex Institute Historical Collections.

Kirkpatrick, George R., Rich Rainey, and Kathryn Rubi. 1986. "An Empirical Study of Wiccan Religion in Postindustrial Society." *Free Inquiry in Creative Sociology* 14: 33–38.

Krippner, S. 1988. "Parapsychology and Postmodern Science." In *The Reenchantment of the Science: Postmodern Proposals,* edited by David Ray Griffin. Albany: State University of New York Press.

Lee, Richard Wayne. 1995. "Strained Bedfellows: Pagans, New Agers, and 'Starchy Humanists in Unitarian Universalism.'" *Sociology of Religion* 56: 379–96.

Lewis, James R. 1992. "Approaches to the Study of the New Age Movement." In *Perspectives on the New Age,* edited by James R. Lewis and J. Gordon Melton. Albany: State University of New York Press.

Lofland, John, and James T. Richardson. 1984. "Religious Movement Organizations: Elemental Forms and Dynamics." *Research in Social Movement, Conflict, and Change* 7: 29–51.

Lozano (Griffin), Wendy G., and Tanice G. Foltz. 1990. "Into the Darkness: An Ethnographic Study of Witchcraft and Death." *Qualitative Sociology* 13 (fall): 211–34.

Luhrmann, Tanya M. 1989. *Persuasions of the Witch's Craft: Ritual Magic in Contemporary England.* Cambridge: Harvard University Press.

Malinowski, Bronislaw. 1954. *Magic, Science, and Religion, and Other Essays.* Garden City, N.Y.: Dover.

McArthur, Margie. 1994. *Wicca Craft for Families.* Langley, England: Phoenix Publishing.

Melton, J. Gordon. 1992. *Encyclopedic Handbook of Cults in America,* rev. and updated. New York: Garland Press.

Meyer, Suzanne P. 1994. "Courting the Baby Boomers." In *Salted with Fire,* edited by Scott W. Alexander. Boston: Skinner House Books.

Michelet, Jules. 1939. *Satanism and Witchcraft.* Secaucus, N.J.: Lyle Stuart.

Moody, Edward. 1974. "Magical Therapy: Contemporary Satanism." In *Religious Movements in Contemporary America,* edited by Irving I. Zaretsky and Mark P. Leone. Princeton: Princeton University Press.

Murray, Margaret A. [1921] 1971. *The Witch-Cult in Western Europe.* Oxford: Clarendon Press.

Niebuhr, Gustav. 1999. "Witches Cast as the Neo-Pagans Next Door." *New York Times,* October 31: A1, 28.

O'Gaea, Ashleen. 1993. *The Family Wicca Book.* St. Paul, Minn.: Llewellyn Publications.

Orion, Loretta. 1995. *Never Again the Burning Times: Paganism Revived.* Prospect Heights, Ill.: Waveland Press.

Orsi, Robert A. 1996. *Thank You St. Jude: Women's Devotion to the Patron Saint of Hopeless Causes.* New Haven: Yale University Press.

Palmer, Susan J. 1994. *Moon Sisters, Krishna Mothers, Rajneesh Lovers: Women's Roles in New Religions.* Syracuse: Syracuse University Press.

———, and Charlotte E. Hardman. 1999. *Children in New Religions.* New Brunswick, N.J.: Rutgers University Press.

Patten, Drake M. 1992. "African-American Spiritual Beliefs: An Archaeological Testimony from the Slave Quarters." In *Wonders of the Invisible World: 1600–1900.* Dublin Seminar for New England Folklife Annual Proceedings, edited by Peter Benes. Boston: Boston University.

Piersen, William D. 1992. "Black Arts and Black Magic: Yankee Accommodations to African Religion." In *Wonders of the Invisible World: 1600–1900,* edited by Peter Benes. Dublin Seminar for New England Folklife Annual Proceedings. Boston: Boston University.

Pike, Sarah M. 1996. "Forging Magical Selves: Gendered Bodies and Ritual Fires at Neo-Pagan Festivals." In *Magical Religion and Modern Witchcraft,* edited by James R. Lewis. Albany: State University of New York Press.

———. 2001. *Earthly Bodies, Magical Selves: Contemporary Pagans and the Search for Community.* Berkeley and Los Angeles: University of California Press.

Ranck, Shirley Ann. 1995. *Cakes for the Queen of Heaven.* Chicago: Delphi Press.

Raphael, Melissa. 1996. "Truth in Flux: Goddess Feminism as a Late Modern Religion." *Religion* 25: 199–213.

RavenWolf, Silver. 1999. *Teen Witch: Wicca for a New Generation.* St. Paul, Minn.: Llewellyn Publications.

Reid, Sîan. 1996. "As I Do Will, So Mote It Be." In *Magical Religion and Modern Witchcraft,* edited by James R. Lewis. Albany: State University of New York Press.

Reisberg, Leo. 2000. "Campus Witches May Wear Black, but Don't Look for Hats or Broomsticks." *Chronicle of Higher Education,* October 20.

Richardson, James T. 1985. "The 'Deformation' of New Religions: The Impact of Societal and Organizational Factors." In *Cults, Culture, and the Law: Perspectives on New Religious Movements.* Chico, Calif.: Scholars Press.

Roof, Wade Clark. 1993. *A Generation of Seekers: The Spiritual Journeys of the Baby Boom Generation.* San Francisco: Harper Collins.

Rose, Elliot. 1962. *A Razor for a Goat.* Toronto: University of Toronto Press.

Rose, Wendy. 1992. "The Great Pretenders: Further Reflections on Whiteshamanism." In *The State of Native America,* edited by Annette M. Jaimes. Boston: South End Press.

Russell, Jeffrey Burton. 1972. *Witchcraft in the Middle Ages.* Secaucus, N.J.: Citadel Press.

———. 1980. *A History of Witchcraft.* London: Thames and Hudson.

Scarboro, Allen, Nancy Campbell, and Shirley Stave. 1994. *Living Witchcraft: A Contemporary American Coven.* Westport, Conn.: Praeger.

Serith, Ceisiwr. 1994. *The Pagan Family: Handing the Old Ways Down.* St. Paul, Minn.: Llewellyn Publications.

Starhawk. 1979. *The Spiral Dance.* New York: Harper and Row.

———. 1982. *Dreaming the Dark.* Boston: Beacon Press.

———, and M. Macha Nightmare. 1997. *The Pagan Book of Living and Dying: Practical Rituals, Prayers, Blessings, and Meditations on Crossing Over.* San Francisco: Harper Collins.

———, Dianne Baker, and Anne Hill. 1998. *Circle Round: Raising Children in Goddess Traditions.* New York: Bantam.

Shehan, Constance L., and Kenneth C. W. Kammeyer. 1997. *Marriages and Families: Reflections of a Gendered Society.* Boston: Allyn and Bacon.

Shumaker, Wayne. 1972. *The Occult Sciences in the Renaissance: A Study in Intellectual Patterns.* Berkeley and Los Angeles: University of California Press.

Stark, Rodney, and William Bainbridge. 1985. *The Future of Religion.* Berkeley and Los Angeles: University of California Press.

Thomas, Keith. 1971. *Religion and the Decline of Magic.* London: Penguin Books.

Trevor-Roper, H. R. 1969. *The European Witch Craze of the 16th and 17th Centuries and Other Essays.* New York: Harper and Row.

Troeltsch, Ernst. 1960. *The Social Teachings of the Christian Churches.* 2 vols. New York: Harper and Row.

Unitarian Universalist Association. 1992. "Reader Profile Study." *World.* Boston: Unitarian Universalist Association.

United States Census Bureau. 2001. "Historical Income Tables (Table P-36). Full-time, Year-Round Workers (All Races) by Median Income and Sex: 1970 to 2000." October 22.
http://www.census.gov/hhes/income/histinc/p36.html

Wallace, Ruth. 1992. *They Call Her Pastor: A New Role for Catholic Women*. New York: State University of New York Press.

Webb, James, 1974. *The Occult Underground*. La Salle, Ill.: Open Court.

Weber, Max. 1963. *The Sociology of Religion*. Boston: Beacon Press.

Wen, Patricia. 2001. "The New Superstitions." *Boston Globe*, January 2: 1, 3.

Wuthnow, Robert. 1978. *Experimentation in American Religion*. Berkeley and Los Angeles: University of California Press.

York, Michael. 1995. *The Emerging Network*. Lanham, Md.: Rowman and Littlefield Publishing.

INDEX